An Evangelical Family Revealed

The Bickersteth and Monier-Williams letters and diaries 1880–1918

Margaret Ford

Foreword by Bishop John Bickersteth and
His Honour Evelyn Faithfull Monier-Williams

Published by Ford Publishing

ISBN: 978-0-9567218-0-8

Dust Jacket designed by Humphrey Stone

Index compiled by Sue Dugen

Prepared and printed by:

Pasttimes Publishing Ltd
64 Hallfield Road
Layerthorpe
York YO31 7ZQ
Tel: 01904 431213

Website: www.pasttimespublishing.com

Dedicated to Wyn Ford and Rosemary Bickersteth

in affectionate remembrance

CONTENTS

ILLUSTRATIONS

Family Tree

A condensed family tree is to be found in the pocket of the back cover. Priority is given to the key figures mentioned in the text of this book. It is anticipated that a link to a much more detailed genealogy, building on the work done by Roy Monier-Williams (1951), Ursula Bickersteth (1965), Arthur Wilson Bickersteth (1966) and Bishop John Bickersteth (2001) will be included in the website: www.ford-bickersteth.co.uk.

FOREWORD

There are not many books of which one can say: 'This kind of subject has never been tackled before'. *An Evangelical Family Revealed* is one of them. Nor do we make such a claim simply because one of us is the grandson of the two main characters in the study, and the other is the great-grandson of Sir Monier Monier-Williams and great nephew of Ella Bickersteth; we do so because we know it is a detailed true story of one such family. Attractively written, it certainly rings true to us, and not by hearsay, we were thirty-four and thirty-three respectively when Ella died; Sam's death was seventeen years earlier. We both saw Ella frequently up to her own death in 1954, which is one of the reasons why so much of the original research evidenced in these pages is immensely personal, and in consequence so enthralling for to-day's Monier-Williams's and Bickersteths.

But this book is for a far wider audience than one family. It will have an appeal to today's evangelical Christians world-wide, both anglicans and free-churchmen: 'how did they tick, these influential churchmen of mid to late Victorian times?' One book of Edward Bickersteth of Watton (ob.1850), his *Companion to the Holy Communion*, was in its 37th edition by the time of his death; and the same year his *Family Prayers* was selling, says the title page, their 13,000th copy; both these books incidentally are on the internet all these years on. But there is also a great deal in what Margaret Ford has written for both social and church historians, covering as it does such a turbulent period in British history, and for academics (Sir Monier Monier-Williams' scholarship was prodigious); and also to some extent for military people, ranging across fighting in North America, India and the North West Frontier, South Africa and Flanders over a period of more than a century.

Vivid, with a light touch, extremely well-documented, *An Evangelical Family Revealed* gives in thoroughly readable style a unique picture of both the professional and private lives of an English Victorian middle-class clerical household; and, with the extended family being so large, there are fascinating offshoots which emerge from the author-compiled family trees.

We cannot commend it too warmly.

Bishop John Bickersteth
His Honour Evelyn Faithfull Monier-Williams

ACKNOWLEDGEMENTS

I should like to acknowledge the generous help given me by members of the Bickersteth family, in particular the never-failing enthusiasm and support of Bishop John Bickersteth, a grandson of Samuel Bickersteth. It is thanks to them that so many intriguing records have emerged. In particular, Michael Bickersteth allowed me to borrow his copy of the War Diary and East Sussex Record Office kindly stored all nine volumes for me. Judge Evelyn Monier-Williams has been equally helpful, giving me access to his archive of family material and allowing me to borrow the unique volumes of the reminiscences of Sir Monier Monier-Williams and his eldest son, Monier Faithfull Monier-Williams.

'An Evangelical Family Revealed' is based on my PhD thesis 'Intimate Records: Faith, Family and the Call of Duty. The Bickersteth Family 1880-1918'. That research was funded by the University of Chichester and to them, and my supervisor, Dr Susan Morgan, I owe a debt of gratitude.

This book represents the end of a long journey. It has been a remarkably enjoyable one, revealing a family where there was much happiness and remarkably little angst. It has been made even more pleasant due to the help of so many individuals who over the years have watched the original thesis develop, and then, when they thought the worst was over, been confronted with drafts of this book. My thanks go especially to those who, with gritted teeth, have fought their way through the mass of Edward Bickersteths and their innumerable relatives and spotted my many errors. Archivists and librarians who have helped me are too numerous to list, but special thanks must go to the staff at the Department of Special Collections and Western Manuscripts at the Bodleian Library, Oxford, John Coulter, archivist at Lewisham Local History Centre and to the librarians of West Sussex County Council who provided a superlative service through my small, local library.

My special thanks also go to Dr Malcolm Lambert, a historian who was prepared for confirmation by Julian Bickersteth. He spurred me on from the day I accidentally came upon the name Bickersteth in the British Library when experimenting with their computer system, and stayed with me to the end. I have been fortunate in having so many delightful travelling companions.

Margaret Ford. Keymer, Sussex. 2010.

PROLOGUE

The big things belong to history and will be familiar enough, but afterwards, the next generation will search back for the intimate records and the psychology of men who lived in it. Philip Gibbs. War Diary. 1915

Sir Philip Gibbs, the War Correspondent of the *Daily Telegraph* was writing to twenty-eight year old John Burgon Bickersteth, then serving on the Western Front. He had just read some of the letters exchanged between the Bickersteth family in the early years of the First World War. He was urging him to encourage his mother to continue to record the details and the hopes and fears the family were experiencing in their day-to-day lives. Within this family no such encouragement was needed. From 1882 the Bickersteth parents had recorded the physical and spiritual progress of their six sons and their own joys and anxieties, and had preserved the family papers of previous generations. But Gibbs' prescience was accurate. Over a century later, the 'intimate records' not only illuminate life in the mud of Flanders, but they reveal the pleasures and pains of life in a vicarage household during the late Victorian/early Edwardian period.

The Bickersteth family has many branches. Here the focus is not on the more senior branches but on the Revd Dr. Samuel Bickersteth (1857-1937) and his wife, Ella née Monier-Williams (1858-1954), and their six sons: Monier (1882-1976), Geoffrey (1884-1974), Julian (1885-1962), Burgon 1888-1979), Morris (1891-1916), and Ralph (1894-1989).Their uncle, the Rt. Revd Edward Bickersteth (1850-1897) was Bishop of South Tokyo. Their grandfather, the Rt. Revd Dr Edward Henry Bickersteth (1825-1906) had been Bishop of Exeter and their great grandfather, the Revd Edward Bickersteth (1786-1850) had been one of the first Secretaries of the Church Missionary Society, a founder of the Parker Society and, in his latter years, the major force behind the creation of the Evangelical Alliance. To help steer the reader through this maze of Bickersteths, the Revd Dr Samuel Bickersteth is always referred to as 'Sam'; the Rt Revd Dr Edward Henry Bickersteth as 'Bishop Edward Henry', the Rt Revd Edward Bickersteth as 'Bishop of South Tokyo' or 'Uncle Bishop', and the Revd Edward Bickersteth as 'Edward of Watton'.

When Ella Monier-Williams married Sam Bickersteth she linked his family to another wide network, spread over Wales, Newfoundland, and Canada and, through the East India Company, India. It included distinguished soldiers, magistrates, architects, an astronomer and an artist. The boys' maternal great-grandfather served in India under Colonel Wellesley, afterwards the Duke of Wellington, and later, as Surveyor General, completed the 'Great Map of India'. Their grandfather, Sir Monier Monier-Williams, born in Bombay, was an orientalist who became Professor of Sanskrit at Oxford and was a devout evangelical. The Monier-Williams archive was assembled by Ella's nephew, Roy Monier-Williams, and survived the London blitz, being dug out of the ruins of his home in 1940. Memoirs, written by his grandfather, Sir Monier Monier-Williams and by his father, Monier Faithfull Monier-Williams, still have traces of grit among the pages. Both are based on their diaries and so give a picture of the way Ella was brought up, and incidentally throw light on her mothering of her sons. Unfortunately, just like the Bickersteth family, it is only too easy to become confused by their names. The family name is Williams. George Williams married Mary Monier in 1762, the daughter of the doctor in St. John's, Newfoundland. Although no written records have been traced, it is a family belief that the Moniers came from France as Huguenot refugees following the Revocation of the Edict of Nantes in 1685. Monier was used as a Christian name down the generations, but in 1880, a few years before he was knighted, Ella's father assumed the additional surname of Monier by deed poll. For the sake of simplicity, he is referred to here as Monier-Williams, unless his life as a young man is being discussed, when he remains plain Monier Williams.

The Monier-Williams archive remains in private hands, but the bulk of the Bickersteth family records is in the Bodleian Library Oxford, though a number of miscellaneous papers, photographs and memoirs have emerged from family attics whilst this book has been written. The Oxford archive covers the period 1815-1976 and contains the correspondence, personal notebooks and diaries of five generations of the family. It includes the letters exchanged between some of the Bickersteth children and their parents from eight years of age to the end of their university careers. Only papers up to 1918 have been examined for this book, and research has always been focussed on family life, leaving much that would merit further examination. The nine large and heavy volumes of the First World War diary, compiled by Ella from the letters sent home from France by her sons, plus newspaper cuttings, which are held in Churchill College, Cambridge, complete the sources used for the research on which this book is based.

Philip Gibbs was right. In many ways, these 'intimate records' do indeed reveal the psychology of the main characters. Ella was no 'angel in the house'; Sam was no martinet of a father. The boys' home life, in which their mother had such a key role, played a much more important part in their upbringing than their public school education. The records shatter the stereotype of the typical evangelical family. The paradox is that Sam and Ella had their own family stereotype. The children's grandfather, Sir Monier Monier-Williams, who had a gift for catchy doggerel, encapsulated it in a rhyme he wrote in 1889, when Sam was vicar of Belvedere. As the potter moulds his clay, the boys must be 'moulded' to become 'children of the Lord'. The 'intimate records' reveal how this was achieved, and also how 'children of the Lord' became synonymous with 'soldiers of the Lord'.

The 'mould' in which the children were formed was within the evangelical tradition, but was essentially broad-based, with a bias towards sacramentalism and inclusivity. It is shown to be rooted both in the evangelicalism and missionary zeal of their ancestor, Edward of Watton, and in the Williams' tradition of Bible-based worship and Christian mission in India. Within this mould there is a dazzling record of achievement by both sides of the family: in the Church, medicine and the law in this country, and throughout the Empire by missionary and colonial service. It is a record which today might be considered to be almost guaranteed to dishearten as well as inspire, or to induce rebellion rather than conformity. That never happened. Their family background confirmed the boys' sense of identity and self-worth. The children's diaries and letters show, over twenty years, the sheer happiness of a family life where the parents were as keen on sports as their sons, hiking, skating, climbing and bicycling with them at home and on the continent. Bickersteth, anxious and affectionate, is shown to be adept at comforting a sick child. Ella, sunny, energetic and directive, dances through the records. Despite agonies of home-sickness, the children's school days were, for most of the brothers, enjoyable, their university days idyllic, and they went light-heartedly to war, faced death and danger with courage, and eventually had satisfying and socially useful careers. At the end of their long lives they were all still communicant members of the Church of England.

To understand the children's background, chapters one and two sketch the lives of their forebears. On both sides of the family, success came through their own efforts, often against formidable odds. Of inherited wealth, there is little trace. As Sam told Monier on his twenty-first birthday, he had 'no interesting interview to arrange with you and our family lawyer as sometimes happens when eldest sons come of age'. Ella's family story starts in Newfoundland. It includes a twelve-year-old who fought in the American War of Independence, then in following generations moves to India with service with the East India Company, arrives in England shipwrecked and fatherless, and in a sense returns to India when Ella's father becomes a distinguished Sanskrit scholar. Sam's story begins with a doctor's family in a small market town in Westmorland, moves in the next generations to Africa, India, Ceylon and Japan, returns to parishes in England and an episcopal palace and then to the parishes of Lewisham and Leeds where Sam and Ella's children grew up, and finishes in Canterbury. And, amongst all these moves, in generation after generation, indomitable evangelical women are revealed.

The following chapters trace the development of Sam and Ella from childhood onwards. Ella is revealed as a loving mother, though an advocate of 'tough love', who becomes not only her husband's support but works through him in introducing imaginative social welfare services. Sam's 'intimate records' reveal a devoted father. They provide a picture of urban parish life at the turn of the nineteenth century and the agony of conscience endured by a sensitive, driven, parish priest. The following three chapters trace the boys' progress through their nursery days, school and university using wherever possible their own words, either reported in their parents' diaries or notebooks, or in their own letters and diaries. Finally, the story moves through the Great War and its aftermath, based on the letters the boys sent home and their mother's diaries. New experiences and changing attitudes are revealed. An epilogue brings the story up-to-date.

It also leaves a lot of unanswered questions. 'Intimate records' can conceal rather than reveal; inevitably they shed uneven light on different family members. The records of the childhood of the first son, Monier, are, not surprisingly, far more comprehensive than those of his brothers. When war came, Monier and Geoffrey both remained in this country, so the War Diary predominantly reveals the attitudes, opinions and experience of the four brothers who served in France. The youngest boy, Ralph, succeeded in ensuring that historians knew as little as possible about him by dumping most of his papers at the bottom of a well. Geoffrey's papers remain closed to researchers. A family argument will be carried on in a series of letters but is only resolved – if it ever is – by a face-to-face discussion in the holidays which is not recorded. Frustrating gaps include the lack of any clear response to the Victorian debate on the authenticity of the Old Testament. Sam promised to explain 'all about Genesis' to Monier – but in the holidays. Despite his being a distant relative of Bishop Colenso and at one time head-hunted as Bishop of Natal, all is silence. As late as 1904, Ella was wary of a vicarage guest who was 'an Advanced Thinker on the Higher Criticism', but she promised Monier 'to tell you all when you come home'. We do not even know what Ella thought of the suffragette movement, though she had no doubts about female enfranchisement. As on one occasion she dressed Ralph up as a suffragette for a children's fancy dress party, maybe she endorsed the aim but not the means? Throughout the records, one senses a cautious, middle-of-the-road approach. This generation of Bickersteths was not in the vanguard of change. They were foot soldiers, a few ranks back, hoping for promotion, doing their best to gain it by hard work and knowing the right people, but in the meantime concentrating on doing their everyday duty.

Why then devote a research project to such a wholesome, happy and not particularly distinguished church family? One answer is provided by Elizabeth Turner, an archivist at the Bodleian Library. The Library considered the Bickersteth papers significant because they uniquely recorded, in dense detail, a family that was neither aristocratic nor, in the main, at the top of the ecclesiastical hierarchy. As a result, they are housed in the Department of Special Collections and Western Manuscripts, and were the first family papers to be catalogued electronically. This book therefore attempts to weave together a mass of different sources to reveal how one vicarage family grew up at the turn of the nineteenth century. It does not attempt to psycho-analyse them, but tries to present them 'warts and all'. It does not try to slot them into any ecclesiastical formula; even that useful adjective 'evangelical' is shown to have a Bickerstethian interpretation. It does show that, although children of their time could be 'moulded', eventually the mould will crack and the spirit range free. The result is no doubt 'messy'. That is because it reflects real life: complex, contrary and always fascinating.

Finally, to make as sure as possible that this account holds close to the actualities of the boys' family life, the chapters are arranged around their grandfather's rhyme. The verses may sound trite and alien today, but they meant enough to Sam and Ella for them to preserve them in the family papers. They may help us enter a world and a way of life that has now disappeared.

Sources

Catalogue of the papers of the Bickersteth Family 1915-1976. University of Oxford, Bodleian Library. (www.bodley.ox.ac.uk/dept/scwmss/)

The Bickersteth War Diary. 1914-1945. A copy is held at Churchill College, Cambridge.

The Monier-Williams Archive is held by His Honour Evelyn Monier-Williams.

Lines written in 1889 by Sir Monier Monier-Williams, the children's grandfather

I'm of Belvedere the Vicar
Loving work and hating liquor
And I have a darling wife
Help and sunshine of my life
Prompt to warn, advise and cheer
Loved by all at Belvedere

Then of children we have four[1]
Each of love a living store
Monier, Geoffrey, Julian, Johnny[2]
Each in form and feature bonny;
All with characters like clay
To be moulded day by day

All with faculties of mind
Varying in force and kind
To be drawn out carefully
And be fashioned prayerfully
So that all in act and word
May be children of the Lord,
Growing, waxing, strong and true
Daily as our Lord once grew.

---

[1] The two youngest boys, Morris and Ralph, were not born until 1891 and 1894

[2] Burgon's first name was John

PART I

THE FORMING OF THE MOULD

THE BICKERSTETH FAMILY

*'I am glad to have the inspiration of the three Edwards, but it is
a responsibility to keep up the standard they have set'. Monier.
1907*

Monier, a young curate in Lambeth, was writing to his clerical
father, Sam Bickersteth, and referring to three of his late relatives:
his great-grandfather, Edward Bickersteth, one of the best known
evangelical divines of the mid-nineteenth century, his grandfather,
Edward Henry Bickersteth, Bishop of Exeter, and his uncle Edward
Bickersteth, Bishop of South Tokyo. From childhood, Monier had been
familiar with the oil painting of his great-grandfather: the young face,
lit by a half-smile, gazing into the future. He had been confirmed by
his grandfather, Bishop Edward Henry, in the Palace chapel at Exeter,
whilst Uncle Edward, when he was home on furlough from India
or Japan, would stay with Monier's parents in Lewisham. Moreover,
every time Monier looked in the mirror, it was obvious that he also was
a Bickersteth. His face told the story. He had inherited the distinctive
nose which featured so prominently, generation after generation, in
the family photographs that he had carefully mounted in the album
his father had given him on his tenth birthday. For Monier and his five
brothers, there was no getting away from their past. Nor is there any
sign that they wished to do so. Their ancestors had lived such exciting
lives, had achieved such eminent positions. The name Bickersteth
resonated in so many circles: clerical, medical and legal. It might at
times be a strain to live up to it – Monier, the most sensitive of the boys
obviously felt this – but his robust, energetic brothers took it in their
stride, proud to be Bickersteths and confident of their place in the
world.

They had reason to be proud. They were the latest generation of
the remarkable family of a country doctor who practised in Kirkby
Lonsdale, Westmorland in the latter part of the eighteenth century.

Dr Henry Bickersteth, apothecary-surgeon, and his wife, Elizabeth Batty, had both come from medical families. Little is known about their life, but they moved in County society and although Dr Henry had a flourishing practice, inevitably in a rural practice many of his patients must have been poor. Certainly his income was sufficiently limited for him to augment it by a method not uncommon for a medical man – by looking after 'a lunatic' in the family home. He seems to be the first Bickersteth to have seriously put pen to paper. His *Medical Hints designed for the Use of Clergymen and others* was published, anonymously, in 1820 just before his death. Sick visiting was an essential part of the duty of an evangelical clergyman and his book, with its summary of human anatomy, was written 'to assist in places where professional advice cannot be immediately procured'. His wife, Elizabeth, was attractive and charming. Known as the 'Queen of the Assemblies', she shone at balls and parties. With regrettably little detail, a grand daughter described her as being 'cast in no ordinary mode ... no peril could affright, no misfortune dismay her. On more than one occasion of great personal danger when others were paralysed with terror, her calmness, her promptitude, her wisdom, were alike conspicuous'. Disappointingly, this probably refers to road traffic accidents, rather than anything more spectacular. The early Bickersteths, always travelling, survived a number of very nasty coach crashes. Elizabeth and Henry were a devout couple, Elizabeth, influenced by her sons, moving to a stronger evangelical position in mid-life. Their eldest son, James, died at sea as a young man. His brothers, John, Henry, Edward and Robert all attended the local free school, Kirkby Lonsdale Grammar, which, although being in a relatively remote country village, was known as 'the leading seminary of the North'. Their two sisters, Mary Anna and Charlotte, were mainly educated at home, though Mary Anna spent one year 'at the best school the country afforded' and she was sent to stay in London for a further year 'to have the advantage of masters'. Her brother Henry would help her with her Latin 'making a written translation of the syntax of the Eton Latin Grammar' for her.

When the boys left school, in their early teens, they had to make their own way in the world. Their father helped with college fees as much as he was able, but his sons needed to rely on strict economy, their elder brothers' earnings, scholarships and support from patrons for their further education. Despite this, all four had distinguished careers in their chosen professions. The eldest, John, was eventually ordained, and became Rector of Sapcote and Rural Dean of Peterborough, author of a range of devotional works. Henry, a lawyer, became Master of the Rolls and was ennobled as Baron Langdale. The youngest son, Robert, was a distinguished doctor, founding a dynasty of surgeons who served the Royal Victoria Hospital, Liverpool for over a century. Edward, the great-grandfather who was so much on Monier's mind, became Rector of Watton, a small village near St Albans, now known as Watton at Stone. Their sisters, Mary Anna and Charlotte both married clergymen, but taught both in England and Ceylon.

It was probably the stories of their great-grandfather, Edward of Watton, that would have fascinated the Bickersteth children. At fourteen, he had been sent from Kirkby Lonsdale to London to join his brother John. Their father's plan was that if they became self-supporting there would eventually be enough money to meet their university fees and at the same time they would be able to help finance their brothers' education. Both worked as clerks in the Dead Letter section of the Post Office, an undemanding job which gave them time to educate themselves. John finally went off to university and was ordained, but Edward stayed in London having met another young clerk, Tom Bignold, also far from his home in Norwich, who was articled to a firm of solicitors. Edward obtained an evening job in the same firm. His employers were so impressed with the energetic young man that they paid for his articles and, self-educated, he became a solicitor. Tom invited him home to Norwich where he joined a household as evangelical as that of his doctor father in Westmorland. There he met and married Tom's sister, Sarah, set up in practice, but became increasingly involved in promoting the missionary movement. Never satisfied with 'doing good' at second hand, he turned again to self-education, struggling to master Hebrew with a view to ordination and missionary work. His bishop initially had some qualms about him as he felt that 'his zeal outran his learning', but in 1816 Edward was ordained and was sent out to Sierra Leone on a tour of inspection for the new Church Missionary Society. The stories Monier and his brothers were told about his dangerous canoe journeys, the 'devil's houses', the storms at sea, rivalled anything they were reading in the *Boys Own Paper*.

On his return, he became the Society's first secretary and embarked on nation-wide tours, preaching to huge crowds – in a typical year he would preach over one hundred sermons in about fifty different towns and villages. At the same time, he wrote constantly: his booklets, pamphlets and commentaries achieved huge circulations and continued to be published after his death in 1850. Often the titles dealt with the topics of his time: 'popery', Judaism, and the imminent approach

3

of the millennium. Many others were guides to understanding the Bible which was now so often proudly displayed, but often unread, in parlours up and down the land. Other titles, including his constantly reprinted *On the Lord's Supper,* where he describes the sacrament of Holy Communion and gives practical advice to help the communicant reverently to receive it, are still in print today. In it he tried to address what he felt to be one of the major problems facing the church: the lack of interest that most Christians placed on this sacrament and its infrequent celebration in most Anglican churches. When he left CMS in 1830 to become rector of the small country parish of Watton his travelling and writing continued unabated. In addition, a constant stream of leading English and European clergy, as well as politicians, including Lord Shaftesbury, called at Watton Rectory. By the time of his death in 1850, the name 'Edward of Watton' had become a household word in evangelical circles.

The 'second Edward', whose clerical reputation weighed upon Monier, was Edward of Watton's only son: Edward Henry, Monier's grandfather. For over thirty years he was Vicar of Christ Church, Hampstead, promoting retreats and quiet days – a very new concept to his evangelical brethren. More conventionally, he regularly occupied a soap box on the Heath. He was also a poet, much admired in his day and widely published. In 1885, when three bishoprics became vacant, Gladstone decided to appoint an evangelical, a high churchman and a broad churchman. Edward Henry was the evangelical, and became Bishop of Exeter. In his theology, his open-air preaching and in his hymnody, Edward Henry followed in his father's footsteps. His composition 'Peace, perfect peace' is still sung and his *Hymnal Companion to the Book of Common Prayer* remained in use until the 1960s. Like his father he had clear views of the importance of the sacraments:

> About the Evangelical view of the Lord's Supper, though of course some few hold unworthy views, I have been so accustomed from my childhood to hear my blessed father speak of it as the loftiest privilege of holding tryst with Christ... that I confess all distinctively High Church views have seemed to me poor and thin in comparison.

He wrote his own version of *On the Lord's Supper*, predictably a more poetic approach than that of Edward of Watton.

It is hardly likely, however, that Monier's most vivid recollections of his grandfather would have been his theological views. Memories

The Bickersteths of Kirkby Lonsdale, Westmorland

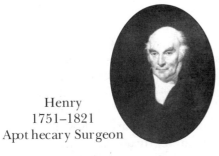

Henry
1751–1821
Apothecary Surgeon

Elizabeth (née Batty)
1758–1832

John
1781–1855
Rector of Sapcote

Henry
1783–1851
Master of the Rolls

Edward
1786–1850
Rector of Watton

Robert
1787–1857
Surgeon

Mary Anna
1789–1849

Charlotte
1791–1846

Bishop Edward Henry and his family

Edward Henry
Bishop of Exeter
1825–1906

Ellen Susannah (née Bickersteth)
1830–1917
'Madre'

Ashley, Sam, Robert,
Edward, Henry (Harry)
Hugh
c.1881

Effie, Mary (May), Amy (standing)
Rosa, Elizabeth (Lily)
Edith
c.1881

of huge Christmas celebrations at the bishop's palace in Exeter and family summer holidays must have taken pride of place. Edward Henry was a family man. He had sixteen children, of whom twelve survived into adulthood. He liked to gather them altogether with their wives, husbands and children. It was no mean feat, but he achieved it by renting a number of houses in some village near the sea and, presumably, sending out invitations in the firm expectation that everyone would respond, regardless of difficulties. In 1888, with four children under seven, Monier's parents, Sam and Ella, took eleven hours to travel from Belvedere in Kent to join Sam's five brothers and six sisters and their families in Lynton in Devon. It involved two rail journeys, crossing London, and finally taking the back seats on a coach, where it was so cold that Sam had to pay an extra 7/6d for inside seats for 'Nurse and the babes' – his youngest son was only six months old. A group photograph shows the assembled family, together with the Bishop and his second wife, in the Valley of Rocks. Five years later, there was a similar gathering at Nefyn, North Wales and this time the party numbered thirty-nine: twenty adults and nineteen grandchildren. When they played cricket they were able to field two bishops: grandfather and Uncle Edward.

Three of Bishop Edward's six sons were ordained: Edward, Sam and Henry, his eldest son, Edward, true to his namesake, Edward of Watton, serving as a missionary. He became the founder and first head of the Cambridge Mission to Delhi and later was sent out to Japan by the Archbishop of Canterbury to bring together the various missionary strands into a single church. In 1886 he became Bishop of South Tokyo and drew up the constitution used today for the Holy Catholic Church of Japan (Nippon Sei-Ko-Kwai) bringing together Japanese, British and American Christians to become the indigenous Anglican Church in Japan. More relevant for the children was the fact that this 'third Edward' was a good, generous uncle, remembering his nephews and delighting them with toys and cheering their financially stressed parents with money for their clothes. They knew him well as he was not physically robust and, badly affected by the climate, would often stay with them when he came to England for recuperation.

Back in Westmorland at the close of the eighteenth century, Dr Henry, though no doubt happy that John and Edward had both decided to enter the Church (and, incidentally, to father 'clerical Bickersteths' throughout the nineteenth and twentieth centuries and beyond) must have also hoped that his third and fourth sons, Henry and Robert, would follow in his footsteps. Henry did go off to London to study medicine but then moved to Cambridge where he had a distinguished academic career and decided to switch from medicine to the law. In 1811 he was called to the bar. A liberal and friend of Jeremy Bentham, he became a King's Counsel and a member of the Privy Council. In 1836 he succeeded Pepys as Master of the Rolls and founded the Public Record Office. In evangelical circles his major claim to fame was his contribution to the Gorham Judgment. Gorham, an impoverished evangelical clergyman in Devon maintained that to become morally regenerate, conversion was necessary. His bishop insisted that the liturgy of infant baptism, which ensured the spiritual regeneration of a child, was sufficient. The case wound its way through the ecclesiastical courts, fomenting huge national publicity. Conflicting views between evangelicals and high churchmen became entrenched. The Court's final judgment was in favour of Gorham for Henry, now Baron Langdale, insisted that its role had not been to try to define the truth of the doctrine of baptism, but only to establish whether Gorham had contradicted the Thirty Nine Articles. A crisis was thus avoided. Much had been at stake: the possible secession of a powerful body of high churchmen or the secession of many evangelicals from the Church of England. From the family's point of view, the influence of Henry, Baron Langdale, persisted through the following generations. When a Bickersteth was not a cleric or a doctor, he was almost certainly in the legal profession.

It was Dr Henry's youngest son, Robert, who linked the Bickersteth name with the medical profession for the next hundred years. Robert was happy to join what his father called 'the shop', becoming an apprentice when he was fourteen years old. He then studied in Edinburgh and London. He came to Liverpool as assistant to a practitioner who 'attended the best society in Liverpool', so Robert was required to look after the remainder – the poor. But his ability was soon recognised and he was elected as surgeon to the Liverpool Infirmary when he was twenty-three and served there for forty-two years. When rich and successful, he built the family home in Rodney Street. Hubbard's silhouette of Robert, his wife and seven of his ten children indicates the spacious charm of its interior. Robert, however, felt that he 'owed a debt of gratitude to the poor' and added a special out-patients department to his home. He took no fees for treating poor patients and, according to family tradition, the queue would stretch 'to the end of Rodney Street and round the corner into Mount Pleasant'. Both his son and grandson were to live at 2 Rodney Street which is now part of John Moore University. In addition, Robert bought a

The Liverpool Bickersteths in their drawing room
2 Rodney Street, Liverpool

Robert Bickersteth, FRCS, dances Emma Katharine on his lap, whilst six year-old Edward Robert, who will become 'the second Dr Bickersteth', is ready to roll his hoop with his older brother, John. Mary Henrietta, eighteen months, toddles towards her mother, whilst Henry, almost four, plays with his toy horse. Clara, the baby, is almost hidden on her mother's lap. In the right hand corner, Ellen Susannah, who will marry Bishop Edward Henry Bickersteth, talks to her big sister, Agnes, the eldest daughter. Another two daughters will be born before the family is complete.

The silhouette was cut by hand by Master Hubbard on 28th March, 1835.

country estate, Casterton Hall, near Kirkby Lonsdale from the local MP, Carus Wilson, a friend of his father. Wilson's son, the evangelical Revd William Carus Wilson, was, in turn, a friend of Edward of Watton who called Casterton Hall 'the Evangelical Hotel of the north' and described the 'retired hamlet' as 'a centre of interest and blessedness to our whole land'. Generations of Bickersteth children were to spend holidays there, and up to 1957 it was the home of Bickersteth maiden aunts.

Robert's son, Edward Robert, also trained at Edinburgh. Lister was a friend and fellow student. Edward Robert began to follow Lister's techniques in the antiseptic treatment of wounds. During a period when there was intense debate over the methods and principles of Lister's antiseptic surgery he wrote a paper in the *Lancet* supporting Lister. He cited cases amongst his patients where amputations had been avoided due to 'suppuration in the knee-joint [being] washed out with carbolic acid lotions'. Perhaps more significantly, he reported that he had successfully used catgut sutures, 'prepared by Lister's methods', when operating on two of his patients with aneurisms, something that Lister had only done on animals. Edward Robert's distinction as a surgeon was marked by his election as FRCS, and he became President of the Surgical Section of the Liverpool branch of the British Medical Association. Like his father, he remained on the staff of the Royal Infirmary and was Consulting Surgeon until his death. His lucrative private practice enabled him to purchase both a yacht and the extensive estate of Craig-y-don in Anglesea. His son, Robert Alexander, was the contemporary of Sam's six sons and so the Bickersteth boys were introduced to a way of life very different from that of their parents. Robert Alexander followed in the footsteps of his father and grandfather, gaining his FRCS in 1891. He became a distinguished clinical teacher and lecturer on surgery, specialising in urology. He served as a major in the RAMC in the Great War and subsequently returned to Liverpool where he remained on the staff of the Royal Infirmary until 1921, thus completing his family's connection with the hospital for over 110 years. All three surgeons are commemorated in the medical window in Liverpool Cathedral.

Dr Henry's sons became so well known and influential that it is easy to forget that he also had two educated and enterprising daughters. His youngest, Charlotte, met her future husband, Robert Mayor, when he was a medical student with her father. He then decided to take Holy Orders, became engaged to Charlotte and immediately swept her off to Ceylon where they were the first CMS missionaries. She had twelve children, among them three boys, Robert, John and Joseph. Charlotte's full life story has yet to be discovered, but there is no doubt that she was a remarkable woman. Of her sons, Robert was a mathematician and became a Fellow of St John's College, Cambridge, John Eyeton became Regius Professor of Latin and President of St John's College Cambridge and Joseph became Professor of Moral Philosophy at King's College, Cambridge. John Eyeton was the sixth of the twelve children, and when he was eleven years old he was at home for three years following scarlet fever. During that period he studied under his mother. 'Not exactly taught' he claimed in a memoir 'for I knew more than she did, but she learnt Greek and Latin in order to help me with my lessons'. A little more generously, he claimed that these three years were the most productive of his life.

Her elder sister, Mary Anna, started her adult life more conventionally, for she left Kirkby Lonsdale to become housekeeper for her brother Robert when he was setting up his practice in Liverpool. There she married a curate, John Cooper, who eventually became Rector of Coppenhall, Cheshire. John had been widowed twice, and had a seven year old daughter, Margaret, on whom Mary Anna lavished love, care – and admonition. When her own babies began to arrive, four (including twins) in two years, her health began to fail. Although her doctor attributed her poor health to 'a failure of vital energy' it would seem that from her sofa she ruled the house, teaching her children, leading Bible classes for local girls, devising programmes of instruction for them and at one time supervising a small school where her older children were teachers. Her theories of child education were ahead of their time and contrasted with the rigid discipline found in some evangelical households. When a child misbehaved, she endeavoured 'to act upon the certainty that he has somewhere a heart, a conscience, or a reasoning faculty – perhaps all three'. Her philosophy was that a child should see that for his teacher 'religion is everything'. A teacher needed grace, love, firmness. At a period when that sequence was still often reversed, she insisted that the teacher should 'always try soothing and encouragement first, forgiving as long as possible'. It was important 'not to expect too much, not by any means to punish every fault and to let warning precede punishment, and prayer for the offender precede reproof.' In short 'by tenderness influence is gained, and good habits formed'. However, such was her personality, that when a Sunday school boy was 'refractory … it was customary to bring him to her sofa and such was her power to win or awe him to submission, that no instance is remembered, in which her influence failed.' On Sundays she attended church, being 'drawn in a garden chair up the aisle to a pew where a couch was prepared'. Of her own children who survived to adulthood, young Mary Anna and Rosa entered religious communities and her eldest daughter, Charlotte, married a clergyman, the Revd John Blucher Wheeler. It is thanks to Charlotte's book *Memorials of a Beloved Mother* that we know so much about Mary Anna. Its success seems to have given Charlotte a relish for literary work and, based on her experience of teaching in her husband's vicarage schools, she produced book after book, mainly Bible-based stories for children. They sold well, and were constantly reprinted.

If all Dr. Henry's children had remarkable careers, the trend continued with his grandchildren. The successful career of Robert and his family in medicine was easily matched by the achievements of Henry, Edward, Robert and Elizabeth, the children of his eldest son, the Revd John Bickersteth, Rector of Sapcote. Henry, named after his grandfather, went out to the Somerset Hospital, Capetown in 1832 when he was nineteen, having 'walked the wards' at St Thomas' Hospital, London. He was associated with the hospital for thirty years, returning briefly to London to qualify as a surgeon, and then going back to Capetown to become Resident Surgeon and a founder of the New Somerset Hospital. His cousin, Charlotte, wrote a sad little memoir of John Lang Bickersteth, Henry's eldest son, who was sent to England to attend Rugby School. His letters home convey his miseries. Dr Arnold was headmaster, though John only spoke to the famous man once. He never reached the top of the school, and died when he was seventeen, his short life having been marked, if Charlotte is to be believed, by remarkable piety.

Henry's brothers, Edward and Robert, were both ordained, Edward becoming Dean of Lichfield, whilst Robert was consecrated Bishop of Ripon. The Bickersteth boys may not have known them, but they could hardly help knowing about them. Dean Edward Bickersteth was responsible for the restoration of the west front of Lichfield Cathedral, and it would be strange if Monier's parents had not attended the dedication in 1884. As incumbent first of St John's, Clapham and then St Giles-in-the-Fields, a huge London slum parish, Robert Bickersteth drew large congregations and set up elaborate schemes of pastoral visiting. He was so popular that in Clapham there is still a road named after him. In the Ripon diocese, he was a preaching and pastoral Bishop, constantly travelling by horseback, endlessly active in proclaiming the Gospel. During his episcopate, he consecrated 157 new or rebuilt churches, and founded the College of Ripon and York

St John. When young Sam Bickersteth, Monier's father, was appointed chaplain to a later Bishop of Ripon, his famous cousin's episcopate was still remembered. Sam's children, Monier, Geoffrey, Julian and Burgon, would all be invited to parties at the Palace and their mother became a firm friend of the bishop's wife. Not surprisingly, Burgon decided he would be a bishop when he grew up. When he was then asked 'What must you be first?' his questioner received the expected answer: 'I must be a good boy', but the six year-old was sufficiently aware of the church hierarchy to add that he supposed he 'must be a Dean first'.

Yet it is among Dr Henry's grand-daughters that some of the most remarkable and unsung Bickersteth achievers can be revealed, overshadowed as they have been by their illustrious brothers. Earnest, hardworking evangelicals all, they were either married to impoverished clergymen or else had clergy husbands who died young and left them with a large family. They all tended to be constantly pregnant and constantly worried about money. Nevertheless, the highest academic achievers of the Bickersteth family can be found among their children, and they have also left behind them a range of books which provide vivid testimony that a Victorian vicar's wife or daughter was well aware of the destitution that was part of both urban and rural life and may well have been more effective than her male relatives in taking enlightened action.

Dr Henry's eldest grand-daughter, Elizabeth, married a priest: Leonard Ottley, Rector of Richmond, Yorkshire and a Canon of Ripon. He died aged fifty-three and left Elizabeth homeless with twelve children, seven of them under fifteen and an 18 month old baby. She moved to Hampstead, probably to be near her cousin Edward Henry where he was vicar of Christ Church, and opened a school, presumably to make a living for her family. Her eldest daughter, Alice, worked there as a teacher. When her mother's school finally closed, she went on to be headmistress of what is now known as the Alice Ottley School, Worcester, Vice-President of the Association of Head Mistresses and a member of the archbishops' central church council on secondary education. Her brothers included Henry Ottley, Canon of Canterbury, Edward Ottley, Canon of Rochester, Robert (Robin) Ottley, Regius Professor of Moral and Pastoral Theology and Canon of Christ Church, Oxford and Sir Charles Ottley, Rear Admiral and Head of Intelligence in the Great War. They were all known to the Bickersteth boys, but perhaps Robin was the closest to them, spending some holidays with them, advising Monier and felt by his mother to be 'a good influence' on Julian at Oxford. No memoir of Elizabeth has been found and the story of how she managed to bring up such a distinguished family remains untold.

The daughters of Dr Henry's second son, Edward of Watton, more than lived up to their father's admonition when, as small children, they asked him if he had any errands for them and were told: 'Do all the good thou canst'. Elizabeth, Charlotte, Emily and Harriet, all became well-known writers and were involved both in missionary work and in social welfare in their own right. Edward of Watton believed in education for women, and he ensured that his daughters were taught by his curate, who was to become a professor of moral philosophy. The girls read their New Testaments in Greek, and their Old Testaments in Hebrew. They had governesses and, where possible, they were sent to boarding schools in Bristol and London. Emily wrote a range of books with titles like *Plain Sunday readings for plough-boys, founded on the Catechism* and *Women's Service on the Lord's Day*. When married to a British officer stationed in India she showed her versatility by publishing *Hindustani verses set to music* and demonstrated her evangelical zeal in action by persuading her brother (Edward Henry) to finance the first CMS missionary to Kerwahla, North India. Her youngest sister, Harriet, married a family physician, Dr Cook, and needed all her Bickersteth energy and determination throughout her long life. She endured fourteen pregnancies in eighteen years, and lost four children in early childhood, six never reaching adulthood, nursing them through typhoid fever, diphtheria, measles and pneumonia. At the same time she ran a Sunday school for girls, a lending library and a clothing club for the poor and began to write religious tracts. Her husband died when their youngest son was eleven, and the family finances which had always been tight became even more constricted. Harriet took in lodgers; the boys' Uncle Faithfull Monier-Williams stayed with her as a young man. He found the household 'too chaotic' for his taste, but admitted that Harriet was 'a very clever woman'. Competent in Greek, French and German, she educated her own children and advertised for more pupils:

> A daughter of the Revd Edward Bickersteth of Watton wishes to hear of one or two little girls to educate with her own daughter between 7 and 8 years old. She offers every educational advantage and a happy Christian home. Terms 100 guineas for one, a reduction for two sisters.

Writing from her wealth of personal experience *Plain Words About Sickness Addressed to the Mothers and Wives of Working Men* became a best seller at a time when such books were rare. Full of economical first aid advice it also reveals her first-hand knowledge of the lives of poor people. In old age, she busied herself in editing the letters and journals of her distinguished medical missionary son, Sir Albert Ruskin Cook. The Bickersteth boys were children when Albert first went out to Uganda in 1896 with his future wife, Katherine, but old enough to hear about their three month overland journey from Mombasa to Mengo, near Kampala where in a shed that had once been a smithy, their cousin opened the first hospital in East Africa. With his medical missionary brother, John, Albert was the first to diagnose sleeping sickness in East Africa, and the Mengo hospital flourishes today. Harriet's third son, Arthur, also had a notable career, becoming professor of classical archaeology at Cambridge.

Harriet, in turning to her pen to supplement the family income, followed in the footsteps of her two older sisters: Elizabeth and Charlotte. Elizabeth was responsible for the first of the two volume biography of their father, Edward of Watton, although the whole work is usually attributed to her husband, T R Birks. It is considered to be one of the better of the many two volume biographies of divines published during that period. She also edited an evangelical magazine. But we see her most clearly in *Doing and Suffering*, a collection of the letters she sent to her younger sister Frances and which were edited by Charlotte. Frances, or Fanny, was in poor health from the age of fifteen when she seems to have developed tuberculosis, but some years later became even more seriously ill with what was probably a form of epilepsy. She died at twenty-nine, seemingly having been in continual head pain, with periods of unconsciousness and convulsions for much of her life. As an invalid, confined to her bed, life seems to have been a constant battle with black depression. She had no control over the thoughts that kept entering her head. She felt that her faith was being tested and she was found wanting: the devil was winning the battle for her soul. Every Sunday Elizabeth wrote to her, sympathising, encouraging and always trying to move her sister's thoughts to the positive, whether in Bible passages or in her daily life. She quoted Isaiah: 'Thy children shall be taught of the Lord, and great shall be the peace of thy children'. 'Observe', wrote Elizabeth 'it is a teaching of peace. Dwell not on temptations, not on the enemy's cavils, not on your sins but on the story of peace'. Although the letters are packed with texts – showing an encyclopaedic knowledge of the Bible – they are also full of simple things to lift the spirits. Elizabeth needs some small items for a parish sale, can Fanny make some mats? Her toddler wants to see 'Auntie in bed'. Could Fanny teach some simple needlework to a village girl? She could empathise with Fanny's frustrations: yes, some visitors were hard to bear, small children could be trying and even father's never-ending cheerfulness could be wearing. At a time when pain relief was virtually nil – Fanny responded badly to chloroform and the other remedy, leeches placed on her head, had only a limited effect – the book must have spoken to the needs of many evangelical women, God-fearing and good-living all their lives, who bore a burden of constant pain and the guilt which extreme evangelicalism could so easily instil. It became a best seller, constantly coming out in new editions. Probably at least 24,000 copies were published. It was reissued in 2009 by an American publisher.

Her editorial success in *Doing and Suffering* in 1860 seems to have started Charlotte on a career of non-stop writing. For years she had been Fanny's main nurse, hardly leaving her bedside. Her father had to insist that she join a family meal at least once a day, in order to have some respite. Now she was free and, going to live with her sister Harriet, she began to help the Cook finances by constantly writing. Books flowed from her pen, mainly Bible-based, though one title stands out. *Lending a Hand or Help for the Working Classes. Chapters on some vexed questions of the day* was published in 1866. It was the year she married the Rev Edward Langton Ward, Vicar of Blendworth in Hampshire, a widower with at least seven children. In *Lending a Hand* she tackled some of the major problems of the day, many of which have a contemporary ring: the decline of family life, homelessness, housing policy, Sunday observance, the servant problem, the indigent poor and the sick poor in workhouses. Each chapter attempts a comprehensive review of the present situation. Was it, she asked rhetorically, appropriate for a lady to write on such subjects? Not if her interest was only political or merely to be able to converse intelligently with brothers or husband. In Charlotte's view, it was the duty of the Christian woman to appreciate the difficulties of the lives of the working class. It was not enough to help them so that the 'seeds of Christianity' might germinate, desirable though that was; nor even because they had a duty to warn the feckless that there was 'an evil to be feared more than social degradation'. There was another reason. They should help because 'the evils under which the [working man] suffers have grown out of the neglect, the selfishness, the indifference to his wants, of society generally: we mean the classes of societies above his own … in our keen pursuit of commerce and manufactures, the interests of the operative have been sacrificed to the wealth he was the means of acquiring for us.' She was sending an uncompromising, radical message. The book ends with a chapter written by Harriet's husband, Dr Cook. It is a plea for the separation of the able-bodied from the sick poor in the workhouses. The sick should be treated separately, and the workhouse in Hampstead, which he attended, could be a model. For a woman who had spent much of her life in a country vicarage, nursing a sick sister, it is an amazing work. How much had she learned at Watton? It seems almost certain that her father must have included her in the discussions that raged to and fro in his library as visiting clergy, politicians and philanthropists called to discuss the problems of the day. How else could she have included a detailed description of housing in Milhous, Basle if it had not been through her father's many European contacts as he worked for the Evangelical Alliance?

How impressed were the Bickersteth boys by all these aunts? Not, apparently, as authors. When working in the Bodleian Library in 1915 Monier's brother, Geoffrey, seems to have disregarded them. He noted that he had found

> 238 books of various kinds by Bickersteths ... Of course, most of the items are sermons, charges and theological and religious works by various Bishops, Deans and smaller fry during the last century and a half.

If his aunts were small fry, they achieved impressive sales figures! They were also very long-lived! Aunt Lottie of *Doing and Suffering* and Aunt Harriet Bickersteth Cook (she insisted on the inclusion of her maiden name) were certainly known to the boys and probably lived in old age in Westbourne Terrace, London with other widowed or elderly unmarried Bickersteth ladies. It was there that Bishop Edward Henry passed his last invalid years with his wife. The boys certainly visited, and when they were older and in London, they would stay at the 'London house'. There are letters as late as the Great War which show how closely they kept in touch with these elderly relatives. Julian wrote to his grandmother from the trenches. 'I can't tell you how much Aunt Edith's cake was appreciated ... From the Colonel downwards, everyone in the HQ Mess of the battalion praised the cake. So please thank Aunt Edie for it very much. Personally I never tasted a better one'. It was a letter guaranteed to please the old ladies.

However, the children had two other 'aunts' or more accurately, cousins by marriage, who could probably never be described as 'old ladies' and who probably did not bake cakes. Harriette Bunyon and Lucy Bignold were formidable women whose connection to the Bickersteths came from that first momentous meeting of young Edward Bickersteth and Tom Bignold in a solicitor's office in London. Edward of Watton married Tom's sister, Sarah, but the two families became more entwined when Sarah's niece, Rosa, became the wife of Bishop Edward Henry and mother of his sixteen children. Tom's other sister, Frances, married Robert Bunyon, Head of the London Office of the Norwich Union, and had two daughters: Sarah, who married John Colenso who would become Bishop of Natal, and Harriette who married Francis McDougall who became Bishop of Labuan. She and her husband went out to Borneo as pioneer missionaries. They worked in Sarawak for twenty years, and although Harriette lost five sons in five years her correspondence and journal show her to be a woman of great strength of character, whose role was crucial as she managed the mission single-handed when her husband was ill or away. It is claimed that 'the mission could never have succeeded without her quiet wisdom'. Her memorial in Winchester Cathedral has the simple inscription: 'She first taught Christ to the women of Borneo'. But the Bickersteth boys must have loved the story of Harriette and her daughter being invited to a native feast and retreating 'in horror on finding served up at it three human heads on a large dish, freshly killed, and slightly smoked with food and sirih *(sic)* leaves in their mouths'.

It is a moot point as to how the other Bignold 'aunt' that the boys knew and loved would have reacted, for she was another strong character. Aunt Lucy Bignold was the youngest daughter of Sir Samuel Bignold, after whom Sam Bickersteth had been named. His father had founded the insurance company, the Norwich Union, which is now known as Aviva. Sir Samuel was elected Mayor of Norwich three times as well as being the Member of Parliament. Aunt Lucy involved herself in every social cause in Norwich: the Police Court Mission, the School Boards, University extension lectures and, above all, her Bible class for working men which she held in her own home in Surrey Street every Sunday afternoon for sixty-four years. She kept the family home, next door to the Norwich Union main office, exactly as her father had left it and it became the focus for County events. There she entertained every leading citizen and visitor to Norwich, displaying what the Bignold cousins described as 'the whole goldsmiths' and silversmiths' alliance'. When the Church Congress was held in Norwich in 1895 the house was buzzing with bishops and clergy, as well as guests as varied as Sir John Gorst, Solicitor General, and General Sir Charles Warren, fresh from leading a military expedition to Bechuanaland. Ella and Sam were enlisted to help with the entertaining. At Christmas and New Year their boys would be invited to Christmas parties and balls where they could demonstrate their dancing skills laboriously learned in the vicarage dining room. Aunt Lucy funded trips to the pantomime and circus for the children when they were little and when they were older slipped them the occasional and very welcome £5 tip. In old age she was still visiting the vicarage 'so active and interested in everything', noted Ella, and in 1918, aged 83, she was photographed standing on a tank urging the citizens of Norwich to buy war bonds. Shortly before her ninetieth birthday her 'working men' carried her coffin for her funeral service in Norwich Cathedral.

In the last quarter of the eighteenth century, one of Wilberforce's ambitions, apart from the abolition of the slave trade, was 'the reformation of manners'. By the middle of the nineteenth century it has been claimed that the evangelical movement had virtually achieved this. Christian influences and Christian ethics were embedded in Victorian society. In two letters from his father to Monier we catch a glimpse of that world that has vanished. The first described the funeral of his cousin, Sir Charles Bignold, Sir Samuel's son, in 1895. Norwich came to a standstill. For two miles the streets were crowded with people as the cortege wound its way to the church. In the church yard the path was lined with soldiers. On the coffin was placed Charles Bignold's open Bible, the one his mother, Lady Bignold, had used till her death. It was open at the words 'I know whom I have believed' from S Paul's letter to Timothy. That civic service echoed the certainty and splendour displayed by the Church a year earlier when the Church Congress was being held in Exeter. His father described it in another letter to Monier, then twelve years old.

> There were 650 robed clergy in the procession, and 26 Bishops and one Canadian Archbishop after whom came at the end of the long procession your Grandfather. Before him was carried by Uncle Harry the beautiful ivory pastoral staff, and behind him, by the tallest clergyman in the Diocese, the magnificent banner which has been made for this Exeter Congress. On every hand pictures of Grandfather were being sold and he has been universally praised for his gentle and courteous manner even by those who do not agree with his opinions.

Such assurance did not last. Even whilst Sam Bickersteth was writing, secularisation was on the march, and Biblical criticism and Darwinism had been making deep inroads into evangelical belief. But change does not come overnight. In the sheltered world that the Bickersteth children grew up in, such doubts were brushed aside. The churches they attended were full, and had been full for a generation. The family had an inner assurance of both their place in the world and in the stability of that world. Bickersteths had breeding; they were gentlemen. They had standards and a duty to lead, to work hard and long, and to achieve. It was against this background that Samuel and Ella Bickersteth were to mould their sons.

Background reading

Bebbington, D W *Evangelicalism in Modern Britain. A history from the 1730's to the 1980's.* Routledge (1989)

*Aglionby, E K *The Life of Edward Henry Bickersteth DD, Bishop and Poet* Longmans Green & Co. (1907)

*Bickersteth, C *Memoir of John Lang Bickersteth.* The Religious Tract Society. (1851)

* Bickersteth, S *Life and Letters of Edward Bickersteth, Bishop of South Tokyo.* Sampson Lowe (1889) Paperback edition Bradley Press (USA) (2008)

Bignold, R *Five Generations of the Bignold Family 1761-1947.* Batsford (1948)

*Birks, T R *Memoir of Rev Edward Bickersteth.* Two volumes. Seeleys (1832).

Bramston, M *An Early Victorian Heroine: the story of Harriette McDougall* SPCK (1910)

Foster, W D *Albert Ruskin Cook 1870-1951* Prestbury, published by author. (1978)

*Hardy, T D *Memoirs of the Rt Hon Henry Lord Langdale.* Two volumes. Bentley (1852)

*Wheeler, C B *Memorials of a Beloved Mother.* Cooper, Wertheim & Macintosh (1866) Paperback edition. Publisher unknown. (2009)

*Ward, C (née Bickersteth) (ed) *Doing and Suffering: Memorials of Elizabeth and Frances.* Seeleys (1860). Paperback edition. Publisher unknown. (2009)

*   indicates the book can be read in full on the internet. An increasing
    number of pre-1900 publications by the Bickersteths, including
    most of the titles mentioned in this chapter and many of Edward of
    Watton's pamphlets can also be read in this way.

Bishop Edward Henry and family 1888

'It was delightful to see the Bishop with his twelve children around him, and Frank and Lottie and me ... 30 in all'. Ella's diary 8.8.1888. Sam stands behind his brother, Edward, holding baby Burgon, whilst Ella is in the front row with Geoffrey on her lap. Monier is next to his cousin Dolly Rundall, and Julian sits on the lap of his aunt Lily. All three have to keep their hats on!

The Golden Wedding of Sir Monier and Lady Julia Monier-Williams, 1898

Torrie, Gordon, Evelyn, Monier, Alice (Cyril's widow), Sam, Geoffrey, Stanley with Hugh, Outram, Montie Mildred, Bernard, Georgie, Monier Faithfull, Dame Julia, Sir Monier, Ella, Mary, Isobel, Florence Ralph, Jack

Lionel, Reginald, Roy, Crauford, Angela, Morris, Julian, Burgon, Lawrence, Brewse, Clare, Randall.

The Monier-Williams Family

Mary Brown
1780–1858

Lt. Colonel Monier Williams
1775–1823

Hannah Sophia Williams
(née Brown)
1793–1877

Sir Monier Monier-Williams
1819–1899

Lady Julia Faithfull Monier-Williams
1826–1908

2

THE MONIER-WILLIAMS FAMILY

O that thou wouldst bless me indeed, and enlarge my coast, and that thine hand might be with me and that thou wouldst keep me from evil. I Chronicles 4.10

Like many small children, Sam and Ella's eldest son used to enjoy signing his letters home with his full name: Edward Monier Bickersteth. In fact, he was always known by his second name 'Monier' or, when a baby, 'Mona'. No doubt his mother had a hand in that. She was a Monier-Williams, and proud of it. From the children's point of view, it had a much more exciting ring than that of Bickersteth. Brave young soldiers fighting in foreign lands, a heroic death and a bandit-infested journey all featured in the stories she told them about her side of the family. Even Captain Hedley Vicars, so often held up as a model to small boys in the Victorian period, was a distant relative. He had gone down in history as the 'soldier saint' who gave up his tent to his men, and died bravely in the siege of Sebastopol. Through her stories two more strands were added to the inheritance of the Bickersteth children: the demands of military duty and an awareness of Empire. A third strand, evangelicalism with its strong emphasis on active, personal service, reinforced Bickersteth belief. And, as with the Bickersteths, glimpsed amid the tales she told of manly bravery, were stories of the courage, and hints of the influence, of strong, devout women.

Ella could take her children back to the days of their great-great grandfather. George Williams left Swansea in 1761 and settled in Newfoundland. By 1796 he had become Chief Magistrate and his large family included two sons, George and Monier. Their lives were guaranteed to catch the interest of the Bickersteth boys. In 1776, George, aged twelve, went with his uncle, Major Griffith Williams, to serve as a volunteer with Burgoyne's Royal Regiment of Artillery in the Northern Campaign of the War of Independence. He soon saw active service, for in the same year he was present at the Battle of Stillwater when five hundred British soldiers lost their lives. Such was the shortage of men that George, despite his youth, was commissioned as an ensign.

According to family stories, he carried the flag of truce when General Burgoyne surrendered after the battle of Saratoga – though maybe this was something the boys would have preferred to forget. They would have been pleased to know that the regimental records instead suggest that it was probably a Lieutenant-Colonel Robert Kingstone who carried the white flag. Later, George served with the 20th Regiment in Nova Scotia, St Domingo and Jamaica, Ireland and Holland before retiring in 1800 with the rank of Major. He settled in Liverpool, commanding the Liverpool Volunteers, with the rank of Lieutenant-Colonel. There he cultivated his land, and was a notable JP who, despite being the terror of all drunken offenders, was known as 'the poor people's magistrate', for he would hear cases at five in the morning so that a labourer would not lose a day's work. In 1832 he was invited to stand as MP for Ashton-under-Lyme, his supporters finding him 'with a spade in his hand and good strong clogs on his feet, working on his farm'. He refused on principle to run a campaign, and without any canvassing on his part he was returned as Member for Ashton in the first Reform Parliament. When attending the House, he used to stay with his niece in London. Many years later, the boys' grandfather Monier Monier-Williams remembered the honest, unconventional Colonel who stayed at his mother's house. He recalled that, at the age of thirteen, he had been 'somewhat scandalised by [Uncle's] radical opinions'.

The story of the Colonel's brother, Monier, was equally exciting. He was the 'first Monier', the fifth son of George Williams and the Bickersteth boys' great-grandfather. Born in Newfoundland, he was probably named after his mother, Mary Monier. He served as a cadet in the Honourable East India Company, going out to India in 1798. Rising through the ranks, he saw active service under Colonel Wellesley, afterwards the Duke of Wellington, and was promoted to Lieutenant Colonel. From 1807 to 1823 he was Surveyor General for the East India Company and completed the 'Great Map of India', begun by his predecessor, Colonel Reynolds. As the name suggests, the map was huge. With a scale of eight miles to the inch, it measured four hundred square feet and was the first attempt to compile a comprehensive map of India. It represented years of fieldwork by East India Company staff. Annotated 'finished copy by Monier Williams' it hung for many years in East India House, the Company's London headquarters. It was whilst he was serving in India that Monier met and married Hannah Sophia Brown. A young English woman, born in India, she was the only surviving daughter of her father's first marriage. John Thomas Brown had spent most of his life in India, probably with the East

India Company. She, however, had lived mainly in England, having been sent home with her ailing mother to go to boarding school. After her mother's death, her father finally returned to England where he married again. His new wife, Mary Sneade, conscious of her delicate position as stepmother, wrote to her stepdaughter, trusting that she would 'not find me very disagreeable' and hopefully adding that 'the large portion of good humour which your father possesses, my love, cannot fail to make us happy together'. Her hopes were realised and Mary Brown would become an important and influential figure both in Hannah's life and in the lives of her children. In the meantime, Mary and the Sneade family took Hannah to their hearts and Hannah soon acquired a half sister, Ellen, and eventually two half brothers. Then, when she was seventeen, her parents felt that Hannah, pale, awkward and shy, would have a better chance of marriage in Bombay than if she stayed in England. It was arranged that she should return to India in the care of her Uncle, George Brown, who was taking up a prestigious appointment with the Bombay Council. It sounds an incredibly harsh decision, and the Sneade/Brown family as a whole were undecided about its wisdom, but there is no evidence that it produced any rift. The loving relationship between Hannah and her relations by marriage would withstand the test of time and be crucial in the future.

Hannah arrived in India in August and there she met the thirty-three years old handsome Lieutenant Colonel Monier Williams. A whirlwind romance followed, and they were married at Christmas. Hannah was just nineteen. Her father was delighted. He remembered Monier from his own India days and wrote to his daughter with 'tears of joy' that she was to marry 'a gentleman whom but to know is to esteem'. They settled down to family life and soon the babies began to arrive. But her husband's health began to fail, and in 1821 he was forced to return to England with his pregnant wife, their daughter and four small boys. It was a horrendous journey of five months, and the ship encountered a violent storm off the Azores. The mate was drunk, the captain exhausted, the ship was old. Monier took command and 'steered the ship safely home'. They landed in Penzance early in 1822 and made for Hannah's father's home in Bath. Their arrival went down in family history: 'It was highly picturesque. A train of Indian servants in turbans and tunics carried in four little dark-eyed boys – George, Charles, Monier, Alfred – and one little girl, Mary'. In due course, Hannah's last baby arrived, another Hannah Sophia. The family was now complete. It included the Bickersteth boys' grandfather, later to be known as Sir Monier Monier-Williams.

Unfortunately, their troubles were far from over. The Colonel's health worsened, and in the autumn he decided to return to a warmer climate. The family travelled overland to Marseilles to set sail for Naples, via Toulon. They had booked a passage on a Neapolitan brig which was anchored outside the harbour. Despite storm force winds, the captain insisted that the family were rowed in a small open boat to reach the brig. Monier Williams was so ill that he was laid on a mattress at the bottom of the boat, and his wife and children sat around him. Three year-old Monier never forgot it, or the 'crowds [that] collected on the quay to see us swamped'. Once on board the brig, the weather worsened, 'the Italian sailors were paralyzed with fright' and again his father had to take over the navigation. The passage from Toulon to Naples took two weeks, but Monier Williams was so exhausted that he died the day after landing. Hannah was left with the problem of bringing her five children and baby back to England from Italy. She managed it with the help of the British Consul and by hiring a large coach and the services of a Swiss courier. Their epic journey became part of folk lore; there are at least three different accounts in the family memoirs. They had to cross the Pontine Marshes, at the time 'a nest of brigands', and were stopped by 'a band of ruffians', but were allowed to pass unmolested when told that the coach carried only a widow and her children. They then found the Simplon Pass blocked by snow, and crossed it by sledge. Eventually they reached London, Hannah maintaining that the name of their Swiss escort, Louis Mignard, 'should be written in letters of gold.' Once safely in England, the Brown family were ready to help, and Mary Brown and her daughter, Ellen, again filled the gap as Hannah began a new life for herself and her children. Fortunately, her late husband had set up a trust for his family. As a result, their lives seem to have been of unostentatious comfort.

They settled in one of Nash's newly-built houses in Cambridge Terrace in Regents Park, not far from Uncle Benjamin Brown's London house in York Terrace. In Spring they could listen to the nightingales, but from the Park entrance gates, the boys watched the first London omnibuses go by. Mary and Hannah, Monier's 'two clever sisters' would seem to have been educated at home, their mother encouraging them 'to revel freely in Walter Scott's novels, Pope's Homer, Dryden's Virgil and the Arabian Nights'. A French master called two or three evenings a week until all the children were fluent speakers. School fees for the boys were paid by the trust, though Hannah had no choice of school. She wanted her second son, Charles, to go to a private school in Laleham run by Mr Thomas Arnold (Dr Arnold of Rugby to be). The trustees would have none of it, and Hannah had to abide by their decision. Monier and Alfred went to King's College School, in the basement of King's College, walking there each day, carrying their books and their lunch. In due course, Charles studied for the law and George became an architect, a legacy from Aunt Farrar, a Sneade relative, meeting the cost of their articles. Both had successful careers in their chosen professions. Monier was undecided, but had leanings towards the Church, so that his mother felt he would fittingly be 'the clergyman son' without which no respectable upper-middle class family could be complete. He was a clever boy and as Oxford was the first step towards ordination, Hannah decided that should be his destination and put his name down for Balliol. Alfred, her youngest, had no doubts. He wanted only to join the Army and return to India. He enlisted and served as an ensign in the 2nd Grenadier Guards, Bombay Infantry. Monier was sent off to stay with a clergyman in Sussex to be coached for university entrance. There he was shocked by the indolence of his tutor who left all the parish work to his curate. It was not Monier's idea of the way a clergyman should behave – was not his half-brother Joe wearing himself out with non-stop activity in his first London parish and risking a nervous breakdown? But his Latin improved greatly and he matriculated and entered Balliol in October 1837. Despite his Indian birth and some initial prejudice, he had 'eighteen happy months' at Balliol. His classical studies had to compete with rowing where he was a founder of the Oxford Rowing Club, and, as he phrased it in middle age, he revelled in 'the companionship of joyous and high-spirited comrades'. Alfred's letters made him long to join him in India and when Alfred tactfully wrote that he felt his brother's 'tastes and inclinations [at Oxford] would be likely to unfit [him] for the clerical profession', Monier thought he might well be right. He wrote home to his mother that he did not know what career to follow, but he was sure he was wasting her money and his time in trying to prepare himself for the Church.

Hannah immediately turned to the career path that she knew best: the Indian Civil Service. She forwarded his letter to a contact in the East India Company. The result was that Monier successfully sat the next entrance examination for the Company's college at Haileybury, near Hertford. He was told that if in the next two years he passed four examinations, he would go out to India as one of the Company's civil servants. That might lead to his becoming a Judge of one of their Supreme Courts or the Lieutenant-Governorship of 'a province as big as England'. It would be a huge change of career. It was from this time that Monier claimed that he began to awake to the earnestness of life, and the necessity laid upon me of battling with its difficulties, and the effort needed for the simple duty of acquitting myself like a man in the conflict.

The difficulties were formidable. Not only did he have to learn Persian, Hindustani, Arabic and Sanskrit, but classics, mathematics, law and political economy were also on the timetable. Monier had never heard of Sanskrit, the ancient and sacred language of India, and nor had anyone at Balliol. His tutor referred him to the Greek philologist, Robert Scott, who told him 'It is the most difficult language in the world, but once mastered, it opens the way to a knowledge of all the languages of the world.' Scott admitted that he 'never could even master the letters. They seem to warn off the intruder like a barbed fence'. But he did give Monier an introduction to the Oxford Sanskrit professor – 'a dried-up old gentleman not quite sixty years of age, seated at a big table, surrounded by big books, and pouring over an abnormally big book'. He was not encouraging. 'He appeared to sprinkle a little cold water on my youthful ardour', noted Monier many years later. Rightly convinced that there was no-one in the whole of the University who had any knowledge of the Indian Civil Service, Monier found a private tutor in London, and worked with him non-stop for a month before he went to Haileybury. It gave him a head-start, and he consistently excelled in oriental languages.

Then in his second year came news of Alfred's death. Their mother told the Bickersteth boys the story of her uncle Alfred and showed them the ring her father had given her to wear in his memory. Alfred had died bravely, aged nineteen, in the First Afghan War. He had been part of a detachment ordered to relieve four hundred men who had been besieged for two months by hostile tribesmen in the fort of Kahun in Nepal. The storming party approached the fort through the narrow Nuffoosk Pass where the ascent was so steep that if a man lost the track he had to crawl on hands and knees. Alfred was among the leaders and was shot through the heart. His mother was shattered at the death of her youngest son, and for her sake Monier decided to abandon his hopes of Indian service and return to Oxford to complete his degree. The complexity and intricacy of Sanskrit, however, had captivated him, and he continued to study oriental languages. Despite a breakdown in health, he graduated and returned to Haileybury, this time as a teacher. Now a serious young man, active in parochial activities and concerned for the moral and spiritual welfare of his students, he married Julia, the youngest daughter of the evangelical Rector of Hatfield, Joseph

Faithfull. Thoughts of ordination, planted by his mother, never left him, but he soon had a young family to support. When Haileybury closed, he moved on to Cheltenham College, again teaching oriental languages, and then made the major move of his life to Oxford where, in 1860, he stood for election as the Boden Professor of Sanskrit.

The professorship was a prestigious and well-paid position, founded in 1832 by Colonel Boden to promote 'the more general and critical knowledge of the Sanskrit language, as a means of enabling Englishmen to proceed in the conversion of the natives of India to the Christian religion'. It would thus help satisfy the urge that Monier still felt towards full-time church service, and also give him scope to use and develop his specialist knowledge. The election period lasted seven months as candidates from India needed that length of time to travel to England. In the event, the only other candidate was Max Müller, Oxford Professor of Modern Comparative Philology, a distinguished Oxford Sanskrit scholar who had just published *A History of Ancient Sanskrit Literature* and was now working on his six volume translation of the *Rigveda*. Monier, who by then had been Oriental Professor at Haileybury College for fourteen years, had already published the first Sanskrit-English dictionary and had written a new Sanskrit Grammar as well as translations of other Sanskrit works. He won the election by a majority of 223 votes, 1,433 members of Convocation having voted.

It had been a long, bitter and expensive battle. All 5,000 members of Convocation had a vote, and had to be canvassed. The Williams family raised £862, Hannah contributing £400. Every college in Oxford had two committees, one for each candidate. In London a further two committees were formed, keeping the election in the public eye through the *Times*. The Bishops of Durham, Chichester and Salisbury supported Monier Williams. Max Müller also had distinguished supporters including, in Oxford, Dr Pusey and the Dean of Christ Church. Thousands of leaflets were circulated, extravagant claims and counter-claims made. The election became vicious, developing along religious and political lines. Both men supported the purpose of the professorship. Both believed that their translations helped missionaries in the field to serve more effectively. However, massive Press publicity meant that Monier Williams began to be presented as a Conservative both in politics and religion, whilst Max Müller was seen as a Liberal and a representative of German theology. His German birth was a matter of disquiet. Yet was it possible to vote for an evangelical, suspicious of recent Biblical research, still clinging to the old certainties about the authorship of the Bible? Monier Williams was clear that evolution theory could not be applied to the Christian faith; between Christian and non-Christian religions there was 'a bridgeless chasm which no theory of evolution can ever span'. Müller took a broader view. Was it so broad that it was suspect? asked his opponents. Müller saw the Bible as being above all other sacred books, but argued that Christianity could be supplemented by other faiths, extracting 'sweetness and light from all kinds of theology, reconstituting those essences within its own body'. Monier Williams had been born in India and his links with the prestigious East India Company carried weight. He was both a Sanskrit teacher and examiner. Müller's reputation rested on his distinguished work as a translator, writer and lecturer. Today it is thought that he was probably the man best qualified for the position. Certainly Monier Williams' clear-eyed daughter, Ella, the mother of the Bickersteth boys felt this. Her father, she wrote, had 'outstanding ability [but] it must be admitted that Müller possessed far greater brilliance'. For the rest of his life, Müller deeply resented the outcome of the election. Not only did the two men never speak to each other, but no Oxford hostess could invite both to her dinner parties.

The election confirmed Monier's standing within the evangelical wing of the Church of England. How had he arrived at this position? Not all the links in the story have been identified, for although Monier considered a conversion experience was essential, no mention has been found of his claiming this for himself, though there were a number of texts, including the prayer of Jabez, which he felt were milestones in his spiritual life. The main impetus seems to have come through a group of strong-minded women: his mother, Hannah Sophia, 'a veritable incarnation of combined energy and wisdom', his godmother, Mary Brown, his half-sister Ellen and his wife, Julia. Geography also played its part: Haileybury College was in a corner of Hertfordshire encompassing Ayot St Lawrence where John Olive, his half-sister's husband, was rector. The Hatfield living, where his future father-in-law, Joseph Faithfull, was rector, was about twelve miles away. At nearby Watton, the rector was the Revd Edward Bickersteth, 'Edward of Watton'. All were within the riding distance, and often the walking distance, of an active, athletic young man like Monier.

Monier always claimed that his 'earliest religious impressions' were owed to his mother. She had begun to prepare him for a clerical life just before his sixteenth birthday. He was required to take morning family prayers and, on Sundays, to take notes of every sermon he heard, a habit which he continued long into his life. The family attended the proprietary St John's Chapel in Bedford Row where the services were conducted by the Honourable and Revd Baptist *(sic)* Noel. It was a fashionable church to attend and Baptist Noel, son of Sir Gerard Noel Noel, brother to the Earl of Gainsborough, was a powerful evangelical preacher. He was one of the few Anglicans who, true to his name, became a Baptist and caused a sensation when he was publicly baptized in 1849. He was twice elected chairman of the Baptist Union. Monier Williams never forgot those evangelical services of his youth, and after a life-time of studying oriental religions his memory dwelt

> on the simple worship and simple psalm-singing by a united congregation, without surpliced choirs, without chanting, without intoning and followed by earnest heart-stirring sermons and no collections except on rare occasions.

No wonder that in later life he detested the 'hideous idolatry' that he saw in the Hindu temples in India and appreciated the 'severe anti-symbolism conspicuous in all the surroundings of Muhammadan *(sic)* mosques'.

Yet it is in a description of his stepmother, Mary Brown, that Monier draws his most vivid and formidable picture of the influence of an evangelical woman. Mary Brown, in 1826, had listened to a sermon preached by Dr. Wilson, brother-in-law to Bishop Sumner, which reassured her that the new evangelicalism was consistent with her Church of England faith. She took it to heart. Monier described her in a memoir as:

> ... very kind-hearted, and gifted with a vigorous mind, strong common sense and still stronger religious opinions. Her bête-noire was Popery and her great aim was to instil evangelical doctrine and a horror of the Pope and of all his works, into the minds of her children and grandchildren. Every day she read a chapter in the Bible to us two boys [Monier and Alfred] commenting on every verse, and doing her best to sow the seed of uncompromising Protestantism in our youthful minds. I can remember in this way she read through the whole of the Gospel of St John and the Acts of the Apostles and on our leaving her entreated us with tears in her eyes never to forget them – and I never have forgotten that parting injunction.

Mary Brown's views were shared by her daughter, Ellen, Monier's half sister. Monier was very fond of Ellen:

A remarkable person, quite unlike any other woman in the world, very handsome, but rather of the gypsy type of beauty, full of affectionate impulses and intellectual activities, enthusiastic in her religious opinions and quite as pronounced in her denunciations of Romanism as her mother, Mrs. Brown. ... I trace back the first stirrings of real spiritual life in my heart to the emotions, awakenings, and convictions produced in me by Mr and Mrs Olive.

When she married the Revd John Olive the Williams family had been delighted. Never, wrote Hannah, had she met 'so agreeable and elegant a young man'. 'Handsome, elegant, musical, refined in manner and mind and conduct' was the verdict of the Brown family. He was also wealthy – and he played the flute. Ayot St Lawrence was a poor living, but true to their evangelical convictions, John and Ellen visited the poor, read to the sick until, Ellen said, she became hoarse, and organised a school. Not all were grateful; an anonymous rhymester at the time gives a rather different impression

> Clergy of Ayot St. Peter and St. Lawrence too,
> Mixture of Piety and Tally-ho;
> Builders of Churches by way of Gammon,
> To keep on terms with God and Mammon,
> Preachers of Love, Apes of Humility,
> Proud as Lucifer, lacking his Ability.

Whatever their failings to connect with the 'lower classes', there is no doubt about John and Ellen's hospitality. They welcomed Hannah and her children to their home, and many holidays were spent there. It was a 'most picturesque little parish, beautifully situated among fields, lanes and woods, fragrant with wild flowers and resonant with the notes of birds' recalled Monier; it was where he 'passed some of the most delightful days of [his] boyhood'. At John Olive's suggestion, his father and brother were commemorated in the newly-built parish church for both Lieutenant Colonel Monier Williams and Alfred had been buried abroad. All the family drafted possible inscriptions, and Monier's was chosen. Far in the future, Ellen's daughter, another Mary, would marry into the aristocracy and in years to come one of her descendants, the Earl of Cavan, would be a helpful friend to the family of Monier's daughter – Ella Bickersteth.

Already, though, the Olive family and the Bickersteths were no strangers. Ayot was about ten miles from Watton, and Edward of

Watton and his wife were among the newly weds' first visitors in 1831. John had been warned that Mrs Bickersteth was: '... a downright goody [although of] sterling piety and worth' and Ellen regretted that the two daughters who accompanied their mother were 'not very good-looking', but friendship flourished. Edward would sometimes stay overnight at Ayot and on at least one occasion he met Mary Brown who seized the opportunity to tell him how helpful she had found his *Essays on Prayer*. Both John Olive and Joseph Faithfull became members of Edward's circle of local evangelical clerics. A constant interchange of visits between Ayot, Watton and Hatfield rectories seems to have resulted, with the annual Church Missionary Society garden parties at Watton and Hatfield being the high spots of the summer season. The five Faithfull daughters and Edward of Watton's five girls already knew each other. Ellen, for a number of years childless, must have been delighted to have female company of her own class. What did they talk about when they met? All the women were involved in sick visiting, and teaching poor children, often in schools that they had helped to found. Charlotte Bickersteth, as has been shown, was seriously thinking about the responsibilities of her class towards the least privileged. It is impossible to believe that the problems they came across, as well as church matters, were not discussed. From childhood, Edward of Watton had shared his impressions 'on the character of public men, or the tendency of public measures in Church or State' with his daughters as well as his son. The Faithfull girls were also well-informed. They were frequent visitors at Hatfield House, for their father as a young man had been a companion of the old Marquis of Salisbury at Oxford, and the Hatfield connection had been maintained over the generations. Lord Robert Salisbury, the local Member of Parliament, who would eventually be Prime Minister, had been a pupil in Faithfull's school in the rectory. Admittedly, he had been so desperately unhappy there that he described it as 'an existence amongst devils'. Nevertheless, the school still flourished, attracting the sons of leading evangelical politicians and the local aristocracy, preparing them for Eton or Harrow. The Faithfull girls helped with the teaching and so their contacts with the political world as well as with evangelical circles increased. They were included in regular invitations to Watton for 'an early dinner' when, after the meal was ended, the guests continued to sit round the table and listen to one of their number talk about his special interest. When Edward's curate, Thomas Birks (who would later be a Professor of Moral Theology) was the speaker, Cecilia Faithfull admitted that 'the effect produced was like the flow of a deep river ... on and on flowed the river with, I fear, the result of closed eyes and nodding heads among the hearers'. Her sister, Emily, could also bring news of a wider world. She was the confidante and companion of Sir Robert's daughter, Lady Blanche Balfour, the mother of a future Prime Minister. Another Emily Faithfull, a cousin, was working in London to 'promote the employment of women' and in 1860 would open the Victoria Press, employing female compositors. On a lighter note, every curate in the area must have been discussed; nearly all the girls married clergymen. Was it only by chance that Monier's brother George also married the daughter of a local vicar and that the youngest Faithfull daughter, Julia, married Monier? Intriguingly, Monier's two sisters broke the rule. They both married prosperous business men. Perhaps their mother could not find them affluent clergymen to equal John Olive?

It was at Ayot that Monier first met Julia. In November 1847, he called at the rectory and found Julia was staying there as a house guest. Monier had been teaching at Haileybury College for three years, his *Elementary Grammar of the Sanskrit Language* had just been published, and he was beginning to think that he could now afford marriage – no longer was it necessary to hold to his resolution that 'Sanskrit must be my wife'. Hatfield was about ten miles from Haileybury and, delightfully, Monier found it was near enough for his white Arab mare to 'carry her master [there] quite cheerfully' within an hour. In May of the following year Julia and Monier were engaged, and they were married a few months later. It was a very happy marriage. Six sons were born and, to Monier's great joy, a daughter, Ella, the mother of the Bickersteth boys.

When Monier and Julia returned from their wedding tour, they resolved, noted Monier. 'to mould [their] lives according to the pattern which my wife brought with her as her best dowry from her father's home at Hatfield Rectory'. That pattern was one where 'family prayers, religious instruction, the love and fear of God, were the rule of conduct.' True to his word, he recorded that from the first day of his marriage he 'began a practice of explaining the Bible to my servants and, as time went on, to my children every morning at prayers'. It was thirty-five years before he finally admitted that 'force of circumstances, old age and infirmity obliged me to seek spiritual consolation in my closet'. Together husband and wife formed and taught in a Sunday school and Monier held a class for 'poor men from the neighbouring cottages'. They helped the local Rector of Hertford with sick visiting and reading to the poor. They started a clothing club, though the Sunday School superintendent ran off with the money and Monier had to find £30 from his own pocket to make good the loss. Looking back, he could 'only think with sincere humiliation of our inconsistencies and of the little good we were ever able to effect'. Nevertheless, when the family moved to Oxford, much of the same regime continued, though as their children grew up, there was some relaxation. At Hatfield, Julia had never been allowed to go to the theatre; card-playing and smoking were unthinkable. Smoking and card-playing were at first banned in Oxford, but slowly her sons 'instilled in [their mother] very different ideas. She actually became fond of going to the theatre and of playing a game of cards herself, and a smoking-room was always provided'. Family life was far from restrictive. Their father had an extraordinarily wide range of hobbies, which he shared with his children. He could fascinate them with his conjuring tricks, and entertained by playing his concertina. He excelled as a skater and was a keen photographer and amateur astronomer and involved his sons and his daughter in all these interests. Their Oxford home became an open house to a steady stream of students. There was Bible reading and prayer on Sunday evenings. Young Edmund Knox, later to be Bishop of Manchester, described it as 'a little home sanctuary in a life otherwise shut off from all ladies' society'. Nor were the students all nascent clergymen. Francis Benson, later to be Sir Frank Benson, a distinguished actor, came to Leeds many years later to speak at the celebrations for Shakespeare's tercentenary. His speech ended 'with a fine peroration declaring his belief in God and man'. He whispered to Ella: 'I learned a good deal of that in your Father's house at Oxford.' Amongst the visitors was young Samuel Bickersteth, invited because of the Watton connection. As a result, he met Ella. They became engaged and married in 1881.

Two large family networks had been brought together, both of which cherished the evangelical view of the family. Of course, 'all people should love each other', but

> people belonging to the same families should stick to their relations. God made us of the same family, and meant this like a gold chain to bind us to each other.

In the Bickersteth/Monier-Williams family this meant that post-natal care, child care, respite care, school mentoring, medical care, financial support and geriatric care – every modern welfare service – could be supplied through the 'golden chain' of relatives. From the point of view of the Bickersteth children, their six Monier-Williams' uncles supplied a crowd of cousins, nearly all boys of roughly their own age. Whichever schools the Bickersteth boys attended – Summer Fields, Oxford, St.

David's, Reigate, Charterhouse or Rugby, a cousin, or even an uncle had preceded them. Burgon was the first of the brothers to go to St. David's Preparatory School – but cousin Roy Monier- Williams was there already. 'How kind Roy seems to you' wrote his father to the homesick child. Possibly less welcome was the huge supply of elderly aunts. Some they met, but others they only heard about from their mother. Ella knew personally the older generation of Faithfull great-aunts – her mother's older sisters. She had visited them in various vicarages up and down the country, for her father and mother were meticulous about keeping in touch. As a result, Ella could tell her boys about their curious quirks: Aunt Georgiana was 'a most alarming person and all her nephews and nieces were afraid of her ... she was very precise. She had four pins put in the carpets to indicate the exact position of the four legs of each chair, and woe betide the visitor who moved a chair.' She had married a clergyman, George Renaud, and Ella claimed 'My uncle had only one lung. Aunt Georgie was a very small eater, and starved him. After her death he became fat and well liking'. (sic) Aunt Cecilia, in contrast, was 'the most saintly woman' that Ella had ever met. Aunt Emily was 'a most interesting and racy person, an artist and an author', though contemporary accounts portray Emily as discreet and virtuous as her sister Cecilia. The boys best knew the next generation of Faithfulls. Lillian Faithfull became Head Mistress of Cheltenham Ladies College and was a frequent visitor. When Monier Bickersteth had a party to celebrate his engagement in 1907 the Faithfulls 'arrived in detachments'.

As the Bickersteth boys grew up, and career choice became crucial, the galaxy of male Monier-Williams relatives became more important. Uncle Monier Faithfull Monier-Williams was now a well-established and successful solicitor, with a growing reputation in the City, Uncle Stanley was a successful architect and Uncle Monty a leading doctor who had a large private practice in Onslow Gardens, London. A member of the British Psychological Society he brought Emile Coué to London and introduced auto-suggestion as a form of psychotherapy. Uncle Monier was always generous with gifts such as a new bicycle and he offered to pay for Morris or Ralph's articles – 'an offer equivalent to three hundred guineas' noted their mother, though the offer was not taken up. In 1914 when Morris wanted to be transferred from the Leeds Pals to the Guards, Uncle Monier enlisted the support of his brother-in-law, Colonel Churchill 'who holds a high position in the War Office and who is ready at Uncle Monier's request to do what he can for Morris' wrote Ella. When the Guards were ruled out as too expensive, cousin Roy, already a Lieutenant in the 7th Battalion of the Buffs, arranged for Morris to see his Colonel with a view to a transfer. Nor had the relationship to be close for the families to keep in touch. Lord Cavan, related to Ella only through the marriage of the daughter of Ellen and John Olive, made enquiries on openings in Canada on the railways on behalf of Monier. It cannot be only by chance that the youngest Bickersteth boy, Ralph, and the only one to follow a career in commerce, chose insurance. Another cousin by marriage, Sir Charles Robert Bignold was a director of the Norwich Union.

Nevertheless, it must have been their grandfather who left the most lasting impression on the Bickersteth children. The three older boys knew their maternal grandparents very well, as from babyhood they had stayed with them during holidays and family emergencies both at Oxford and at their holiday home in Ventnor, Isle of Wight. Sir Monier must have impressed them when they saw him in full crimson academic dress – perhaps not quite so magnificent as grandfather Bickersteth but, with his bushy black beard, maybe a more imposing figure. A quick glance at any of his books was enough for them to be daunted by his scholarship. It was a rare year that he did not publish a book and he was working on the final revisions of his huge revised Sanskrit-English dictionary a few days before his death. It has still never been superseded. All the boys visited the Indian Institute at Oxford, an imposing stone building designed in the style of the English Renaissance, but with a weathercock formed by an elephant and howdah. It housed a unique collection of literature and artefacts. It was the culmination of Monier-Williams' lifework, and its existence was due solely to their grandfather's initiative. His aim had been to provide 'a centre of union, intercourse, inquiry and instruction for all engaged in Indian studies'. The *Times*, reporting the official opening in 1896, put it more succinctly. The new Institute existed 'to put the intellect of India into communion with the intellect of England'. Monier-Williams funded it through his own exertions over twenty-one years, travelling up and down the country, holding meetings and giving lectures to raise support for the scheme. He secured the interest of the Court, and Queen Victoria became one of his supporters. Three tours of India resulted in gifts from native Princes, Viceroys and Governors. The foundation stone was laid by the Prince of Wales. Soon afterwards Ella was delighted that her father was knighted KCIE (Knight Commander of the Indian Empire). Her father, in contrast, when writing his letter of acceptance to the Prime Minister, regretted that it was not a KCG (Knight of the Garter). Nevertheless, after he added the extra 'Monier' to his name, there was no denying that 'Sir Monier Monier-Williams' had a distinguished ring when mentioned in Bickersteth conversation. If the Bickersteth name gave the boys standing in the clerical world, the Monier-Williams name linked them to the academic world and to Empire.

As the years went by, so did the size of the two families. By the time of Sir Monier and Julia's Golden Wedding in July 1898 Ella had a major task on her hands in organising the family celebrations. Of her six brothers, Cyril had died childless the year before in the West Indies, but she managed to assemble his widow, her remaining five brothers, with their wives and children, at the family home in Chessington. Her father paid Outram's fare from Capetown. With the six Bickersteth boys, the final tally was 20 grandsons and one grand-daughter, her brother Stanley proudly holding the latest addition: Hugh, who had just celebrated his first birthday. Only one thing marred Ella's day. Her son, Morris, fell down the day before 'and cut his head open. It had to be all plastered up, a trial to me, as he is a beautiful child and his good looks were spoiled'. She made sure that, in the family photograph, Morris and Julian sat sideways, looking at each other, so only Morris' 'good side' showed. Otherwise, all her arrangements went smoothly.

> At 10.30 we gathered in Father and Mother's room, where he offered a beautiful prayer, and we knelt in groups round him and mother. Then the giving of presents, then the photographing in the garden, then the happy stroll over the fields to Church, Father and Mother driving in a phaeton, and the beautiful service of thanksgiving, taken by Sam. ... lunch was a great success ... the garden party followed. Mother looked like a queen as she sat in her chair and received her guests with Father looking so young and active near her.

Although he looked 'so young and active', her father's days were numbered. He and his wife always spent the winters in the south of France and a year later, a heart condition led to pneumonia. Sir Monier had always tended to be preoccupied with his death. Even as a young man, every year his diary entries for his birthday were tinged with apprehension.

> I was thirty-five to-day. Never did I allow myself to imagine that I should live to reach so great an age. ... If it please Him to preserve me, may He make me more prepared for death, though it be through suffering, pain, sorrow and humiliation.

At eighty he was still apprehensive. He dictated his last prayer.

My God & Father has taught me that if I am
a true believer in His beloved Son I
must be a new creature in Him &
if I am a new creature in Him I must
have Christ formed within me. I must
have Christ living in me & if I have
Christ living in me, I must have life
in myself. I cannot really die.
What is called death will only be trans-
mission. But my last prayer is that
I may have Christ in me at my last
hour. I may not be forsaken by Him
at the last as Christ was himself forsaken by His Father —

My Saviour forsake me not at my
last hour fullfill Thy gracious promise —
:I will never leave thee nor forsake thee

My Father accept this my last
prayer for Thy dear Son's sake

written by Sir Monier Monier-Williams,
who had death the realized
in his presence, when he
himself was dying — Dictated to Catherine Grosse his Swiss
secretary correction in Sir Monier's handwriting.

The note added at the end reads: 'Written by Sir Monier Monier-Williams who hated death to be mentioned in his presence, when he himself was dying. Dictated to Catherine Gasser his secretary. Corrections in Sir Monier's handwriting.' Sir Monier seems to have returned to the comfort of the hymns of his childhood. The words 'I will never leave thee nor forsake thee' recall the closing lines of 'Jesus, Friend of little children:'

> Never leave me, nor forsake me
> Ever be my friend
> For I need thee on life's journey
> To its end.

Sir Monier clung to his faith despite his fears and remained sure that death was 'only transition'.

Monier-Williams has been described as 'a devoted representative of the evangelical wing of the Christian church and an acknowledged authority on Hinduism'. At that time, an evangelical who was also an academic was something of a rarity. How did it come about? Perhaps part of the answer lies in his account of a service he attended in 1850 at Ayot. The sermon was based on a text found in I Chronicles 4.10. Jabez, a man of whom little is known, prayed that God 'would enlarge his coasts'. The unknown preacher interpreted this as a plea by Jabez that he would be enabled to find 'new opportunities for usefulness'. Monier-Williams never forgot it. It could be argued that his decision to work for the foundation of the Indian Institute was a direct result. It was sufficiently significant in his life for him to copy the text into the flyleaf of his daughter's Bible when she was ten years old. It was so impressed on Ella's mind that she asked her eldest son, Monier, to make sure he read it on his thirteenth birthday and she repeated it, almost one hundred years later, on her ninetieth birthday, as her wish for the coming generation. It was the traditional evangelical call to activism. But Monier-Williams had another 'distinctive character trait' to pass on to his grandsons. It was 'enthusiasm'. By this, he did not mean the over-zealous preaching and piety of some evangelicals, but whole-hearted concentration on the work in hand. It had its dangers. As he admitted: 'it was in my nature to overdo everything I undertook. I overdid study, I overdid athletic exercises, I overdid pleasure, and overdid sight-seeing.' But he never regretted it. Ella passed the words on to her sons. If she had also intended them to be a warning, there is no evidence that any of the Bickersteth grandchildren paid any attention. Brimming with energy and 'enthusiasm', they grasped their own 'opportunities of usefulness' as they met the challenges of the new century.

Background reading

Oman, C *Ayot Rectory. A Family Memoir* Hodder & Stoughton (1965)

Hedges, Paul *Preparation and Fulfilment: Studies in the intercultural history of Christianity.* Peter Lang (2001)

Sources

Bickersteth, E C F *Memoir* (1938) Untitled. Held by the Bickersteth family

Monier-Williams, M F *A Long Life's Reminiscences 1849-1925.* Held in the Monier-Williams archive

Monier-Williams, R T *Historical Notes relating to the family of Williams* (1950). Compiled by Roy Monier-Williams and held in the Monier-Williams archive

Monier-Williams, M *Notes of a Long Life's Journey* (1895) Photocopy held in the Indian Institute, Bodleian Library, Oxford

Storr, Cecilia *The Faithfull Memoir.* Held by Hatfield Public Library

Williams, George. *Descendants of George Williams 1728-1803* www.southsidefamilies.com Includes a copy of Lt. Col Monier Williams' will.

Williams, George. Major, 20th Regiment of Foot. www.62ndregiment.org/George_Williams.htm

Wednesday

Morning.

Ps. 25 & 63 and 32.
M.E. prayer & Psalm

Collect for Ash Wednesday, 3rd for Good Friday.

My husband
Prayer for true repentance.

Intercession for Missionaries especially for Coloured. see /page f. 36.
Prayer commencing "O God who hast made of one blood:
The Japan Guild Intercession papers
f. 145 - 198. 210 9 Before the throne
Special prayer for Tommy, & his wife & children
Julian
(4 children to train: work that I may have grace to give him up;)
Hugh, Dottie & children
Hilda, Amy children

Evening.

Ps. 139. Magnificat.

Prayer for the hastening of God's kingdom.
Prayer at end of Burial Service beginning "Almighty God with whom do live."
Prayer of Father commencing "O my God & Father ... Help me to lay the axe." p. 31.
Prayer in preparation for death
f. 230. 231. (before the throne)

Self-examination

Special prayer for Nurse & servants, & that I may be an understanding mistress
For our G.F.S. girls & our G.F.S. prayer

A page from Ella's Prayer Diary, circa 1896

3

THE MOTHER: ELLA BICKERSTETH

We all went to Sir Moynihan's fancy dress ball – Morris as Prince Charlie in dark purple velvet, wig and sword and Ralph as a jester. I had my hair powdered and went in black velvet.

Bury your will in the field of duty – to think, to do, to fulfil a duty, to resist a temptation, to conquer a passion – you must will and will with energy.

Ralph is like me, we dance through life.

These glimpses into the life of the wife of a Victorian Church of England clergyman are found in Ella's diaries and correspondence. Only by turning to one of her husband's notebooks do we find a remark made by the Bishop of Rochester which conveys a more usual view of the conscientious vicar's wife: 'Ah, Mrs. Bickersteth knows how to do her very best for her sons and yet work hard in the parish'. Yet even that comment can be somewhat misleading. Two years later at a reception in Leeds when he had secured the prestigious appointment as Vicar of Leeds, Sam overheard the same Bishop saying to his wife 'Why, Mrs. Bickersteth, you are one of the great factors in determining that it [the living] was offered to him'.

Ella does not fit in comfortably with any of the conventional pictures of dutiful Victorian wives: submissive, domestic, passive and pious. She sparkles across the stereotypes. Light-hearted and charming, with an inner core of steely resolve to be a faithful servant of her Lord, she was also an enthusiast for all things sporting and patriotic. Of independent thought, sometimes implacable, often more dominant than her husband in domestic life, and at least his equal partner in social life, she was not someone to be patronised. Her faith and her role as the wife of a vicar enabled rather than constrained her as she extended her activities beyond the parish to the community. With the confidence that came from an inner conviction of self-worth, she was able to work through, as well as alongside, her husband. Of piety, in the sense of hypocritical virtue, there is no trace. She was unquestionably devout. The nurture of her sons and the care of her husband were her first priorities. The Bickersteth archive reveals how these qualities developed and the way they influenced the 'moulding' of her sons.

Ella had six brothers and was the fifth child in the Monier-Williams family. When the fourth boy, Stanley, was born Monier-Williams wrote in his diary 'I confess that I felt disappointed when I heard that another boy was born, as I had set my heart on a little girl; but I have learnt the lesson that things most desired are not always sources of happiness, when obtained'. Two years later, in 1858, he obtained his source of happiness: 'a precious, precious little daughter was born to us today'. She was christened Ella Chlora Faithfull by her uncle, the Revd James Faithfull. Her mother, Julia, chose her first name and her second name was chosen by her father 'because it is the name of my favourite English wild flower [yellow-wort]'. His 'source of happiness' was life-long. Ella grew up to be close to her father. When Monier-Williams published *Hinduism* in 1877 he dedicated it to 'The best of little daughters whose love makes her the best of little secretaries'.

The picture of Ella's childhood which the family memoirs reveal is one of privilege and stability, with the evangelical ethos at its heart. The atmosphere was not as repressive as the Faithfull home in which her mother, Julia, grew up, but there were still clear boundaries set. Card-playing was forbidden, though family games such as Spillikins and Happy Families – the latter itself a card game but without any connection to gambling – were enjoyed. Her mother read to all the children but would not let them sit in idleness whilst they listened. It was compulsory to 'occupy their hands'. Ella did embroidery and her brothers made nets. A generation later, when Ella was reading the story of Nansen's expedition to the North Pole to her boys 'they all worked me some toilet covers while I read'. Perhaps the most distinctive note in the Monier-Williams' family life was the continuous flow of distinguished visitors through their home in Oxford; a steady stream of students and officials from India, University colleagues, many of the Faithfull and Williams relatives and, occasionally, even royalty. Prince Leopold, the youngest son of Queen Victoria lived nearby when he was a student at Christ Church. He came for afternoon tea and talked about 'his late father, Prince Albert, and his admirable plans for the education of the Royal Princes'. He was said to be 'delighted' when Julia's pet dove suddenly settled on his head. 'What a jolly bird!' he exclaimed. As a result, when Ella married and left home she had a wide range of contacts from which her husband and her sons were to benefit.

It is thanks to Lewis Carroll (Dr Charles Dodgson) that we have a series of photographs of Ella taken when she was about eight years old. Dodgson, a mathematics lecturer at Christ Church, Oxford was on calling terms with Ella's parents. In all he took at least eight photographs of Ella, and a further twenty-one of her parents, uncles and cousins. In July 1886 he wrote in his diary that he had 'taken a good many [photographs] of little Ella, of whom I did several pictures with no other dress than a cloth tied round her, savage fashion'. 'A visit to Mr. Dodgson's rooms to be photographed was always full of surprises' recollected Ella in old age. In one photograph he posed her as a soldier, holding a stick as a rifle. It contrasts sharply with some of his pictures of feminine little girls as, serious and absorbed, standing rigidly to attention, she gazes steadily at the photographer. Below the picture is her autograph in immaculate copper plate handwriting. It is tempting to think that Dodgson chose the pose to suit her personality.

From childhood, Ella had a mind of her own and a strong sense of right and wrong. One of her earliest recollections was of her seventh birthday when her brother Stanley gave her a small purse. Her godmother 'made me a present of a pale blue leather purse, tooled in gold' – on condition that she exchanged the small purse for it. 'I refused to do so mean a thing' recalled Ella, the memory of the incident still rankling over fifty years later. No doubt, as the only daughter, she soon learned to stand up for herself, though she was not always successful. Her brothers naturally thought they knew what was best for girls. They took her round the annual St Giles' Fair, held outside their house in Oxford, but, she recalled, they would only let her go into the booths which 'they thought proper for me to see'. It meant, to her disgust, that she never did see 'the fat lady'. On the other hand, having six active brothers did have advantages. They taught her to climb, to row, and to skate. All the men in the family were keen skaters. Her father had been an early member of the exclusive London Royal Toxophilite Skating Club whose members skated on the Serpentine or, less successfully, on the green used for archery which was flooded for the skaters when the winter was sufficiently cold. In the evenings the members would skate dressed in their swallow-tailed coats, and Monier Williams would be wearing the skates he had himself designed. Ella's younger brother, Montie, who became a doctor, patented his father's design. Somehow he found time from his medical studies to become an expert on figure skating. When he was twenty-three he published *Combined Figure Skating, being a collection of all the known combined figures, systematically arranged* which came out in three editions between 1883 and 1892.

He recommended that gentlemen should wear knickerbockers for country skating, though his preference was for trousers. For skating in town he considered that 'no costume looks better [than] tall hats, black coats and trousers [though] frock coats look uncommonly well'. Ladies should always wear 'well fitting tailor-made dress'. No wonder that Ella, presumably suitably dressed, could skate during a hard winter 'for miles along the Cherwell' and her figure skating was of a sufficiently high standard to qualify her for membership of the prestigious Wimbledon Skating Club. She modestly described the test as being 'somewhat severe.'

In many ways her upbringing was ideally suited to her future as the mother of six sons. On the other hand, it probably made her not the easiest of children to deal with. Her behaviour when she was out for a walk with her governess in the country was never forgotten. They were stopped by the police and told to go home. Ella would have none of it.

> There was a criminal concealed in the corn … the agitation of my governess was extreme! I, on the other hand, was curious to see what was meant by a "criminal" and refused to move until the head of the man appearing in the distance above the corn was pointed out to me.

When her father was sufficiently established at Oxford to build his own house, he included an 'observatory with a revolving top' His brother, George Williams, who became a Fellow of the Royal Astronomical Society, equipped it with 'a refractor telescope'. Ella recalled that 'many a time did I coax my mother to let me sit up late by declaring that I wished to study the stars'. She could soon 'pick out constellations and stars of the first magnitude, while the glory of the planets was a continual wonder'. Her father, she recalled, gave her 'many a lesson in geography, science, geology and astronomy'. Her brothers remembered them too. They called them 'Father's Courses' and had mixed feelings about them, as her eldest brother, Monier Faithfull recorded. 'He used to give us lectures on astronomy as he did on all other subjects, scientific, historical and geographical … as children and even in after-life, we did not appreciate this as we ought to have done [but] notwithstanding our reluctance at being set down to listen to an hour's lecture he managed to knock a good deal of general knowledge into our heads.'

It is clear that although Ella never went to school her education was far from neglected, though she felt that her governess, Miss Wilds, 'was not a clever teacher'. This was hardly surprising. Agnes Wilds came as a governess to the little boys in 1857 when she was about seventeen years old and stayed on long after the boys went off to public school. She seems to have become Ella's companion in that very masculine household and Ella kept in touch with her until at least 1904. No doubt to compensate for their daughter's lack of formal education, her parents arranged for her to take advantage of a range of other educational opportunities outside the home. By the time she was twelve years old she was staying in Dieppe for the summer, working with a French master and 'could as soon take up and enjoy a French story book as an English one'. In February 1875, she wrote to a cousin that she was 'studying very hard' and attending 'some most delightful lectures on the Crusades,' as well as French and German lectures for women. These were arranged by Mrs. Humphry Ward and led to the founding of the first colleges for women in Oxford: Lady Margaret Hall and Somerville Hall. Ella studied art at the Oxford School of Art when 'Ruskin himself came in and overlooked my drawing, adding a few strokes of his own'. With her best friend, Maud Price, destined to be the wife of her sons' housemaster at Rugby, she sang in the Oxford Philharmonic Society choir. At seventeen, she wrote with some apprehension that her music master had 'expressed his intention of taking me through every single sonata of Beethoven's. He brings the most difficult one tomorrow.' Mathematics was not pursued at the same level. The two girls studied arithmetic 'with the help of a National School master'. In later years, she tried to cheer up her eldest son by telling him that she had 'worked on Euclid [as] a little girl and got just over the *Pons Asinorum*!' (The theorem proving that the angles opposite the equal sides of an isosceles triangle are also equal.) She hopefully added 'I believe although Euclid seems hard, it is really all common sense, and a good master makes it very plain.'

As she grew older it would seem that she increasingly worked for her father as his secretary. Details are very sparse, but in his memoir he describes the method he used throughout his 'life-long lexicographical labours' which culminated in his *Sanskrit-English Dictionary*. He had begun, as a young teacher at Haileybury College, by employing a clerk to copy out all the English entries from a 'good English-Latin dictionary', leaving spaces to be filled in by the equivalent Sanskrit. He then wrote 'every English word with its corresponding Sanskrit on separate slips of paper' and whenever his mother and sisters came to visit him, they helped 'in the arrangement of the slips'. No doubt Ella was also eventually enlisted to help with the task which continued for many years. Some indication of the work involved can be seen in the size of the second edition. Published just after his death, it added 60,000 Sanskrit words to the original 120,000 entries with 'accentuation of nearly every Sanskrit word to which accents are usually applied'. It must, at the very least, have been tedious work demanding meticulous accuracy. How far his 'best of little secretaries' was involved is unknown and whether she learned Sanskrit remains a tantalising, unanswered question. A clue may be found in the fact that when she was married with a young family, she was still at her parents' beck and call, and seems still to have been needed for proof-reading. Nor was her father always the easiest of employers. Just before her marriage, despite her protests, he insisted that she accompany him to Germany as he was making a presentation to 'an Oriental Congress in Berlin'.

Every year her parents seem to have taken her abroad for a lengthy holiday. She was thirteen years old when she visited Germany for the first time and at Dresden was taken to see Raphael's *Madonna di San Sisto*. 'I shall never forget my sense of awe as I sat for a long time opposite it' she wrote in her diary. Nevertheless, she disliked Berlin. 'Everything had to give way to the military; swaggering officers thought it no shame to themselves to remain on the pathway and push us or any other woman on the road'. Ella and her father both settled down to lessons in German, something which became a regular feature of their European holidays. In old age, Ella looked back on these tours and claimed that they 'greatly increased my being able to talk fluently with all I met in either French or German. My only regret is I never learnt Italian'. As her sons grew up, she was able to coach them in French and German conversation. The culmination of her foreign tours came when she was sixteen. Her parents took her on a six-month tour of India. This was Monier-Williams' first visit to India both to study and to raise money for the Indian Institute. Here they enjoyed

> ... an open sesame to places not usually seen by an ordinary traveller. Priests vied with each other to show [my father] parts of their Temples not open as a rule, and Pandits came from afar to meet him. They would sit cross-legged talking about Indian lore and mythology and quoting from their sacred books ... talking in Sanskrit which, in their hands, became a living language.

Their tour coincided with the Prince of Wales' first visit to India, and on several occasions they were invited to join the royal party. According to her brother, the Prince was present at her coming-out ball at Government House in Calcutta. Surprisingly, Ella makes no mention of this except to say that the 'State Ball was a lovely sight, and the supper room with the Throne-room at one end had the entire floor of marble'. She seems more concerned with the fact that the Prince of Wales 'sought out my father and they had a long talk, HRH consenting to be patron of father's Indian Institute'. In contrast, she describes in detail the magnificent receptions she attended. At the Chapter of the Most Exalted Order of the Star of India she recorded that she had watched Rajahs invested as Knight Grand Commanders.

> I have never seen such a sight again, nor shall I ever forget how splendid the blue mantles, the full uniforms of the Englishmen and the gorgeous apparel and diamonds of the natives looked under an Eastern sun.

It was on her return home from India that Ella experienced what she described as 'perhaps one of the greatest trials of my life'. The Revd John Burgon, Gresham Professor of Divinity, Fellow of Oriel College and Vicar of St Mary's, the University Church, had left Oxford to become Dean of Chichester. It is one of the enigmas of Ella's upbringing that she claimed that up to her seventeenth birthday, he had guided every step of her life. Part of the answer must lie in his personality. Dean Burgon loved children, was full of fun and it was impossible to be dull in his company. He first met Ella when she was seven years old, and she reminded him of a little sister 'he had lost and tenderly loved'. Every Sunday, after the 4 o'clock service at St Mary's, she would walk with him and her governess to Oriel College where six Charity girls were waiting for him to distribute cakes and buns. Then, for the next ten years, sitting on his knee or on a stool at his feet, Ella recalled that

> he taught me Divinity ... or Church History, Church principles, the Harmony of the Gospels and other Bible study ... he would show me old manuscripts, explain Codex A, or Codex B, point out the beauties of some picture of the Madonna or some sculpture with which the walls of his rooms were adorned and would send me home with a mind awakened to every kind of interest.

Every Friday, he held a Bible class for 'the ladies of the University' at the Monier-Williams' home. Ella recalled that:

> I, even when a child, was admitted. I sat on a stool at his feet, and had to look up all his references. And very quick and particular he was, expecting me to know the order of the books in the Bible as well as my alphabet.

She was an apt pupil. The Principal of the Oxford Diocesan Training College remembered her as a child, who 'sitting at the feet of the revered teacher, did her best to atone for the shortcomings of us older ones: "Now, Ella, what do you say?" being the usual last resort in the general silence.' If she happened to meet the Dean during the week there would be games of hide and seek, or a visit to a College garden where he could tell her the name of every plant or tree, or she would be taken with 'a small crowd of ragged children' to a pastry-cook's for 'handfuls of cakes'. Yet this 'tall, thin man with black hair and dark eyes' was the most controversial clergyman in Oxford. He was 'a High Churchman ... who was as opposed to Romanism and ritualism as he was to rationalism and every form of liberalism' and could be relied upon to support any lost cause. He insisted on a literal interpretation of the Bible. When Ella was thirteen, a woman was elected a member of the Oxford School Board. Burgon's opposition was fierce. He 'loathed this new development'. He warned his congregation against 'the unfeminine, the unlovely method of these last days' and published his sermon as a tract entitled *Women's Place*. Burgon, a bachelor, educated Ella in some detail on the domestic skills he felt she needed to fill her 'Women's Place'. She should learn sufficient cookery skills in order, in the future, to be able to instruct her cook. 'I really judge a Lady very much by the way her dinner is served up'. Ella must know how to avoid 'watery spinach, mashed potatoes ... and pastry as heavy as lead'.

How far was she influenced by Burgon? It would have been unbecoming for a young girl not to respect him. For all his eccentric, controversial ways, Burgon was a very distinguished clergyman. In later life, Ella became a competent housekeeper and, after a shaky start, an employer whose staff worked for her for many years. As Burgon advised, she first instructed herself – her early notebooks meticulously note baby care details for future reference. She was never foolish enough to allow herself to be Burgon's anathema – 'a bustling, forward, inconvenient rival' of her husband. But neither did her work in the community, her presence on the platforms of so many charitable organisations, and the addresses she forced herself to give, make her feel in Burgon's words, that she was acting as 'an inferior kind of Man'. Throughout her life she remembered him with great affection. He conducted her marriage service and that of her eldest brother, and one of his final acts was the baptism of her fourth son, named after him. Yet it is difficult not to believe that Ella did not sometimes have a private chuckle at the expense of 'our much-abused Vicar', as she described him in a light-hearted letter to a cousin.

How far she acceded to Burgon's wish that woman should 'rejoice in the sacred retirement of her home and the strict privacy of her domestic duties' is very doubtful. Ella was never a home-based 'ministering angel'. She was 'serious' in the evangelical tradition. From childhood she had absorbed her parents' convictions that she had a duty to be a responsible steward both of her time and her money. Her days should be filled with worthwhile activity, and income should be tithed. Holidays were needed for rest and recuperation, but they should widen horizons and pave the way to a fuller life, rather than just be an escape from day-to-day routine. Her life was founded on family devotions, private prayer and Bible study. Although there is no account of Ella's childish devotions, there is no doubt that she was earnest in private prayer. When she was a wife and mother her well-worn prayer notebook lists her private intercessions – compilations of morning and evening prayers for every day of the week. On Monday mornings, there would be psalms and collects to be read, followed by a prayer 'for blessing on my week's work. A special prayer for poor and needy, for hospitals and homes'. Then there would be prayers for different members of the family followed by prayers 'For those I have injured by word or example' and 'For those who have injured us, or think badly of us, Miss G, Miss B, Miss S'. It would be difficult not to conclude that in her prayer life she was following a pattern laid down in childhood. It was the pattern she taught her children.

Perhaps Dean Burgon's influence can also be seen from the fact that from an early age, she was aware of the significance of the Sacraments, something that was not always an essential part of evangelical 'seriousness'. When she was eight years old, and had known the Dean for a year, she went to church with her parents whilst on holiday in Llandudno.

> I walked up the Great Orme's Head with my father and mother to attend the service at the church there. The Holy Communion was celebrated, and my father and mother communicated, leaving me sitting in the pew. I have never forgotten the solemn impression made on me by this service, which I witnessed then for the first time.

The Dean prepared her for confirmation and she always remembered the

> Holy Communion services in the chancel of St Mary's, where according to old custom we did not leave our seats, but the

fair linen cloths were placed all round the chancel, over the broad book desks. Mr Burgon would come down, and as he administered the Sacred Elements, he would tenderly lay his hand on the head of each lad who might be present, or on the hand of each girl who knelt there.'

Ella became a conscientious wife and mother. Before their first child was born she and her husband agreed how the infant should be reared. Their child would 'be given to the Lord' and their responsibility would be to train him or her to 'stand up for what is noble, true and manly'. It was a solemn responsibility and one she diligently fulfilled.

The stereotype of evangelical seriousness – solemnity, ostentatious piety, mean-spirited frugality, so vividly portrayed by Trollope in the Barchester novels, cannot be applied to Ella. Rather she possessed 'a spirit of Christian joyousness'. She described herself as 'someone who danced through life' and felt that Ralph, the most extrovert and gregarious of her sons, was the one who most closely resembled her. When ten year-old Monier was due home from school she wrote 'I feel like singing and shouting at the thought'. When her youngest son, Ralph, went off to preparatory school, aged eight, her husband sat in his study, grieving. His wife would not give way to her feelings. He jotted in his notebook 'Ella has just passed down the stairs, singing!' She shared the children's interests and joined in their activities. She would play golf with them and go for long cycle rides. On holiday she could be found in a home-made dark room, helping develop their photographs. Her boys watched with admiration as she tackled recalcitrant French railway officials – and won the argument. During the war, when there was very little to be cheerful about, she made a note of all the best funny stories that she had heard so that she might include them in her letters to her sons. When Morris died in France she could write 'I cannot say much about this in the Diary, but we were in a way prepared for it. It is a joy to think that the three brothers had their happy meeting two days before Morris went into action'. Even as a young woman her recall of the death of Dean Burgon had no trace of Victorian morbidity, though, as Sam wrote in his diary 'she felt it much'. Instead, she could chuckle over one of his last requests: 'When I am dead, place my head on a copy of the Gospels for which I have fought so consistently during my life … mind, only a shilling copy'.

On a different note, it is not possible to equate her 'seriousness' with prudery. On her trip to India she noted that having been brought up 'very quietly as an only girl, never having even shared a bedroom with anyone else' she found it 'extraordinary how indifferent one got as to what déshabillé the officers or the passengers saw one in'. Nor did she conform to the current expectations of respectability – she was ready to push the boundaries just a little further. Her eldest brother recorded that as 'the Duke of Connaught and his suite' were on board 'my sister naturally had a good time on the voyage out'. Ella herself noted that there were shipboard romances, with 'many opportunities for flirtation during the voyage, of which I took full advantage'. With James Wilson, a civilian returning to work in India who had been one of her father's students, she had

> Many interesting talks, especially at night, sitting in a quiet corner
> in the prow of the ship watching the phosphorescent light, or,
> what was still more beautiful, the moonlight on the water.

Admittedly, the subjects of the talks she chose to record were very unromantic. 'He was a Presbyterian and I a staunch member of the Church of England, and we differed on many points of theology, as well as on the question of votes for women'. Yet we must suspect that their moonlit conversations strayed on to other subjects. Her mother saw that 'she was quite aware he loved her, and she returned his affection'. Parental pressure put a stop to the match and she was forbidden to write to him. Mrs Williams made sure that her daughter 'saw well our horror and dread of an Indian life for her' and a year later recorded that Ella had 'made up her mind that it was her duty to beg me to write to him and tell him she must be perfectly free.' On her twentieth birthday, Ella received a bracing letter from her mother:

> ... long may you [remain] the bright sunny thing you still are, in
> spite of some troubles and some trials, all of which are working
> real good for you. I know you wouldn't be what you are if life
> was entirely sunny.

Two years later, the sun came out again when Ella fell in love with young Samuel Bickersteth, though her mother still felt that 'the right person and the right time' had not arrived. Again there was the problem of Ella leaving England. Sam hoped, after his ordination, to follow his brother to India as a missionary. Mrs Williams did not feel Ella was 'physically fitted for an Indian life', though there is no evidence in the records that she was anything other than robust. The final decision, she told Sam, must be made by Ella, but the life of a missionary's wife is not the one which we in our hearts desire for her, neither can we think of such a parting, as that would involve, without the most bitter pain. We shall always entertain a warm regard for you, for your own sake, and for your father's [Bishop Edward Henry] and there must be a peculiarly warm and grateful corner in my heart for one who loved my dear child, even though I cannot feel it at all likely she will ever be his.

Sam turned to his father for comfort. Bishop Edward Henry tried to cheer him with the assurance that 'this joy of a heart all your own is only delayed not denied'. But he also wrote to Ella's mother, though no copy of the letter has been found. Somehow matters were resolved. Sam had an interview with Mrs Williams and told her that his father had undertaken to provide an allowance 'while God blesses the circulation of [his] hymnal', the best selling *Hymnal Companion to the Book of Common Prayer*. On his own part, he would undertake that Ella would not live outside England. A year later, they were engaged. Ella wrote to her fiancé: 'It was worth being sad and troubled to experience the bliss of being comforted by you'. It proved to be a very happy marriage, though Sam continued to yearn for missionary service abroad. Twenty-five years later at Early Celebration before the High Altar of the University Church, Oxford where she had been married, Ella recorded 'My heart overflowed with thanksgiving for my twenty-five years of blissful married life'. Then, characteristically, she added that the evening before, at a family party 'I wore the same dress in which I was married.'

As Dean Burgon would have wished, in the early years of her marriage and as a young mother, home and children were the centre of her life. It was, however, a natural progression that, when the children had started to attend boarding school, she began to share her belief in the sacred importance of home and family life by setting up new branches of the Mothers' Union. At the same time, it must have been through parish activities that her organising skills were honed. The administration needed to hold a two-day pin-cushion sale to which very few people came and which only raised £30 might not have been arduous, but encouraging disappointed helpers must have called for tact and diplomacy. In contrast, a three-day bazaar, raising £566 11s 6d, was opened by HRH Princess Christian. It was the culmination of weeks of work, and inevitably would have called for endless organisational and conciliatory skills. It was when her husband became

Vicar of Leeds in 1905 that Ella began to undertake more dynamic activities outside the home. She seemed to collect Presidencies. The Preventative and Reclaiming Mission of the Diocesan Temperance Society, the Ladies' Association for the Care of Friendless Girls, the Parents' National Education Union were a few of the organisations in which she was involved. At least one imaginative new initiative, started 'without much popular support' can be seen as coming to fruition partly by the joint efforts of Sam and Ella. Sam, in public speeches, publicised details of the high rate of infant mortality in Leeds. In 1907 the *Yorkshire Post* reported a speech he gave, spelling out the grim details: 'Babies under a year old die at the rate of 138 a month ... of these, one sixth die within a week'. Ella, through the Leeds sub-committee of the West Riding Nursing Association, working with three other leading women – the chief woman sanitary inspector, the school medical inspector and the matron of the Women and Children's Hospital, helped to provide a practical response. Three cottages were adapted to form a 'Babies Welcome' centre. Training was offered in all aspects of childcare. Mothers were invited to come with their babies. A graduated subscription entitled them to midwifery or nursing support during their pregnancy and confinement. The 'Babies Welcome' movement grew apace, with nine centres open in 1914. By 1930 there were twenty-one branches. It continued to flourish. During the Second World War it was distributing welfare foods and did not close until 1972.

Ella joined the National Union of Women Workers (NUWW) a non-political organisation of middle-class women which aimed to help working women. The sons of the President, Louise Creighton, wife of the late Bishop of London, were friends of the Bickersteth boys, and she often stayed at the Leeds Vicarage. Ella became President of the local Leeds branch and was instrumental in organising a band of ladies to befriend women who were charged with offences in the Police Court. The thinking was that women of good character sitting in the Court would prevent any cross-examination from 'being needlessly coarse'. In addition, the accused women would be reassured to see 'among the crowd of strange faces two or three of their own sex who were present in silent sympathy, and not from prurient curiosity'. The initiative required some courage and, presumably, considerable powers of persuasion to enrol the 'wives of some of the University professors, the clergy, medical men and other leading citizens' to form a rota. It attracted opprobrium in the local Press. It was defended, wrote her husband, by 'Labour women' who 'took up the cudgels ... and extorted an admission from the editor that he wholly misunderstood their motive'.

The Red House Settlement, another social initiative under the wing of the NUWW owed, according to the *Yorkshire Post,* 'more to Mrs. Bickersteth's initiative and enthusiasm than anything else'. It was a residential centre for four professional women engaged in various kinds of social or government work in Leeds and one parish worker. Linked to the Workers' Educational Association, it offered training courses in social science and was used by women students from Leeds University for practical social work experience. In the first year of the war it was providing social evenings for soldiers' wives, as well as play and drill centres for children, whilst seven hundred families were visited once a fortnight by ninety visitors.

In all her many and varied activities there is no evidence that Ella ever found her position as Vicar's wife inhibited her wider role. Rather it gave her an entry to established organisations and to front new ones. It is, however, necessary to put this in perspective. It was not only Christianity that was empowering her, even though for Ella this would have been the all-important motivation. Her own social connections played a part. She was extremely conscious of her rank in Society and ready to exploit it on behalf of her husband and her sons, though it was not until her husband moved to Leeds that she was able to do this to the full. Her Balfour contacts, for example, originated from the days of her maternal grandfather, Joseph Faithfull, and his school in the Hatfield rectory. When Faithfull died the school was taken over by his son-in-law, the Revd Charles Chittenden. Ella often went to stay with her aunt and uncle at the Grange School, Hoddesdon where, for a time, her cousin, Lilian Faithfull was a pupil. The boys came from the local aristocracy or were the sons of evangelical politicians. Amongst them were the Balfour brothers. Arthur, when he became Prime Minister, retained good memories of his old school. He had been a delicate, highly strung boy and Ella's uncle would play the organ softly to soothe his nerves. At the Leeds Musical Festival in 1907, Arthur Balfour, and his sister Alice stayed at the Vicarage, together with

> Gerald [Balfour] and Lady Betty and their daughter Ruth, Lady Frederick Cavendish plus valets, maids and secretaries … It was a great rush for meals. We sat down 14 or 16 to breakfast … afternoon tea was any time from 2.30 and crowds of people came in – such as the Harewoods, Armitages, Lascelles, Lady Don, Lady Jekyll, Alfred and Spencer Lyttelton … Mr Balfour always took me in [to dinner] and very charming I found him.

It meant that a recent Prime Minister, together with his sister and his brother, who had been MP for Leeds Central for the previous eleven years, and the Earl of Harewood were all under the Vicarage roof. Even more satisfying was Miss Balfour's comment. She 'told me that her brother Arthur thought our sons delightful. They were a great help in entertaining and were so simple and natural'. It is only fair to add that Ella's appearance and her personality must also have helped to make the event so successful. Indeed, who could have ignored a petite, charming little woman of five foot two inches, surrounded by six sons and a husband all over six foot tall? It was probably no coincidence that a few months later two of the boys were recommended to the Duchess of Sutherland as possible companions for her eldest son, the Marquis of Stafford, who was to undertake a world-wide tour. Julian was the lucky one chosen, and the Duke gave him £250 to pay for his outfit and other expenses. He was, wrote his mother 'quietly happy'.

His mother was undoubtedly equally happy. She and her husband knew that their sons would have to make their own way in the world. When she married, her mother had made it clear that she would not receive an allowance from her father, and any legacy would be divided equally among his seven children. Nor were any legacies or allowances to be expected from the Bickersteth side of the family. Grandfather Bickersteth (Bishop Edward Henry) might have been a prosperous author, but his earnings had helped finance missionary work, there were his unmarried daughters to support, whilst his married daughters often needed his help as well. Even his aunt Harriet was thankful to rely on him for financial help, including the £5.00 note which he would occasionally press in her hand. A 'well-formed' character was essential if the boys were to serve their Lord, but friends in high places would enable them to serve Him more effectively and earn their living in an independent, prosperous and genteel manner. It was the same philosophy that lay behind William Wilberforce's letters to his son when advising him, on going up to Oxford, to 'get acquainted with any good man or any useful man'. It was a philosophy that Ella fully endorsed. Delightfully, it coincided with her natural inclinations.

Whether the choice of Christ Church, Oxford as the college for all the boys was influenced by Ella's Oxford connections is a moot point. Sam had some reservations when he wrote to Monier about becoming an undergraduate there. 'It is a splendid place … if you had extravagant tastes it might be different. Also it is not entirely a reading College.' On the other hand, Ella must have been delighted as now she could introduce Monier to all her Oxford academic connections made through her father's 'open house' when he was Professor of Sanskrit. She pointed out to her somewhat diffident son:

> You being an Honours man, it is quite impossible for you to know too many people in Oxford, ... whom we send you to Oxford to [know] and to keep up.

Monier dutifully visited Sir William Herschel, an eminent judge and tried, but failed, to cultivate Viscount Lewisham who was the son of the Earl of Dartmouth, who had been the patron of St Mary's Lewisham when Sam was vicar. His outgoing brother Burgon, charming, handsome and a soccer blue, had no such problems. He featured in *The Tatler*.

> Mr. Bickersteth has been the secretary of the University Association Football Club for the last year. He will make a most popular captain of the Varsity side in the future and is as successful socially as he is at marking the various outside forwards whom the team oppose.

There is no doubt that Ella's influence on her children was immense: deeply religious and loving, it permeated all aspects of their lives. However, she was no saint. Prayers for selflessness and humility featured in her private devotions, but in daily life she could be domineering and manipulative and blissfully unaware of the result. Some of her methods of child rearing, described in the following chapters, ring uneasily in modern ears. At times she seems strangely insensitive. When two year-old Monier and eight week-old Geoffrey stayed with their grandparents at Oxford whilst Ella and Sam were on holiday, Ella was delighted to learn that Monier had been so pleased to see a letter from her that he 'kissed it over and over again'. It was, she felt, 'capital news' – she had no reservations. When she first became a mother-in-law, she promptly fell into the most common of traps. She attempted to interfere with her eldest son's career, as well as knowing what was best for his speech impediment. It finally exasperated her long-suffering daughter-in-law. Ella could hardly believe her ears. 'Kitty told me she had borne more from me all her married life [she had been married to Monier for almost four years] than any daughter-in-law ever had borne from a mother-in-law. It bowled me over with sheer astonishment'. She must have learned from the experience, for there are no references to similar altercations with the other young wives in the family. Despite such ups and downs, the family held together to the end and huge family reunions became a feature of Bickersteth life.

Ella, like so many of the family, lived to a ripe old age. When she celebrated her ninetieth birthday, surrounded by four hundred letters, fifty cables and telegrams from all parts of the world, one tribute stood out. It was from her cousin, Lilian Faithfull, retired headmistress of Cheltenham Ladies College.

> We have delighted in your courage, your gaiety, your sympathy, and you have taught us many a lesson, as we follow you on the path of old age. To laugh as we stumble along, to be interested when we incline to be bored and never to give up the fight when we are weary till the work is done.

It was a masterly summary of her life. But perhaps the atmosphere within which she 'moulded' her sons is best sensed through a conversation that her husband overheard her having with eight-year old Ralph. He was going off to preparatory school for the first time, and she was packing his trunk.

> Mother, will you pack this for me?
> Yes, darling, I will pack whatever you like best
> Will you mother?
> Certainly, darling
> Very well, Mother, you must pack yourself.

Background reading

Bickersteth, S *Citizens All. Civic Service: the Churchman's Duty*. A R Mowbray (1918)

Egremont, M *Balfour*. Orion Books (1988)

Goulburn, E M *John William Burgon. A Biography*. 2 vols. Murray (1892)

Family memoirs

Bickersteth, E C F *Memoir* (1938) Untitled. Held by family

Monier-Williams, M F *A Long Life's Reminiscences 1849-1925*. Held by family

Monier-Williams, M *Notes on a Long Life's Journey*. (1895) A photocopy is held in the Indian Institute, Bodleian Library, Oxford

Other primary sources

Bodleian Library: Diaries and correspondence of Ella Bickersteth

Sam Bickersteth, Vicar of Lewisham 1891-1905

4

The Father: Samuel Bickersteth

Mr. Bickersteth is a son of the recently resigned Bishop of Exeter and is exactly like his father in appearance: rather like a great bird of prey, with hooked nose and large overhanging eyebrows. But there is no sign of any fierceness in his disposition: he is of mild and courtly manner, full of sincerity and sweet reasonableness. Charles Booth Collection. Notebook B314 p 29.

Such was the picture painted in December 1900 when the interviewer for Charles Booth's *Inquiry into the Life and Labour of the People in London: Religious Influences* met Samuel Bickersteth, the Vicar of St. Mary's, Lewisham. He then added, with some regret:

> He is a very cautious, diplomatic person who would be chary of discussing general principles and most careful not to give himself or his parishioners away with the freedom which is so common with our interviewees.

The pen portrait, though vivid, does not convey an air of a confident manly Christian, and Sam's lack of self-confidence shows later in the interview. He explained that although he felt 'the religious outlook in the parish is perhaps unusually hopeful', this was due to the 'very large number of natural church-going people who will go unless you repel them'. His interviewer obviously felt that Sam was doing himself less than justice. He commented: it 'has certainly been added to by the fact that Mr B has as far as possible made the Vicarage a great social centre'. Sam only seems to have become fluent when discussing his church building programme and the many community activities listed in the Church Year Book 'which he harped on with rather wearisome detail'.

The matters on which Sam did not 'give himself or his parishioners away' can be found in the Bickersteth archive. Sam summarised 1900 as 'the most laborious and in some ways the most anxious year of my life.' He was forty-three years old, though his interviewer had guessed that he was 'nearing fifty', and had been at Lewisham for eight years. Preferment seemed increasingly unlikely. He was in poor health, suffering from neuralgia and a melancholy that, a year later, would become acute. In the parish, 1900 had been a series of disasters. For some months he had been single-handed. He had appointed a whole series of unsatisfactory curates.

> FSM 'the weakest of men ... no visitor and no power'; ... AH 'wholly without initiative, entirely unable to keep a Sunday school in order, moody and miserable, and heartily disliked'; ... GTM 'gave me most trouble and most disappointment. ... he was oblivious of the fact that he was not worth sixpence. I could not ask him to preach, his visiting had to be given up.'

The last straw was that 'the new organist was incapable as a choirmaster.'

When Philip Gibbs urged Burgon to preserve the 'intimate records' of his family, he was not to know that within Sam's notebooks the details of daily life of a late Victorian evangelical clergyman were already preserved. His claim that they would reveal the psychology of the writers was, however, entirely accurate. They provide an entry into Sam's private and public life and reveal a devoted family man who was also a conscientious parish priest. They show how the claims of parish and family, allied to the need to suppress frustration and disappointment in an endless round of work, threatened his physical and mental health. Unfortunately, 'intimate records' are also limited – not only by the details the writer wishes to record but also by whether they have physically survived the passage of years. Two notebooks have been found in which Sam recorded his impressions of 1900-03, years which, as Vicar of Lewisham, were particularly difficult for him. It is likely that he was using them as a source of catharsis as well as of record. His personal records of Leeds (1905-16) are much scantier and those that refer to the Great War are considered in the final chapters. Nevertheless, when read in conjunction with his early correspondence with his father and Ella's diaries over the same period, a vivid picture of an evangelical Anglican ministry can be revealed.

Sam was the seventh child, and second son, of sixteen children. His father, Bishop Edward Henry Bickersteth, had married a cousin, Rosa Bignold, who died very suddenly when Sam was sixteen. It was particularly sad for Sam, as only a few months before his nineteen year-old sister, Alice, to whom he was close, had also died. Three years later, his father married again. The older children found this difficult to accept. Edward, Sam's elder brother, recalling the wedding, wrote to him:

> ... this seems mournful very – and anyhow the poetry of the old family idea all gone. It is not very easy either to see the why and the wherefore – but such there is, be assured.

One 'why and wherefore' is obvious to the outsider – there was still a young family to bring up. Sam had four younger brothers and three younger sisters. His father had chosen another cousin, Ellen Susannah Bickersteth, a daughter of the first Dr Robert Bickersteth of Liverpool, to be their replacement mother. It must have seemed to him an ideal solution. From the older children's point of view, it was not. Three years after the wedding, the Bishop noticed a book lying on the drawing room table. He recognised it as a gift from himself and his wife, who was known as Madre, to Sam's sister, Lily (Elizabeth), but when he picked it up he saw that where he had written on the flyleaf 'From her loving father and Madre', the last two words had been crossed out. Bishop Edward was horrified. Lily, he felt, 'had much to learn of the vanity and evil of her own heart. The Lord must be her teacher'. He wrote to Sam to tell him how greatly he was 'grieved' and 'wounded' that his words had been 'so stopped and marred.' Sam, now nineteen and at Oxford, attempted to explain his feelings and those of his siblings. The older children felt that Ellen had tried too hard to take the place of their mother. They were unhappy that all mention of their real mother was avoided. He put it to his father as tactfully as he could. He had, he wrote,

> often talked it out with Edward and Rosie, Lily and Amy ... I am sure I could make her [Madre] happy by a thousand little attentions and caresses, if I felt that in all she did for me, or for the others, it was only as our <u>greatest friend</u>, (sic) if mother's name was constantly on her lips, ... only mother's name will unseal all our hearts'.

His father did not agree. Ellen could not simply be regarded as a friend,

> Because your stepmother has a closer bond and claim than any friend just because she is forever indissolubly one with your own father and will be one for ever. ... [If only the children] would

draw out its intense sympathies (often the most precious are the most hidden) that would be the fondest desire of your own sweet mother's heart.

It is here that the 'intimate records' conceal rather than reveal. Only the virtual absence of Ellen's name from all correspondence, diaries and notebooks hints that a coldness still persisted until the end when, in 1917, Ella noted in her diary 'Sam's stepmother, old Mrs Bickersteth. is dying and we fear we may be summoned south any day'.

If Sam as a young man had a difficult relationship with his stepmother, he was close to his older brother, Edward. Both boys attended Highgate School, walking across Hampstead Heath each morning with their father who was then Rector of Christ Church, Hampstead. Both won university scholarships. Edward went to Cambridge and gained a First Class in the Theological Tripos, became a Fellow of Pembroke College and went out to India as the founder and first head of the Cambridge Mission to Delhi. His father was delighted that his 'beloved son [was] numbered with the blessed missionary band of evangelists'. Sam struggled to cope with academic life in Oxford. He suffered from insomnia and could not sleep 'without a soporific [bromide]'. His father thought he was overworking and sent him a timetable. Even so, Sam only managed to obtain a Fourth. Where, he wondered, had he gone wrong? Why did he feel so unconfident or, as he put it, 'fish out of watery'? Part of his problem, he thought, was that so often he felt himself to be an outsider. Later in life, he discussed it with Ella's father, Monier-Williams. We have Ella's account of the conversation.

> My father found it a great drawback not having been to one of the Public Schools. The Public School men were linked together by a kind of freemasonry of kinship and comradeship which was a great source of strength. ... My father-in-law, [Bishop Edward Henry] having been brought up in the very strict Evangelical school, decided to keep all his six sons at home, and send them to a day school. When they reached the University, they all found this a very great disadvantage in making and keeping friends. One of these sons – my husband – decided for the very same reason to send his sons to Public Schools rather than day schools.

It was a decision that had financial repercussions which were to haunt Sam for thirty years. He was determined that, if he had sons, they would be 'public school men' with an entrée to jobs, Society, marriage and, he hoped, even to senior Church appointments.

Down from Oxford, and true to his promise to Ella's parents that he would not take her out of this country, Sam looked for clerical appointments in England. His first position was as curate in his father's old parish of Christ Church, Hampstead and, when the vicar, William Boyd Carpenter, became Bishop of Ripon, he accompanied him there as his chaplain. He moved to Belvedere in 1887, then a rural parish in Kent near Erith and, in 1891 became Vicar of Lewisham. His mother-in-law was delighted. She wrote jubilantly to her cousin, Emily Faithfull, founder of the Women's Press: 'A capital house and garden – £1,400 a year, £1,000 clear – near good places of education … a thoroughly well-organised parish'. The parish church, St Mary's, was flourishing. Sunday services were packed, with extra seats placed down the aisle. Sam's hopes were equally high. The patron was the Earl of Dartmouth, and he and his wife were actively involved in parish affairs. A contact with the aristocracy was always helpful for an up-and-coming clergyman. Moreover, it was a Crown appointment and his predecessor had been made Bishop of Lichfield. The future looked bright. Amazingly, within a year it looked as if history was going to repeat itself. A letter arrived from Archbishop Benson summoning him to dinner at Addington Park 'on a matter of very great importance in which you can help me'.

It was indeed about a bishopric – but the bishopric of Natal. Sam's distant relative, Bishop John Colenso had died there nine years earlier. He had weathered a stormy career, having been excommunicated on a charge of heresy due to his doubts about the authorship and accuracy of the Pentateuch. Then, after a new bishop had been appointed, the decision was reversed by the Privy Council and he was reinstated. As a result, the diocese had split between the 'Bishop of Maritzburg and Natal' and, as Colenso's followers styled him, 'the bishop of the Church of England in Natal'. In 1891 all parties finally agreed that this state of affairs should not continue and the Archbishop of Canterbury should appoint a 'bishop of Natal'. Hence his letter to Sam on the grounds that there was 'a danger – more than imminent – that there will be a perpetual schism between two sides of the Church of England in South Africa'. The offer put Sam in a dilemma. There was the promise he had made to Ella's parents eleven years ago to be considered, and now he was worried about his health. Could he 'stand transplanting'? Would his 'tendency to nervous weakness, to insomnia and inherited and already more than threatened rheumatism' be worsened by a change of climate? He consulted his father and his doctor. His doctor considered his 'nervous organisation [was] peculiarly delicate … this being so I feel sure you will not be able to stand the heat and the relaxing climate. Your nervous system would become unstrung'. Bishop Edward Henry was also very doubtful. Apart from personal considerations, would it be right to leave Lewisham so soon after becoming vicar? If the offer had been of a missionary bishopric, rather than a colonial one, he would have felt 'less hesitation'. He travelled up to Lewisham to discuss it further with his son and gave his verdict: 'I confess I have my grave doubts whether the Lord of Hosts Himself has not already instructed you with a wider influence at Lewisham and in the Church at home, than you could command at Maritzburg as Bishop.' Sam decided to refuse the offer. The Archbishop was not best pleased. He wrote to Edward Henry regretting:

> ... very deeply that your son Samuel does not go to Natal.... I thought he had the special gifts for reuniting them. I thought that both sides would accept him, and he would bring them together and avoid for us the wretched spectacle, and more wretched fact. I felt that I certainly knew no-one who could do it as he could. I cannot say that I am convinced he is right to decline.

Perhaps that letter partly explains why any preferment was so long delayed. Sam laboured fourteen years in the parish of Lewisham whilst he watched 'younger men than myself made Bishops of London, Exeter, Stepney'.

To make matters worse, his new parish was not as attractive as he first thought. Sam and Ella arrived at Lewisham just when improved communication systems were opening up the area to a vast migration of lower middle class workers. Within a few years seven railway lines connected Lewisham with central London. 'It really did seem', reflected Sam, 'that the masses of south-Londoners appear to see the words "All change here" posted up at the entrance of our streets.' Desperate to move in 'before the mortar is dry', they were equally ready to move on 'as soon as the brass handle is tarnished'. As he and his curates methodically visited every house in the parish, they noticed that it was becoming 'impossible to visit right through a long street, such as Howson Street, before many of those first called upon have gone to make way for still more recent newcomers'. Sunday collections told their own story. In 1896, a third of the congregation gave nothing, and although the remaining two thirds gave something, the something was very little. That year, 60,149 coins had been put in the offertory plates, but most of them were coppers: 33,522 pennies, 25,906 half pennies and 721 farthings. It confirmed Sam's opinion that the parish was seeing not only an 'incoming of numbers who are without much of the world's goods and weighted with many expenses, but also the outgoing of many of the better-to-do who have fled before this invasion of bricks and mortar'. The upper classes were indeed steadily moving away from the pleasant rural areas which were now becoming vast housing estates. He had to be thankful when some of his most stalwart parishioners stayed: 'the churchwardens are safely moored in their respective homes, and will, I trust, resist all temptations to drift elsewhere.' Sam and Ella themselves would very much have liked 'to drift elsewhere' – if only they were given the opportunity. They were, he revealed in his notebook: 'painfully aware that we have no really like-minded friends … wifie's power in society seems all frittered away here … the boys growing up have no friends here, no occupations'.

It was a challenge for any young, evangelical vicar and true to his roots that it was no use repining, but that it was 'better to wear out than to rust out', Sam threw himself into parish work and marathon money-raising efforts. At St Mary's he followed the example of his father and grandfather by gradually increasing the opportunities for celebrating Holy Communion, first by a 7 a.m. Celebration on all Saints' Days, then an Early Celebration every Thursday with a mid-day Choral Communion one Sunday a month. The latter, he felt, 'if most carefully and prayerfully rendered, would lift the soul of man heavenwards'. On the other hand, he could not support the desire of parishioners 'to make private confessions in order to secure private Absolution'. He rejected the view that there was 'greater validity in a private than in a public pronouncement of Absolution … Private Absolution may convey greater comfort, but never greater grace. If this were taught it would do much to restrain private confession to those exceptional cases which alone seem to me to be contemplated by our Prayer Book, and for which no loyal Churchman can deny that the Church has made provision.' It was a view that, in years to come, would not be shared by his son, Julian.

With St Mary's packed to the doors and the population steadily increasing, there was a crying need for new churches. In Sam's first ten years at Lewisham, three new churches were built and £24,000 raised to meet the building costs. There was a new Parish Church Hall with a club room, classrooms and kitchen which had cost £5,000 and was now in constant use for Bible classes, youth activities, discussion groups. Sunday evening concerts and entertainments filled the building to overflowing. Sam agreed with Bishop Thorold that 'a young clergyman might do good by playing cricket and football, <u>so long as he played</u>

well' *(sic)* and appointed curates who could encourage youth activities. He was delighted that in one curate 'all athletics interests have an unfailing friend' whilst another was busy organising summer camps and, innovatively, a show of domestic pets 'to interest the children in promoting kindness to animals'.

Sam needed all the help he could get. Although Lewisham had a much lower percentage of working class people than the neighbouring boroughs, there were still areas where most of the residents, he felt, should be classified as casual labourers. 'Such families' he wrote 'always live on the edge of want'. Poor housing, lack of sanitation, overcrowding led to the poor health which seemed endemic in some areas. His response was a team of voluntary District Visitors and the appointment of a nurse whose salary was paid for from the annual harvest thanksgiving offertories. He supervised over fifty social service groups including slate clubs, a sick diet kitchen, a blanket club, a children's shoe club and a coal club. Lord Dartmouth was persuaded to provide land for allotments, and the Fruit, Flower and Vegetable Society was formed. Ella raised money to open a shelter for young women and Sam addressed 'Men only' meetings on social purity and 'on the high chivalry with which all Englishmen should regard and reverence girls and women'. In 1902, long and anxious consultations at the Vicarage led to the creation of the Lewisham Municipal Association 'the members consisting of representatives chosen from the Wards, both clergymen and laymen, including Anglicans, Roman Catholics, Congregationalists, Unitarians, medical men, a journalist or two, women as well as men'. Its concerns included the housing of the poor, overcrowding, sanitation, social purity, and sobriety. It was a ground-breaking example of how inter-Church co-operation or, in Sam's words, 'Home Union', working with statutory services, might meet social needs. Sidney Webb addressed the first meeting, Lord Dartmouth presiding.

The pressure of work was unrelenting and, as Sam admitted, 'really finished me up'. It was made much more acute because he was always worried about his own finances. Sam had held to his resolution to send his sons to public schools and, at Lewisham, his family was completed by the birth of a sixth son, Ralph. To educate six sons at the best public schools was a heavy expense. By now Monier was at Oxford, Julian at Rugby, Geoffrey and Burgon at Charterhouse, Morris at St. David's, Reigate (a preparatory school) and Ralph was still being educated at home as he was only six years old. However, the plan was that he would join Morris at St. David's. Fees alone were costing £600 p.a. (in spite of scholarships), and they were likely to rise to around £700 when Ralph started school. In 1901 Sam's notebooks show the state of his finances. Lewisham was not a poor living. Sam calculated that his net income was £1,524 of which £353 was his own private income. His figures show that their living expenses plus school fees and £300 to charities totalled around £1,510 p.a The boys' clothing was budgeted at a modest £30 p.a. thanks to a careful system of 'handing down'. Apart from schooling, the biggest drain was housekeeping, estimated at £240 p.a., reflecting his estimate that it cost about ten shillings per person per week to feed the household, including £20 per annum to feed 'stray visitors'. It was a tight budget. To maintain the standard of living Sam and Ella felt necessary for the Vicar of Lewisham meant that every penny needed to be counted. Even on holiday, Ella would note in her diary that they had been working on ways to make ends meet. One year, when Sam miscalculated, he explained to Monier that, as a result, they would not be visiting him at Oxford that term. The boys needed permission to buy such things as a chest expander or an Old Rugbeian blazer. Only the first was allowed. Fortunately, there were generous friends and parishioners to help with the cost of holidays. Generous uncles helped with the cost of children's clothes. To the outside world, Ella and her six boys sitting in the vicarage pew at St Mary's in their best clothes would have been a picture of upper-middle class prosperity. But to Sam, worrying in his study, it felt very different and he knew he was in danger of giving way to his feelings. Depression, he told himself firmly, should be 'tackled in its very first stages, and should never be given a foothold in any life – least of all a busy professional man's, with a family dependent on him, and a priesthood to be worked'. He consulted his doctor for 'giddy spells' and 'neuralgia' or what would probably be termed nowadays as 'migraine'. His doctor suggested the cause was overwork and recommended two days' holiday a week. 'A very stupid suggestion' was Ella's down-to-earth response.

It was the promotion of the Revd Arthur Winnington Ingram, the Suffragan Bishop of Stepney, to Bishop of London in 1901 that nearly took Sam to breaking-point. Surely it made a vacancy that he was ideally qualified to fill? He became convinced that it would happen. He wrote in his notebook: 'If a voice had suggested it to me, I could not have had clearer premonitions'. The impression was so strong that he called it 'a most extraordinary hallucination or temptation' and for three weeks could think of little else until 'it all came to an end when Cosmo Gordon Lang's name was announced'. That evening, he described his reaction and how he dealt with it:

'It teaches me that here I am, and here I must expect to stay and here (oh *Deo gratias*) have I work to do for my Lord. ... I have thrown myself into home duties, study, and parochial [work] and now I must go to rest (11.45 pm) ... humbly asking God to give me an earnest and bright spirit, a new start, and unfailing zest'.

He did not go to bed, for despair swept over him again and he added 'It is a practical and known fact that hope ceases with middle life'. The next day he began to recover himself and prayed that he would find in his 'bounden duty our greatest blessing, and the secret of true peace'. He was not to know that he had been pitting himself against an exceptionally strong candidate. Lang spent seven years at Stepney before becoming Archbishop of York and finally Archbishop of Canterbury.

A few months later Sam's hopes were raised again. The Secretary of the Society for the Propagation of the Gospel was due to retire and Sam's name had come up in discussions. At the end of May he received a letter from the Bishop of Winchester asking if he was willing for his name to be added to the list of 'possibles'. It was a position after Sam's heart – a missionary post, but London-based. He and Ella would miss the parish work but the more he thought about it, the more attractive the position seemed. He would be able to help 'lonely men by correspondence, sympathy with returning missionaries, literary work, communication and counsel with leaders of the Church and cordial and sympathetic union with other missionary societies'. The huge draw-back was financial. As no house would be provided it would mean an annual drop in income of at least £300 – a very serious consideration. There were hurried, anxious discussions with the family: brothers Hugh and Robert were against acceptance, brother-in-law Monier Faithfull and cousin Robert Ottley were in favour. Aunt Lucy Bignold was doubtful as was sister Amy. He wrote to his four eldest boys asking their opinion, pointing out that 'the banquet of life is apt to become very insipid, however plentiful it might be, without the salt of self-sacrifice'. Their reaction is unknown, though Sam considered Geoffrey's reached 'a very high standard of analysis and of weighing possibilities for a son only 16 years of age'. Brother-in-law Frank Aglionby told him that the Bishop of Bombay favoured him. Canon Brook, who was canvassing clerical friends, passed on the news that 'the Bishops of Corea *(sic)* and North China 'both wished me to be appointed'. Sam became more and more enthusiastic. The Church of England missionary movement 'should become the focus for imperial Christianity: the "Foreign Office" of the

Church of England.' The secretary of the SPG should be a Canon of Westminster Abbey. That would 'establish a connection between the SPG and the Abbey'. Such a link would be seen as significant because the Abbey had 'an imperial outlook and is felt by all England to belong to the Empire as much as to this island'. He replied to the Bishop of Winchester allowing his name to go forward and if the remuneration would enable him to meet his sons' school fees he believed he 'should accept the post as a call from God'. For the next three weeks he heard nothing and 'lived in expectation daily and hourly, of receiving a call to leave Lewisham'. On the 21st June it was announced that Bishop Montgomery of Tasmania had been selected and only his formal acceptance was awaited. Sam was devastated, mainly because he felt he had been 'lifted up, looked at and dropt as an unsatisfactory specimen' but also that even when he was being asked if he was willing to stand 'the cables had been going and coming between Lambeth and Tasmania offering the work to Montgomery and urging it on him'. Coming on top of the Stepney disappointment it was almost too much to bear. Why had God allowed this to happen? It was, he decided, because he needed to be taught three lessons: the relative unimportance of self, the importance of all work regardless as to whether it was in a small parish or in a world-wide Society and the absolute importance of God alone. He decided that he must no longer pay any attention to premonitions, or the flattery of friends, and accept the fact that 'early and high promotion which undoubtedly brings out all that is in a man is not to be mine'. Instead he would serve Lewisham 'with fire and force' and reconcile himself that 'so far as its unknown elements are concerned our six sons are now the main interest of our life, their education, their success, their first loves, their start in life'.

In the first instance, that meant concentrating on the Special Mission that was planned to mark the tenth anniversary of his arrival in Lewisham. There were over 34,000 papers, letters and leaflets to be circulated in the parish, and 20,000 to be distributed during the week of the Mission. He and Ella 'worked with all our might for six weeks, leaving papers at every house in the parish'. When the Mission began 'every night there were open-air preachers and a procession of the choir in surplices, singing solemn Litanies'. Special preachers were engaged to take 8 p.m. services. They were not an unmitigated success. Sam exasperatedly wrote in his notebook: 'The addresses by Canon Lester are too long [and] far too loud. He has preached three sermons nearly 45 minutes in length, one over 50, on Jereboam, Reuben and his brothers, and Judas'. Instead, he felt 'these folk need the very ABC of the Infant School of Christ, time upon time, here a little and then a hymn and then a little'.

But to continue to serve with 'fire and force' was exhausting, especially when so much of his life was filled with monotonous routine. In 1902, he tried to list all his engagements. In two weeks he had attended or chaired fourteen committees, ranging from the Anglican Men's Guild, to the Bazaar Committee, the Lewisham Municipal League, the Believers' Committee, and the Standing Committee of the Society for the Propagation of the Gospel. He had conducted Sunday services and a Baptismal service, and taught at the Church School and, mid-week, rushed down to Godalming to visit a son's housemaster at Charterhouse. He could not stay long, as he needed to get home for an evening service. Inevitably, the train was late. The only relaxation he seemed to have had was one morning playing golf. After a fortnight, he gave up recording everything. 'Time failed me to add anything to this record'. No wonder that the boys rushed to meet their father as he came through the front door and at times would compete for his attention. No wonder that he confided in his notebook 'I don't think I loathe my work, because it is familiar, but I loathe the recurrence of so many annual or quarterly or monthly services and meetings.'

As we shall see, Sam was fortunate in that his sons never gave him acute anxiety. That was left to the rest of his family. For much of his life, Sam shouldered responsibility not only for his parents but for his siblings. His elder brother, Edward, was rarely at home to help. Of his remaining four brothers, Robert, Hugh, Henry and Ashley, Hugh became a successful solicitor and partner in the family firm of *Ellis, Bickersteth, Aglionby and Hazel*, Robert a prosperous business man, Henry became Vicar of Falmer, Sussex and Ashley had a school of his own at North Foreland, Kent. However, in 1902, things looked very different. Sam listed the family matters that had weighed on his mind during that year.

> We have Father only with us in the flesh, not in the mind or spirit; a real imprisonment and deeply trying to him; Harry in an asylum at Perth, as mad as a hatter about himself, though sane and statesmanlike on every other point; Robert is lying with broken ribs and scratched lungs at Westgate-on-Sea where he had gone to cheer up Effie [his widowed sister] for Christmas, and has great financial anxieties at Fetter Lane [He lost £1,200 in the collapse of the well-known religious publishers, Sampson Low]; Ashley with his wife dying having for a third time destructed (*sic*) his school and pupils, actually earning not a penny.

The stress imposed by mental illness is still today one of the heaviest burdens a family may have to bear. In the Bickersteth family both sides of the family were affected. Ella's brother, Outram, died in a mental asylum in South Africa in 1906. Sam's father died the same year following a slow loss of his faculties – probably a form of Alzheimer's disease. Between 1901 and 1903, Sam's notebooks reveal in some detail the mental illness of his younger brother, Henry Venn Bickersteth (known as Harry) who possibly suffered from a clinical depression. Although the burden of Harry's care was shared between members of the family, the ultimate responsibility remained with Sam, at a time when he was far from happy coping with the endless routine of Lewisham parish life. Harry became mentally ill when he was vicar of Rockbeare, Devon, in his father's old diocese. Early in 1902 he was 'engaged in persistent self-analysis, weeping and acting strangely'. At other times he was preaching and chairing committees effectively. Sam arranged for him to see a specialist in London. It was not a consultation which inspired confidence.

> He pointed out that if HVB retired now from Rockbeare his self-analysis as to his folly and unwisdom in so doing might plague him just as much as now, and even more than the present prospect of it does. He assured me he might quite wholly recover, that to put two stones on him [in weight] is the desirable thing at present. He said, I feel inclined to say 'Let us face the risk and take it'.

In short, felt Sam, his verdict was 'in this state of uncertainty … Let us toss up for it'.

It was decided that Harry should return to Rockbeare, and the family mobilised. His sister-in-law Marion (Edward of Tokyo's widow) offered to go and stay with him; Bickersteth and his brothers Robert and Hugh conferred and decided to keep the whole matter secret from Harry's Bishop. Robert would see Harry off to Exeter, sister Mary Jane (May) would meet him, and Effie would go with him to Rockbeare. The sisters and brothers would organise a rota. Robert would visit from London every weekend; it was not fair to involve Marion. By the autumn, they decided that Harry would be 'either better or worse, and if the latter we are confident that he [will] resign without a bother'. He did become worse and Sam had to tell the Bishop, who suggested a six week holiday. Meanwhile, Harry must go to Lewisham with Sam and get medical advice.

> The next day Harry was in a very weak state of indecision, but at 10.20 I carried him off, poor fellow, with hardly any luggage, to London. Gordon [the doctor] seemed to think that this rapid remove before the next day (Sunday) to be necessary. ... On the journey to town I tried to keep him occupied, but often he knit his brows, smote his knees, clenched his hands and looked distraught.

Sam took him to see another London doctor who

> ... described Harry's state as 'dips of depression', told him nervous conditions were as plain to doctors as bones to a layman, that a sprained bone needed rest, not neglect and more work, and that a strained nervous system must have rest if it was to recover. If not, its breakdown would become chronic.

He recommended 'not an institution [but] a companion in a quiet place, either a clerical or medical friend for a holiday'. Between them, Robert and Sam found a suitable medical man and arranged Harry's admission to Chequer Lawn, St. Albans at £10 10s. a week. At first, Harry improved and discussions started about returning to work. Family influence found a living for him at Falmer, Sussex. But Harry could not cope and was soon again 'in a weak and feeble state of mind and become intensely selfish and jealous'. He returned to Lewisham. 'Harry was with us all Lent in a very anxious state of brain, which took it out of us' was Ella's understated comment on the situation. Finally he had to be admitted to Murray's Asylum in Perth, Scotland, now part of Murray Royal Hospital. Sam made the long journeys to visit him, and was pleased with the care his brother was receiving. He also liked Dr Urquhart, the physician superintendent, who had designed the asylum chapel.

> My impression after seeing Dr Urquhart, the personnel attending, Thornley, the gardener, the lodgekeeper and everybody was that he was cared for and understood (sic). ... I shall never forget Urquhart's loving attitude as he sat by Harry in Harry's own comfortable room, and reasoned with all his vagaries for nearly an hour.

'His rooms are like College rooms with his own private servant' added Ella. Harry, however, was not happy. He started writing to his brothers. Ella described the result:

Harry was miserable at Perth and wrote despairing letters two or three times a day. Sam and Robert both had to go up there during the winter and force Harry to remain ... it took it out of my Sam terribly.

Brother Hugh was certain that Harry should be removed and wanted to send a telegram to Harry to this effect. Sam was horrified:

A better meant but unwise telegram under the circumstances I never read. ... It would have forced on Harry an act of decision of which he is, alas, incapable. Therefore I posted up to Hugh, met Robert there, and explained why the telegram must not be sent. ... Hugh then said in perfect good temper that in that case he must retire from the case ... he there and then wrote a letter to Harry saying he must refer him to me for all matters ... In this of course I assented, Robert again with me, which is consoling as dear old Hugh's action makes it just a little harder to bear that great burden.

Finally, care, rest and quiet were effective. 'By Easter 1903 he was cured' wrote Ella triumphantly. Robert brought Harry back to Lewisham and the brothers helped him to settle in again at Falmer and supported him through the first Sundays. Sam felt that 'a wife not less than 45 years old' would be desirable, but finally settled for his old nurse to live with Harry. Harry remained vicar of Falmer and a bachelor for the rest of his life. Sam gratefully recorded

I can never thank Ella enough for her admirable judgement and strength of character all through this painful year. She has greatly sustained me in my determination to keep [Harry] at Perth and so has Robert's cool judgement ... Well, *Deo gratias*! And let us take courage.

Sam needed to take courage, because he was also looking after his father. Bishop Edward Henry had become steadily more confused and it had been Sam's responsibility to ease his removal from Exeter. Between August and November 1900 his father's conversation had become 'disjointed and impossible to follow at times ... [while] he takes a long time to write a few lines which are perhaps quite unintelligible ... he the busiest of men now does nil.' His doctor thought that 'he had an old man's heart, imperfectly nourishing the brain, hence the loss of memory, lapse of words, etc.' Sam spent many hours at the Palace, sorting and destroying papers, whilst Ella arranged the furnishing of a house in Westbourne Grove, Paddington. There, surrounded by unmarried daughters and his wife, the old Bishop clung both to life and his son. Sam visited regularly, and sometimes found him 'speaking with much greater clearness than before'. Edward Henry seems to have been a placid, gentle invalid, still reading his Bible and his Psalter. On a 'good' day, Sam noted his father's conversation:

> I have nothing that I can follow now but the Word, and that is most precious ... Again and again, he said, it is so good to see you. I love you so you cannot come too often ... I must say goodbye to Ella. She is such a delight.

Over the next five years, Sam watched his father – 'how strange an affliction for him of all men' – becoming more and more confused. He poured out his grief in prayer: 'O God, my Father, lead gently home thy good servant and that quickly, if it seems right in Thy sight. For Jesus Christ's sake. Amen'

The old Bishop died in 1906, and by then it really did seem that Sam and Ella's worst troubles were over. On Ascension Day, 1905 Sam and Ella had gone to Early Celebration with their eldest son, Monier. Ella and Monier reached home first and 'on the hall table saw a long envelope with the name A J Balfour in the corner'. Frustratingly, Ella had to take family prayers, 'knowing Sam would come in and open the letter'. She and Monier were convinced 'it would mean Leeds'. They were right. 'When we came out there was Sam looking as if God had spoken to him'. A whirl of activity followed. The previous vicar who had just been consecrated Bishop of Gloucester had to be consulted, the relatives at Westbourne Terrace visited, Ella's mother told and letters sent to each son. The Bishop of Rochester was contacted and approved. The Bishop of Lichfield sent a wire saying 'yes'. Then, wrote Ella, 'we heard the Bishop of Ripon was hurt at not being consulted by Balfour, so they 'waited till he returned from the theatre at 10 p.m. and smoothed him over'. On Saturday afternoon 'Sam left a letter at Downing Street accepting the Vicarage of Leeds'. There was only one cloud on the horizon, and again it was financial. Their income would drop by about £300 p.a.

It was going to be a tight squeeze financially, and Burgon was going to have to postpone taking up his place at Christ Church, Oxford for a year. On the other hand, there was so much in its favour. Leeds was a prestigious appointment and the Vicar of Leeds was not only regarded as being one step away from a bishopric, he was also a key figure in civic life. The parish church, St Peter's, was huge, being built in the style of a cathedral by an architect who wanted to accommodate the largest number of worshippers possible. Eucharist was celebrated every morning at 7 and 8 a.m and choral evensong sung daily. The choir, composed of thirty men and thirty boys, was one of its chief glories and thought to be the finest Parish Church choir in the country. Sam made no changes, but was careful to point out that he would never forget the advice given him by an earlier Vicar of Leeds, Dr Gott: 'You were brought up among evangelicals. See that you build on it, but never depart from what you were taught'.

In July, Sam and Ella made their first visit to Leeds and went to see the vicarage. 'The house was ugly outside but comfortable inside' noted Ella. Like every other vicarage they had inhabited 'the drainage had to be thoroughly overhauled'. Then they were driven around the City and, passing the Parish Church, had the thrill of hearing the coachman spontaneously saying 'That's been a good training ground for Bishops and Choirmen'. Later in the day they met the Lord Mayor and were invited to stay with him. Sam's induction in September was overwhelming. The service was 'magnificent' and so was the music. In the evening, the church was packed to hear him preach his first sermon, and next day there was a reception in the Town Hall. Ella, who had much experience of this type of event, wrote '… such a sight I never saw. We stood for an hour shaking hands with people who crowded in, and when the Hall was so packed that there was not standing room, then came the speeches. Sam caught the people at once … they shouted and moved handkerchiefs, and gave him such a moving welcome.' Gerald Balfour, the MP for Leeds stayed the night at the vicarage, accompanied by his wife, Lady Betty. 'Such charming people' noted Ella. Soon they were 'constantly at bazaars, meetings or dining out'. In October, Ella was 'at home' every afternoon and had between 300 to 400 callers.

The work load was, however, immense. As soon as he arrived in Leeds Sam was faced with raising £1,200 to pay off the mortgage on the Church Institute and he soon found out that money-raising in Yorkshire was rather different from his experience in Lewisham. However, he succeeded, and there was a big Festival Service with the sermon preached by the Archbishop of York and a grand procession of Bishops and clergy though the streets. The opportunities for new welfare initiatives were endless. There seem to have been few areas of social concern in which Sam did not become involved. Arranging a meeting between Bishop Gore and Arthur Balfour to discuss town planning, heading a deputation to lobby the Prime Minister to introduce legislation to implement the Report of the Royal Commission on the Care and Control of the Feeble-minded, pressing for slum clearance and influencing intransigent City Councillors, all came within his sphere of activities. In addition, his church responsibilities were almost overwhelming. To help him, he had a staff of sixteen curates though, in the early days, this was a mixed blessing as, noted Ella, 'the old staff were very disloyal and tried Sam a good deal'. With the hard-won experience he had acquired in Lewisham, Sam began to appoint his own men and included a friend of Morris: young George Bell (later Bishop of Chichester), whom Morris persuaded to come and see his father about a curacy.

He had to attempt 'the impossible task of controlling the Parish Church with a large staff of clergy, four missions, two thousand Sunday School scholars, Bible classes, Guilds, with perpetual money-raising schemes inevitable in a poorly endowed Benefice and at the same time [try] to meet the innumerable demands made from the biggest undivided Deanery in the British Empire with nearly seventy parishes serving half a million of people.' The solution would be to divide the Diocese of Ripon, with Leeds forming a new See with a bishop who would 'absorb into the office the traditions centering round the Vicar of Leeds, with the Parish Church becoming the pro-cathedral of the new diocese'. In 1907, Sam started discussions with a speech at the Diocesan Conference. For seven years negotiations wound a slow, tortuous and unprofitable way. Pressure groups had to be placated; Leeds members of the Church Association were vociferous in wanting no increase in bishops. Sam wrote to the Archbishop of York: 'I have pointed out to them by increasing the number of bishops they increase the chance of getting men after their own heart and decrease the area in which those men whom they distrust can do mischief.' He had an ally in the editor of the *Yorkshire Post* and there were 'constant paragraphs in the Press'. It made people uneasy, and the Bishop of Wakefield wrote to Ella hinting that she might mention to her husband that 'matters were being pushed a little too quickly'. Financing a new See was inevitably problematic. Sam, a southerner, in a moment of exasperation, complained that 'Leeds churchmen, like all Yorkshiremen, will do their religion, like everything else they do, at other people's expense if they can'. Seven years of constant meetings, constant lobbying, constant delays all took their toll on Sam's health, which was now complicated by increasing deafness. In 1914, the formation of the Bradford See and the outbreak of war postponed the formation of a Leeds See indefinitely.

Sam and his sixteen curates. Leeds 1909

LEEDS PARISH CHURCH.

(*Left to Right*). *Top Row*—Rev. R. Shipman; Rev. D. M. M. Bartlett; Rev. W. F. Long; Rev. G. G. Payne-Cook.
Middle Row—Rev. A. M. Sullivan Rev. N. L. T. Hodgson; Rev. A. C. de Boinville; Rev. W. Parker (Archbishop's
Chaplain); Rev. G. K. A. Bell; Rev. R. Lewis; Rev. E. H. Dykes. *Bottom Row*—Rev. J. B. Seaton;
Rev. H. H. Malleson; Rev. R. G. Glennie; Rev. Canon Wood; His Grace The Archbishop of York;
Rev. Dr. Bickersteth, D.D. (Vicar of Leeds); Rev. O. G. Mackie; Rev. T. H. Bywater; Rev. S. C. Harris; Master Hurdu

This background of inhibited affection, disappointing academic achievement and frustrated ambition could well account for Sam's hesitant and diffident manner, still recalled today by his grandson, who felt it would hardly have been a recommendation for the episcopate. A further contributory factor could well have been the history of mental illness in the family. For much of his life, Sam was dogged by ill health. He estimated that his recurrent neuralgia lost him 60 or 70 days work in 1900. Bronchitis and influenza took an annual toll, and when Vicar of Leeds, he suffered so severely from a type of skin disease that he was unable to work for about six months and was finally sent to recuperate in Sicily. One can speculate that much of his illness was psychosomatic, but there is no doubt that his suffering was acute and was rarely eased by medical treatment. His skin condition was first treated by extracting all his teeth, as it was thought to be triggered by poor digestion. Then bed-rest was prescribed, with bandages saturated in peppermint oil applied to his back and arms, five pints of water to be drunk every day, with chloral to be taken for a sleeping draught. When his wife was called away to look after her dying mother, the rash worsened. Ella telephoned Burgon to say that his father was 'completely unnerved' and 'he really must have someone at home'. Burgon rushed home from Oxford to deal with parish business and look after his father. He slept in the same room and supplied 'beef tea and cocoa two or three times in the night'. Eventually, Sam's brother-in-law, Monty (Dr Montague Monier-Williams), recommended 'electrical treatment' in London. Burgon went with his father to Welbeck Street and reported: 'He lies on a sofa and holds a sort of rod, through which the electricity passes into his body. It is very soothing'. Sam's poor hearing became increasingly handicapping, although his specialist felt 'he need not give up Leeds if he would rest one hour before dinner, and never think about his hearing, and never to speak of it'. To his grandfather's instruction to 'wear out rather than rust out', and his father's dictum that Bickersteths 'must work hard and play hard', Sam now added: 'Grace is not intended to sterilise grit'.

If Sam needed grit to cope with his clerical career, his other 'main interest in life' – his boys – was the source of great happiness. Six healthy, good-looking, self-confident young men, all with promising careers, preferably in the Church, would show that his branch of the family were 'true Bickersteths' and, incidentally, make attending Lambeth Palace garden parties a proud delight. Nor was he disappointed. His less than happy youth does not seem to have impaired his ability to make close, loving relationships with his sons as will be shown in the following chapters. In his own life, the keynotes were self-denial and strenuous living. As a priest, he had to wrestle with his yearning for high office and his duty to conscientiously fulfil his vocation in a lower role. As a father, to ensure that his sons became self-confident, potential leaders, he condemned himself to years of financial anxiety. It would appear that, as a result, he also condemned himself to years of indifferent health. Yet the ultimate result was a conscientious priest loved by his parishioners for his 'assiduous care' and an anxious, affectionate and playful father and grandfather who was greatly loved by his family. His vulnerability strengthened the relationship between him and his sons. On one occasion when his father was poorly and alone, thirteen year-old Monier sent him a comforting letter:

> Dearest, dearest Father. I hope you will be alright soon, do obey the doctor's orders. I wish there was someone to take care of you. Your loving and affectionate son, Edward Monier Bickersteth

Background Reading

Bickersteth, S *Citizens All. Civic Service: the Churchman's Duty.* A R Mowbray (1918)

McCleod, H *Class and Religion in the late Victorian City – London.* Croom Helm (1974)

Sources

Notebooks held by family

Correspondence and papers 1838-1904 of Edward Henry Bickersteth, Bishop of Exeter. Bodleian Library.

Charles Booth Collection. Notebook B314. London School of Economics, British Library of Political and Economic Science.

Annual reports of St Mary's Parish Church, Lewisham. Held at Lewisham Local Studies Centre.

PART II

THE MOULDING OF THE CLAY

5

NURSERY DAYS

'As a family we have indeed wonderful happiness to look back upon'. Julian. 1916.

'I know I'm made of dust, but I suppose it was very poor dust'. Monier, aged 8.

Sam and Ella's first child, Monier, was born in Spring Street, Paddington in 1882 when his father was a curate at St Mary's, Hampstead. Before his birth his parents had made some decisions about how they would care for any family they might have. Their home would be more relaxed than the ones they had experienced. They would play with their children, and even card games would be allowed. Visits to the theatre and pantomimes would be family treats. They would try to make Sunday the most pleasant day of the week. The new baby would be 'a gift from God' and so it would be their joy and privilege, as well as their duty, to do everything in their power to bring up their child within a loving, happy home. Two generations earlier, Edward of Watton, looking at baby Edward Henry, described his son as 'untainted beyond his natural corruption'. That was a world away from Sam's feelings when, 'nursing our really placid little son', he found him to be 'quite a darling'. Nevertheless, in one major aspect of the child's upbringing, Sam and Ella were at one with the previous generations. Their son, like his forefathers, would be enrolled at his baptism 'manfully to fight under [Christ's] banner, against sin, the world and the devil; and to continue Christ's faithful soldier and servant to his life's end.'

Like their predecessors, the children's spiritual care would be their first priority, but as regards daily behaviour, the aim would be 'self-conquest'. Good behaviour should stem from the child's own moral sensibility. Once that foundation had been built, it would lead to self-confidence and independence and feed the inner drive so necessary for a manly Christian and leader of men. Nor was there much time to achieve this, because the children would be leaving home for boarding

Ninny and her 'six perfect pets'

Monier   Geoffrey   Julian

Burgon   Morris   Ralph

school when they were about eight years old. Ella and Sam would have a shared role. To Sam went the more formal training through regular Bible study and private chats with each child. In the background, he would be the ultimate authority. Ella's responsibility would be two-fold. She would continue the daily simple Bible teaching and prayers in much the same way as she had experienced them as a child. But she would also help the children to win 'victories' on the nursery 'battlefield'. 'Good' children shared their toys, they bravely coped with shyness, they did not easily give way to pain and they certainly did not give way to temper tantrums. They conquered themselves. It was these encounters that were to prove to be much more difficult to resolve and her diaries reveal her manful efforts.

But all that was still far in the future, for in November 1882 two questions dominated all discussions: 'Would their baby survive? and 'What action would it be right to take?' The problem was wholly unexpected. Ella could not breast-feed him. Now she was in danger of either losing him or accepting a solution which she may have interpreted as prejudicing his Christian nurture. She recorded in her diary that the baby was

a fine healthy child ...The first week of his life he was a pretty little fellow – they said like me – with a little round face and small features, but want of nourishment soon told on his looks.

She tried to feed him herself 'but it was no use. I had literally nothing'. She was distraught.

It was such pain to see the little red head of my sonny screaming for want of food, that we determined to give it up and give him the bottle ... but day after day he began to grow thinner and smaller, in fact quite to waste away, and he screamed night and day ...we changed him to the Artificial Human Milk, now made in London and said to be a facsimile of Mother's milk, but that proved worse than anything.

If artificial milk failed there was only one course remaining, although Ella and Sam did not even want to contemplate it.

We had many consultations with Mr. Rayley Owen, [their family doctor] who several times recommended a wet nurse. This we shrunk from, but at length Dr Owen gave us to understand that it was not safe to try anything else and that we should lose our darling if we did not have a wet nurse.

89

Sister-in-law, Georgie Monier-Williams, lived nearby and came to the rescue. She went round to Queen Charlotte's Hospital and found 'a respectable married woman' whose baby was 'a beauty'. Both were submitted for Dr. Owen's approval. All was in order. The mother was the wife of an unemployed labourer, whose family was 'starving with everything pawned'. Ella provided comforts for the impoverished family and rejoiced that

> Our poor little thin wasted boy began to thrive from the first moment ... the relief it was to hear him stop crying repaid us for the keen trial it is to have a wet nurse.

The wet nurse, Margaret Lyons, stayed with Sam and Ella 'giving wonderfully little trouble, [though] of course liking a great deal of stout' until, at ten months, Monier was fully weaned.

Only the words 'shrunk' and 'keen trial' allow us to speculate whether his parents resisted the idea of a wet nurse because of risks to the baby's wellbeing or from natural repugnance that a stranger should come between Ella and her baby in such an intimate way. There was also a moral dimension to the problem. At this critical time, they may well have been influenced by the old Puritan belief that it was the will of God that babies should be breastfed, for the Lord had equipped mothers to do this very task. In addition, a wet-nurse, who would almost certainly be lower class, might transmit unwelcome character traits with her milk. It is probably significant that the next three babies survived on varying mixtures of cow's milk and barley sugar water. No wet nurse was employed again. Ella was only able to nurse her last two sons. Morris was born in 1891 and she 'nursed him four and a half months, the first of my babies I have been able to – and it was such a delight'.

Ella was far from alone when her babies arrived. Her mother regularly came to stay, and Sam followed the example of Prince Albert and was present at each birth, growing in confidence with each new arrival. When Julian, the third son, was born Ella recorded that 'Dr Collier gave the chloroform on a bit of lint with oil silk under it. Mother held the lint and Sam poured on the chloroform.' Although sister-in-law Georgie was not present at the birth, she was always around in the early years of Ella's marriage, ready to lend a helping hand. She was the wife of Ella's eldest brother, Monier Faithfull Monier-Williams, an up-and-coming solicitor and lived nearby. She was the same age as Ella and already had two baby sons when Monier arrived. At last, Ella had a female relative of her own age to confide in and her early accounts of her babies are peppered with thankful references to Georgie's help. Georgie, attractive, witty, charming and clever, speaking French as well as Ella and an accomplished pianist, had much more experience than Ella in running a household. She understood the problems in employing staff. Ella had difficulties in finding a suitable nurse for Monier. Her first attempt was disastrous. Ellen Twyman turned out to be 'dirty, slovenly and impertinent'. Her replacement was 'a young Scotch girl, Agnes Kelly'. It solved nothing. At Oxford, Agnes was 'much disliked by mother's servants'. Ella gave her 'a good talking to'. Two months later. Monier was 'suddenly seized with a severe attack of pleurisy'. He was nineteen months old. The weather was 'intensely hot', Ella was heavily pregnant and she was in the midst of moving house to Ripon where Sam had just been appointed Bishop's chaplain. Monier was 'always in a perspiration' and Ella was sure 'nurse deliberately disobeyed my orders as regards windows open and draughts'. She moved him to her bedroom and nursed him herself whilst 'packing the house linen'. Then the new baby arrived at short notice. Georgie came to the rescue – not only with the loan of her old double perambulator but, more importantly, she 'found out what a little villain the nurse was', told Sam and Agnes was dismissed. After that, Georgie 'lent' Ella one of her nurses, a most useful arrangement for when little Monier went to stay with his aunt and uncle in the future there was a familiar face in the nursery.

The nurse problem was not solved until the arrival of Eliza Peters about a year later. Monier was aged three, Geoffrey was two, and Julian had just arrived. She was twenty-nine, and came from Staffordshire. Yet she remains a shadowy figure in the Bickersteth archive. Ella mentions her comparatively rarely in her diaries and always refers to her as 'Nurse', listing her name, amongst others, on outings and holidays. To the children, she was always known as Ninny. It is only when she was in her 60's, writing to Burgon, that we catch a glimpse of her background:

> When I came to your mother I was very much [illegible] with my own sorrow, and you were all such helpless little boys then and you filled up a gap in my heart which no one else could ever do; and it has been one long joy to me to care for you all. I don't think any other nurse could have had such a happy time.

The children leaving home for boarding school was felt as keenly by her as it was by the small boys. She was as homesick for them as they were for her. 'I do so often go and look at the picture in your bedroom of your School' she wrote to Burgon. 'I try to fancy I can see you there. What shall I do when Morris comes [to the school] I don't know'. The children rarely wrote home without sending their love to her, and as adults they remained in affectionate contact. Few details have survived as to the way she cared for them, though the displays she arranged to welcome home the older boys from boarding school went down in family history. Ella described them:

> The decorations for the boys in the nursery and hall are beautiful. Nurse has something new every holidays and last night the whole household was busy helping with flags and garlands. This year [1898] we have the names of the four schools in white letters on a red ground.

Perhaps a clearer picture can be obtained of her role in their lives through the story of Ralph's fifth birthday present. It was a horse tricycle; a tricycle with a horse's head moulded on the handle bars. Ralph wanted it more than anything else in the world and had worked out his own way to obtain it. Wording his request carefully whilst his mother listened to his prayers, every day he asked God: "Please let me have one on my birthday, if you think it is good for me". Later he could not resist adding: "Don't forget the bell and the lamp." His parents seem to have decided that such an expensive gift was out of the question. Ninny decided otherwise, and raised the money herself from relatives and the servants. The older boys, away at boarding school, kept a watching brief. 'Have you found out about the bicycle horse yet for Baby's birthday? Do let me know' wrote Burgon. Ninny kept them updated. 'I have got 9 shillings towards the bicycle horse and I am writing to Aunt Edie [Bishop Edward Henry's daughter] tonight. I will write and let you know the result.' Only 12/6d was forthcoming from Exeter, but finally the horse tricycle was bought and she wrote to Burgon in triumph '… it is a real beauty it cost 34/-. I collected 30/-.' Presumably Ella and Sam made up the difference – or did Ninny?

Fortunately, we know in detail what happened on Ralph's birthday morning, for the few letters from Ninny that survive show how meticulous she was to recount every detail of home life to homesick boys away at school.

> I do wish you could have seen him receive the Bicycle Horse: on Friday evening I took his cot down to mother's room so that he could be in their bed early. [It was a family tradition that the

birthday boy jumped into bed with his parents] He had a few small presents to receive, amongst them a card with a little boy on a Bicycle. He said 'I don't seem to have got many presents Mummy' so father said: 'You must wait till you are dressed'. I ought to tell you Aunt Marion [Bishop Edward's wife] came and slept here on purpose to see him receive the Bicycle Horse. At 8 o'clock the Horse was put in the front hall and everyone stood in the hall and then father brought Ralph downstairs. I wish you could have seen his joy. He jumped about he was so excited, and finally burst into tears. He was so overjoyed. I will send you a list of the smaller presents.

In 1910, when she had been with the family for twenty-five years, Ninny was presented with a silver watch, Ella noting that 'She looks so strong and well and is very happy especially since she got her annuity. It is wonderful how with sheer pluck she has managed to save for it.' As Ninny's salary in 1901 was £7 a quarter, it was certainly an achievement. On the fiftieth anniversary of her employment, Sam paid his tribute.

She served since August 27th 1885 and therefore on August 27th 1935 she is Queen of the day, and we crown her with our Love, with our Blessing, and with our Prayers and Thanksgivings.

In contrast to that formality, the 'intimate records' unveil a more poignant picture. When Burgon was eighteen Ninny wrote to him at the beginning of the summer holidays:

I am feeling rather low spirited today, they have all gone off to the Lakes and I miss them all so. 'What an old Silly I am' (sic) and it is just 21 years today since I entered your home. I dare not look back, with all my many, many failings, I just feel I have only been a disappointment.

It is a sad reflection on a working life that had given great happiness to the children, but which leaves a question mark over her relationship with the parents. As was the custom of the time, Ninny was always treated as 'staff'. Today she is recollected as a quiet figure sitting outside the immediate family circle, not expecting to join in the general conversation. Her living area was the nursery and the kitchen quarters. Joining the family in the dining room was sufficiently unusual for it to be noted in Ella's diary. She expected nothing else. When she had 'a very great treat' she wrote to Monier to tell him all about it. 'I went to see Julian at his school. I did enjoy it so much. I never thought I should ever have seen Summerfields [a preparatory school in north Oxford]. I shall always be able to picture it.' It is quite possible that Ella sometimes found Ninny a rival in her children's affection, perhaps even a silent critic. It is only thanks to Ninny that we have an insight into Monier's childhood: 'he never was childish or boyish enough, he was sombre, and was sad'. The comment was recorded by Sam; no hint of it can be found in Ella's accounts of Monier's childhood, although she described meticulously how she 'drew out' and 'fashioned prayerfully' her six energetic sons.

In the early days the spiritual message was simple. God was a loving, heavenly father. It was not a difficult idea to convey as the boys had a model in their own father. They had watched Sam feeding the latest baby or nursing a new arrival. A loving heavenly Father meant that they themselves must be loving, especially to each other, so that one day they would also each have a 'heart full of love to God and of a desire to please Him.' So the parents encouraged the children to care for each other. As a result, Monier peppered his letters home with requests to buy the new baby a rattle from him or lend Julian his hoop. He was 'so very glad Morris and Burgon have learnt to ride the tricycle. Please will you hire it again for an hour and I will pay for it? When one of the boys was ill at school, his brothers would send him flowers. When Ralph broke his leg, his brothers were sent to meet the doctor when it was time for the splint to come off. There were 'five eager little faces round the bed when the leg was undone and found to be straight and sound'. Training in the Christian faith also started early. Monier was two and a half when, at Ella's knee 'he began to say a short prayer every morning'. She noted in her diary that he could already say 'who kind Jesus is and will tell you that He lives in the sky and likes Mona to be a good boy. He insists on praying 'God bless Mona's own likky (*sic*) dolly and make her a good girl too'. A month later he was 'putting his hand on his own head to show how kind Jesus blesses little children'. By the time he was three, Ella was 'telling Mona about Heaven'. She must have painted an attractive picture for his response was "I hope the little children there will lend Mona their pretty play things" and "I want Mother to take Mona there next summer". He was not burdened by the fear of death, and the children were fortunate that they were very rarely dangerously ill. Seemly behaviour at daily family prayers was taken for granted by adults and children alike. But when the boys were very young, there was also understanding, indulgence and enjoyment. 'Monier [aged four] tried our equanimity at prayers yesterday morning by repeating the Blessing in a grave and audible voice after his Father' reported Ella.

**Portrait in oils of the Revd Edward Bickersteth (1786 - 1850)
by Alexander Mosses, circa 1826**

Portrait in oils of the Rt Revd Dr Edward Henry Bickersteth,
Bishop of Exeter, (1825-1906) by Charles Cope, 1899.

Portrait in oils of Sir
Monier Monier-Williams,
K.C.I.E., (1819-1899) by
W. W. Ouless, 1882

Photograph of Lady Julia
Grantham Monier-Williams,
née Faithfull (1826-1908),
undated

Portrait in oils of
the Revd Dr Samuel
Bickersteth (1857-1937)
by Maurice William
Greiffenhagen, 1928.

Photograph of Ella Chlora
Faithfull Bickersteth,
née Monier-Williams
(1858-1954), 1925

He had already managed to sit quietly throughout Sunday morning service. Ella was delighted: 'He behaved beautifully the whole time ... He began to speak once in the sermon, but only because he forgot'. Grace was said at every mealtime from the earliest days. It would seem that the children were encouraged to use their own words. 'Burgon is now two and a half and very backward in talking. His grace is very characteristic. He likes to thank for everything separately. "Ta meat, ta tate [potato], ta honey, ta lots of honey."'

'Self conquest' was much more difficult to achieve and Ella was fortunate that her first son was by temperament an 'easy' child, sensitive, obedient, 'tall and thin with a sweet expression'. He passed his first test of character with flying colours. When he was two and a half, his younger brother, Geoffrey, was growing fast and learning to crawl. 'Monier gives up his toys to him so prettily' noted Ella proudly. It was not to last. Three months later she noticed:

> He and Monier are beginning to have a few scuffles, for Geoffrey is now old enough to upset Monier's bricks or seize his toys. Sometimes Monier takes Geoffrey's things, but he has a strong will, and is very determined and will not be put upon by Monier. He yells out lustily.

A month later she was worried. 'I hope Mona will soon be able to learn to play unselfishly with Geoffrey'. There is no indication as to how she dealt with that problem, but eight months later she gives a clue in an account of a 'little chat' she had with him.

> You are growing very big, Mona, but you must grow good at the same time. 'Mother', he replied, very earnestly, 'I do try to be good, but I can't be good'. He said it from the bottom of his heart. He has begun to learn the sad lesson of the spirit is willing but the flesh is weak'.

That conversation appears to have left its mark. When he was eight, he was very ill with measles and had a difficult convalescence. His mother wrote:

> He has had to submit to various remedies, and his nurse [Ninny] said to him jokingly: 'Well what a lot of things there are to do for you. You are an extraordinary boy. I wonder what you're made of?' Monier replied in a depressed voice 'I know I'm made of dust, but I suppose it was very poor dust.'

One can speculate as to the message that Ninny was trying to convey when she told Ella about that incident, but there is no indication that Ella felt any cause for concern. It was when their fifth son, Morris, was born that Ella began to encounter problems that she had never before experienced with his more malleable brothers. Although

> a bright, quick, clever child. ... He has a tremendous will, really stronger than all the others ...He never wastes words but is monosyllabic and determined in his replies to questions: I do, I should, I will, I can, being his usual mode of reply. He is passionate and self-willed, but we are helping him to conquer himself.

She had at least two methods. One was standing him in the corner, though his reaction was resigned rather than contrite. 'Such is life. It is so tirely'. The other was suggested by thirteen-year-old Monier. He gave Morris two vases: a shiny gold Benares brass one and a plain terracotta one. They were to be kept on Ella's faldstool, presumably in the Oratory. When Morris had 'conquered his temper, a white bead goes into the gold vase, when he has been naughty a black bead into the ugly vase. It has already had a marvellous effect' wrote his mother. It was certainly a formidable mixture of reward, punishment and spiritual reinforcement. How successful it was in the long term is less certain. Not long afterwards, Ella reminded Morris at prayer time that he had been crying several times that day. 'You must ask God to help you to-morrow'. 'No, I won't' he replied 'I can be good of my own self if I want to'. However, Ella persisted. Some months later she could report that 'Morris has been trying very hard, and has only had one black bead this week. That one was a great trouble to him, but he put it in very honestly.'

Five-year-old Morris might have been strong-willed and determined, but he was also very shy. A little later, he failed miserably to 'conquer himself' and, worse still, he failed in full view of the public. He was required to perform the task which seems to be the prerogative of Vicarage children – especially good-looking ones like Morris – that of presenting the bouquet to the visiting dignitary at the annual Church bazaar. It was a calamity. He could not even be persuaded to climb the steps to the platform. Another little boy had to be recruited at the last moment. What was said, we do not know, though Sam asserted that 'nothing was said to Morris by way of blame'. Instead, a few months later his parents required him to perform a similar task at another ceremony. This time it was even more awe-inspiring – a real Princess was to be the recipient. All went well. Ella noted proudly that 'dressed in a white silk suit with a white silk Liberty hat, he looked supremely handsome, and with great grace presented his flowers, though his face was as white as his coat.'

In looks and in temperament, anxious Monier and timid Morris closely resembled their father, but they were treated in the same way as their more resilient brothers. Burgon cheerfully shrugged off his failings: 'I know if I begin the day thinking I won't have one sin, I generally have about twelve'.

Dressed in a similar fashion to Morris, Ralph had no qualms about presenting a bouquet. He faced the Duke and Duchess of Westminster with complete self-possession and 'gave the Duchess a bouquet with a profound bow and then turned and made the Duke another'. Ella appeared to feel that if their brothers could do it, so could Morris and Monier. Making the presentation might make Morris miserable in the short term, but how much more manly and happier he would be when he had overcome his stage fright. It is unlikely that it would have occurred to her that the price paid for this kind of self-conquest could sometimes be incapacitating. To Ella's distress, Monier developed a stammer which would plague him throughout his school life and beyond. 'Monier is such a very home boy and his tendency to stammer makes him more nervous and sensitive' wrote his mother sadly. On the other hand, the consequences of Ella's training were not necessarily quite as harmful as might be supposed. One morning Monier slipped into her bed.

> As he lay in my arm in bed this morning he said
> "Mother darling does ou [sic] love me so much?"
> "Yes my pet."
> "Well then I will try to be a gooder boy today."
> "Why my darling?"
> "Cause ou [sic] loves me so Mother".
> "Darling, Father loves you too, and kind Jesus.
> "What a lot of people does love me" said the child.

There is no mention of physical punishment in the home, though the children 'minded a word from their father'. It would seem that moral pressure only was used. The Bickersteth family were friendly with Bishop Creighton's family, but there is no evidence that Ella tried to make the punishment fit the crime in a way which Louise Creighton admitted, 'may be considered brutal by some people'. When one of her sons played with fire she 'held his finger on the bar of the grate for a minute that he might feel how fire burnt'. In contrast, one incident is recorded which may show a Bickersteth method – that of reinforcing good behaviour. It is accidentally revealed when Ella described an episode that she has just witnessed. 'Mona gives Geoffrey a toy. "Ta" says Geoff of his own accord. "Oh, ou [sic] darling little boy" says Mona patting him on the shoulder.' Was Monier mimicking his mother's (or Ninny's) positive handling of tricky situations? Yet some of the drastic remedies that were applied when the children were ill must have seemed like punishment. Julian, almost three years old, certainly thought so. Having had a poultice on his chest for bronchitis in mid-summer, his mother reported that his 'favourite retort when vexed with anyone was "Put poultice on you, me will, and very hot'. Julian was the only child to suffer from prolonged bouts of illness. He was two years old when he began to suffer from bronchitis and 'for eighteen months he had it every three weeks' reported Ella. Poultices were eventually discontinued, but the alternative treatment which, Ella thought, was 'wonderfully successful' was also drastic.

> All winter he was rubbed all over his body by Nurse's hand for ten minutes before washing in a warm bath. Then he had two quarts of cold water with Tidman's sea salt poured over him. The remainder of the cure was a dose of medicine every week. Gregory [powder] for two weeks and grey powder every third week, followed by castor oil in the morning'.

No wonder that when another new brother arrived, Monier wrote home hoping that he would not be ill like Julian.

By 1899, as well as teaching the children to read and write, Ella was giving a Bible lesson every morning to seven year-old Monier, Geoffrey aged five, and four year-old Julian. At night she heard each child's prayers separately and told them a Bible story. The children were encouraged to question what they heard. 'Not bad for a five year-old' was her verdict on a comment made by Geoffrey:

> Mother, Jesus Christ could not pray.
> Why not?
> Because if he was God himself, He could not pray to God.

Sam was also sharing in the teaching although apart from very occasional entries it is rarely mentioned in the records, probably because it was so much part of family routine. On a Monday morning: 'Heard children say Psalm'; on a Sunday afternoon: 'Bible story to boys' and, on a Sunday morning: 'Before Church, taught our dear chicks on Genesis I'. Unfortunately no more details are given. It also fell to Sam to help his boys understand what was meant by being 'Christ's faithful servant and soldier'. Ella had some difficulty in explaining this to Morris. At four years old, he may have understood that he should be Jesus' faithful servant, but he was far from clear as to the meaning of 'faithful soldier'. So his mother asked him: 'What kind of things did Jesus' soldiers have to fight against? His reply was prompt: 'Wild Indians'. Perhaps his father remembered this when writing a pamphlet for Sunday School children. It provides a clue as to how Morris' question might have been answered. At their baptism, Sam explained, children were dedicated

> manfully to fight under [Christ's] banner against sin, the world and the devil ... That meant not only that you are to fight when a man but also to fight like a man ... where are your battlefields? The nursery, the school-room, the playground. ... The Banner of Christ is woven like the National Flag of our own dear country ... red teaches us our duty to our neighbour; white reminds us of our duty to God... blue teaches us ... to live on earth so that we may at Christ's coming enter into Heaven.

Sam may have been modelling his pamphlet on a rhyme on the Union Jack written for a grandson by William Boyd Carpenter, his Bishop.

> Now first its triple colours mark,
> High meaning in each hue:
> Red – flame of love; white – blameless life;
> Beneath Hope's heavenly blue:
> Then bear these colours joyously,
> Though threatening clouds be black;
> For you're a little British boy,
> And here's your Union Jack.

Patriotism became embedded in their faith.

It was a philosophy in tune with the spirit of the times: upper middle class boys such as the Bickersteths were expected to be robust and manly Christians, always ready to do battle for those less fortunate than themselves. That meant that they were also expected to be gentlemen. Sam told his sons about the 'Gentleman's Psalm'. Psalm 15 taught them that a gentleman was 'a man of blameless life, who does what is right'. When the boys were little, 'doing right' as a gentleman meant having good manners and showing consideration for others. There were other good reasons for the boys to become 'little gentlemen' as soon as possible. Sam and Ella were very aware of the expectations and the challenges of the world outside the vicarage. Their children would, in some sense, be public property as their upbringing and behaviour would be the cynosure of parishioners as well as the huge extended Bickersteth family. Training in the niceties of deportment would also ease their way in Society if, as they hoped, the boys would be able to benefit from family connections and the ones they would generate for themselves at public school. So training in manners began even before they could talk. Morris was fourteen months old when his mother proudly noted 'He can hold up his baby fingers to say "Hark" and of course claps his hands together for "please"'. Clapping hands for 'please' seems to have been a custom originated by a distant relative, the Revd. Henry William Burrows, who liked his children 'before they could speak, to be taught to put their hands together when they wanted to ask for anything, as he thought it would make them better realise that praying was asking.' When Burgon was six, he also was doing well. 'He has a smile and the right word for all he meets, and tradespeople and poor alike all love him. He never forgets the sweetest thanks for the most trifling service'. Monier was introduced to his role as the Vicar's son when he was nineteen months old. A flower service was being held at his father's church. Monier wore a white pelisse and hat and carried a basket of flowers. After the service, he was taken to St. Mary's Hospital, 'where he delighted the sick people by trotting about from bed to bed with his hands full of flowers'. He was not quite three when his mother thought him sufficiently well behaved to accompany her when she was visiting. A year later he went to his first children's party on his own. It was at the Bishop's Palace at Ripon where his father was the Bishop's chaplain. His mother met him there and watched him proudly.

> He took little Joan into tea and when everyone was seated just before Grace, he amused everyone by saying in a clear voice 'What a large tea party.' He thanked Mrs. Carpenter [the Bishop's wife] so prettily before he left saying 'Dankin very much'.

Monier had remembered his manners! Ella was not, however, always so successful. When Julian was six and Burgon only three years old, they were invited to the Mayor of Lewisham's Fancy Dress Ball. Julian went as a soldier and Burgon as a handyman. 'They found the society rather trying' noted Ella enigmatically. To help them be at ease in company, there were dancing lessons in the vicarage dining room.

There were other special occasions when manners and deportment were essential. The huge summer holidays which Grandfather Bishop organised were particularly sensitive events. In 1893 Ella made sure her four boys rose to the occasion. Monier, Geoffrey and eight year old Julian were dressed in 'white flannels, navy blue blazers and caps with Sam's crest worked in crimson on the pockets and peaks'. Being well presented and fashionably dressed was important in Ella's eyes. When visiting their only close relative with a title, Lady Margaret Bickersteth, Monier was dressed in his sailor suit plus a black fur cape, Geoffrey in a crimson coat, crimson plush hat and a grey fur cape whilst Julian, the baby, was all in white. Burgon wore Liberty silk smocks until he was four. His 'gold curls' were not cut off until he was six. Sam took him to the barber's. 'A sad day, but high time' said Ella. Sam gave Burgon the huge sum of five shillings as a tip. Perhaps Sam was more upset than his boisterous energetic son? When the story *Little Lord Fauntleroy* was the craze, the older boys were dressed like the hero in velvet suits with deep lace collars. There is no hint in Ella's notebooks as to their reaction. It is difficult to believe that it would have been any different from that of their contemporary Compton Mackenzie. He recalled that 'the Little Lord Fauntleroy costume of black velvet and a Vandyke collar was a curse'. Nevertheless, elaborate clothes, often paid for by a relative, were worn on Sundays and passed down the family. Everyday clothes were generally sailor suits – white for summer and blue for winter. The apotheosis came when Monier was nine and attending Sunday morning service. Ella wrote triumphantly: 'He wore his first Eton suit today and looked such a refined little gentleman'.

Fortunately the children, although always expected to be 'gentlemen', did not always have to be 'refined'. On one occasion at least, to the little boys' delight, even their father, normally dressed so respectably in clerical black, 'came home so dirty, and with torn clothes'. In 1897, his mother wrote to Monier to tell him the details: 'Father has had two terrific days beating the bounds of the Parish. [St Mary's, Lewisham]. … they have to go over walls, and through houses, over ponds and in all kinds of extraordinary places'. Holidays, with father wearing his Norfolk knickerbockers (and clerical collar) while chasing butterflies and leading long walks or cycle rides, mother dressed in a voluminous costume, leading a family bathing party at the seaside, and family picnics with Ella presiding with the tea basket and the men lighting a fire to boil the kettle, were joyous occasions. Christmas was the other high spot. The Christmas tree was always in place and Father Christmas was there to hand out presents to family and to staff. Christmas 1888 was a 'most happy day'. The Christmas tree was decorated in secret. It was revealed after Evensong, and there was Father Christmas. None of the three little boys aged six, four and three realised that actually he was their Uncle Stanley. In the evening, wrote Sam, 'we dined happily, all five of us, and talk and games... endless cards and nice presents'. To crown it all, he went out on Boxing Day and 'bought fireworks for our boys, much to their delight'. There are few clues as to the contents of the children's presents. Toys are mentioned very infrequently, and expensive items seem to have been hired. Perhaps that is why the presentation of the tricycle horse was such a momentous event. The evangelical emphasis on Sunday being a day exclusively devoted to religious duties was one convention that had passed away. Ella wanted her 'children to connect thoughts with Sunday as their happiest day in the week' and reserved special toys for Sundays. She felt it worked admirably. '[Monier] is very fond of what he calls "Happy Sunday" and is always so delighted with his ark on that day'.

Letters and diaries give random clues as to the quality of the children's lives. Burgon went running and played fives with his father. All the family played croquet in the Lewisham Vicarage garden and went cycling together. The children had pets. Three year-old Monier was 'almost beside himself' when he was given a rabbit. There always seemed to be one or two dogs. On their own and their parents birthdays, the children all came into their parents' bedroom for a romp. Undoubtedly the boys would also have made their own amusements, for they divided neatly by age into two groups of three, so there was always someone with whom to play and plot. Not surprisingly, no records exist except for one vignette, where the boys are playing 'vicar and visitor', the vicarage version of 'mothers and fathers'. Ralph, aged six and Morris, aged nine, were in Sam's dressing room. Ralph pretended to be Sam. It shows how well the children had grasped one of the main features of their father's ministry in Lewisham.

"Come in and be a gentleman calling on me".
"Very well, what shall we talk about?"
Ralph, with great dignity, "What do you think about all these Churches we is trying to build round about here?"
"A very good thing".
"Yes", says Ralph "I is going to give a million to each, what is you going to give?"

For all the children, these years of vicarage home life were orderly and predictable, interrupted only by visits to relatives and the great annual summer holiday in August. It followed the Church year, with Lent, Easter, Harvest Festival and Christmas being the markers of an unchanging round. The fundamentals of an evangelical household remained in place: family prayers, bible study, regular and frequent church attendance and constant supervision of their spiritual welfare. Although there is no example of the old evangelical nurse's admonition 'dooty fust and pleasure afterwards,' its spirit pervaded the Bickersteth nursery. There is no indication that the children resented it. It was part of the routine of their lives and accepted as such. When they visited relatives, they found very similar regimes being experienced by their many cousins.

From the parents' point of view, the spread of their children's ages meant that they had a child in the house for nearly twenty two years. It was Sam's job to take each boy to boarding school for the first time. It was always an upsetting experience, but especially so when he took Ralph, the youngest.

> Yesterday, I took Ralph to St. David's. ... But this morning, I hardly know how to rule my emotions, or to keep back my tears! As I sit at work now, I feel I <u>must</u> (must I say) have the sight of his lithe little figure, gay and debonair, racing round the garden, or rushing up to my study window to flatten his little face on the window pane, making perhaps some queer grimace, and calling out a slightly cheeky comment on things in general. There, I must work ... to work, and to work!

It was, felt Sam, 'the close of a long and happy chapter of our home life'. Did the children also feel that their childhood had been happy? Julian had no doubts. He wrote from France that 'as a family we have indeed wonderful happiness to look back upon'. Family life recollected from the mud of the trenches is inevitably bathed in a golden glow, so perhaps it is better, in the end, to try to judge their happiness solely through the eyes of the children. Fortunately Burgon had a gift for descriptive writing which showed early. When he was eight, just before he started school, he described a Sunday when the family were on holiday in Kent, and then an overnight visit paid the next day. As far as it is possible to judge, these artless accounts were not written with one eye on his parents' possible reactions, so they give an added dimension to the spirituality, family love, and self-discipline which had been fostered in the home. Sunday was pleasant, but not as much fun as the next day. Ella seems to have tolerated dangerous activities. There is, perhaps, even an intimation of the dark years to come. In 1914 Burgon proved to be an accurate marksman on the Army rifle ranges and 'Nigel' (the Hon. Nigel Gathorne-Hardy) would serve in the Rifle Brigade, become a Lieutenant General and be awarded the DSO.

> After breakfast we play about (I read) till Bible lesson at 10.15 after that we go to morning Church at Saltwood. We get back at 12.30. Then we read till dinner time. After dinner we read. I then took care of Baby [Ralph, age two and a half, with his leg in a splint] till tea. Julian and Ninny went to Sandling in the afternoon. After tea we all had some hymns, after that mother read to us, but before she did so, we went out. After supper we all talked and then all of us boys went to bed.

Next day they all set off on their bicycles:

> ... all very busy getting ready to go to Benenden, where we are going to spend the night. And all of us (down to me) ride to Ashford [about twelve miles], while Mother, Monier, Julian and I take the train to Paddock Wood. Geoff and Father ride the whole way. When we get to Paddock Wood, we change, and get into the Cranbrook [train]. That takes us to Cranbrook station where we get out and then we ride up to the Grange, where we find Lady Medway and Janie sitting in the garden. Then Nigel comes out. Soon he tells us he is going to blow up a wasp's nest in the evening and he is making the different things for them. Then we go and help him, and try the different experiment with the gunpowder. Then Nigel takes us to a field and brings his gun with him, and lets us all have shots at different things... Then we go and blow the wasps nest up, but it did not go off well. Then we all change. And go into dinner. After which we had a very good game. And then we all go to bed.

Background reading

Pollock, L A *Forgotten Children. Parent-child relations from 1500 to 1900.* Cambridge University Press (1983)

Tosh, J A *Man's Place. Masculinity and the Middle-Class Home in Victorian England.* Yale University Press (1999)

Sources

Bodleian Library: Diaries of Ella Bickersteth

Diaries of [John] Burgon Bickersteth

Ella and her six 'manly' sons. (circa 1911)

Monier Geoffrey Julian

Burgon Morris Ralph

6

SCHOOL LIFE

*'I am very happy at school but not <u>nearly</u> (sic) as much as I am
at home'. Letter from Monier, aged 10.*

The Bickersteth children attended boarding schools from 1892 to
1913. By then, Thomas Arnold's ideal of education as an energetic
process whereby the cultivation of intelligence would be perfected in
Christian faith, where a 'school without a chapel would be like an angel
without wings,' had been replaced by more earthy philosophies. Boys
should be responsible and independent, athletic and able to bear pain,
ready to 'walk a thousand miles in a thousand hours'. Muscularity had
become the dominant ethos of the public schools. Organised sports,
the Rifle Corps and patriotism were of supreme importance.

The journey through their school days is most closely recorded in
the correspondence between Monier and his parents. It begins from his
first days at preparatory school in 1892 when he is missing his parents
'so orfalle' and continues through his time at Rugby and then on to his
university days. It has been possible to sort his letters chronologically,
and intersperse them with his parents' replies. There are, naturally,
many gaps but sometimes there is a complete series of letters and
responses. There is no indication that the school censored Monier's
letters. When vital information had to be sent, such as holiday train
times, it was written on the outside of the envelope, presumably by a
master. The letters are in a surprisingly pristine condition, having been
kept in their original envelopes, and one can only surmise that as a small
boy Monier, having read his parents' advice once, carefully refolded
the letter along its original creases, put it away safely and never looked
at it again. The other five boys all kept up a similar correspondence,
but very few letters, apart from a few written by Burgon, have been
identified. Details of their school careers have been gleaned mainly
from references in their parents' papers. The sheer quantity of the
letters relating to Monier, generally three a week during term-time
plus his weekly replies is almost overwhelming, but is not particularly
unusual, at least in clerical families. When William Temple was at

Rugby, he exchanged letters with his mother every day, and once a week with his father. Children were generally away from home for about twelve weeks and, apart from a telegram in an emergency, there was no other way to keep in touch. Within the hundreds of letters sent by Monier, overloaded though they often are with endless accounts of form placements, and the numerous replies sent by his parents, we can watch him being moulded into a manly, robust, young man. These 'intimate records' suggest how far this process was life-enhancing or life-damaging and reveal the intertwining roles of Sam and Ella as they carried out their resolve that their sons should be the 'main interest of our life, their education, their success, their first loves, their start in life'.

The first problem which confronted these conscientious parents was: which school to choose? They wanted their boys to become self-confident, robust, patriotic leaders of men, which they felt could only be achieved through the public school system, but at the same time to model themselves on the 'kind Jesus' presented so consistently in the nursery. Given such views, it is not surprising that Ella and Sam had to look long and hard for suitable placements. In effect, they were seeking to reconcile the inherent contradiction in Christian manliness identified by Norman Vance. 'The secular hero is captain of his fate and master of his soul ... but the Christian hero must acknowledge Christ as captain and master'. They were wise enough not to take the schools at face value, no matter how persuasive the claims of headmasters as to the moral and muscular impeccability of their products. Radley was rejected, and although cousins Gordon and Evelyn Monier-Williams were pupils at Winchester, that school was finally ruled out as the vacancy was in a house that was 'not desirable'. If the discipline was too harsh they were prepared to change schools, and would intervene if they thought the happiness of a son was at stake. Nevertheless, although they took advice from their relatives, the children were not consulted. Once the decision was made, brother tended to follow brother to the same school, a move which helped to ease some of the distress at leaving home for the first time or apprehension at starting at a new school. Monier, Julian, Morris and Ralph went to Rugby and Geoffrey and Burgon to Charterhouse. Two preparatory schools were chosen. The three older boys went to Summer Fields, Oxford and the younger three to St David's, Reigate where Burgon paved the way and looked after his younger brother, Morris, when he arrived three years later. As a result, Morris was nicknamed 'chicken', and when the youngest of the family, Ralph, arrived, he was known as 'bantam'.

Summer Fields, still flourishing today on the same site in Oxford, was chosen for Monier. The principal was Gertrude Maclaren, a classical scholar, who was referred to as the headmaster though the children called her 'Mrs'. One of the masters, Peter Joy, was the ordained son of a friend and would later become one of Sam's sports-loving curates. Gertrude had the reputation of being 'the maker of scholars ... obtained not by cram, but by sound education'. Her husband, Archibald Maclaren, was a distinguished teacher of physical education, who owned the school and had founded the Oxford University Gymnasium which Ella's brothers had attended. There he taught fencing and developed a system of physical training for the army which is still their basis of training today. The school had an excellent academic record, and was regarded as a stepping stone to Eton and Harrow, with a fine record of obtaining scholarships. It could boast that both sons of Thomas Hughes, author of *Tom Brown's Schooldays*, had been pupils. Summer Fields seemed to have the moral and manly attributes for which Sam and Ella were looking, as well as important personal links. Oxford was Ella's home and her parents still lived there. She must have been reassured by Mrs Maclaren's response to her first enquiry:

> We shall be very much pleased to see you and Mr. Bickersteth on Tuesday... I have only just realised that you are little Ella Monier Williams. It does not seem possible that you are the mother of a schoolboy. Yes, it is a real trial to part with one's nestlings, especially the first one. But I am sure he will be very happy at school.

Monier was duly enrolled and Geoffrey and Julian followed.

When Monier arrived, Mrs. Maclaren, in addition to teaching, was closely concerned with the children's welfare, a concern which included their physical and spiritual needs. She would come into the bedrooms as the boys settled for the night, kiss the homesick ones and – so the story goes – ask the others 'Are you all asleep?' Her first mid-term letter to Sam and Ella brims with well-meaning reassurance.

> We are all fond of him [Monier] and find him a winning dear little chap... He and Hugh Wolley [his cousin] continue good friends, and I think the little bedroom party is a very happy one. They are all good boys and careful about their reading and prayers.

His parents, however, were not prepared to accept Mrs. Maclaren's assurance regarding Monier's prayers. They sent Monier a list of questions which the nine-year-old did his best to answer:

> Do you kneel down for your prayers? *I do kneel to say my pray (sic)*

> Has Dr Williams given you any prayers, or do you use the words Mother taught you? *No he has not given me any.*

> Who gives you your Bible lesson and are you doing well in it? *The doctor gives us Bible lesson and I am getting on with it.*

Monier reported that every school day began with prayers at 7.45 a.m., followed by breakfast. Then there was a 'Bible lesson' at 8.30 a.m. and school lessons started at 9 a.m. Later, when Summer Fields had its own chapel, there was Bible reading for the whole school before breakfast, followed by Morning Prayers in the chapel. Lent was observed. The children were not allowed to attend the Gymnasium on Ash Wednesday and amusements were curtailed. 'We have *(sic)* a conjurer and ventriloquist called Mr. Farrington last night it was awfully good. Dr. Williams says we are having all the things now before Lent begins' reported Monier.

Sam and Ella were not, however, content to leave such vital matters as the observance of Lent to the school authorities. The children must consider what personal sacrifices they should make. When Geoffrey had joined Monier, their father sent them some suggestions:

> During Lent you might decide with Geoffrey upon something to give up, perhaps tea as you did last year. But you must not give up solid food, as your long limbs need much food. Tell nobody except Mother or me of your little Lenten self denials, as these matters should be kept a secret between ourselves and our dear Lord, Jesus Christ.

But at Easter, Monier could report with delight: 'We had Easter eggs this morning at breakfast all chocolate and little cream chocolates inside them they are awfully good!!!!!'*(sic)*

The struggle for 'self-conquest', which had begun in the nursery, continued at preparatory school. Home sickness was Monier's first battle. His first letter home shows him doing his best to sound cheerful.

Summer fields
Sept 25th 1892

Dear Farther

Your Latin that
you did with me in the holidays
has helped me very much,
I do not do Latin with Saley
but with Miss Hlis but I think
I am going to & do it with a
master. I tried to remember
what you said about church.
It rained when we came
out of church so when we
got in we had to change.
I am in the quier hear.
I like school pretty much
but I miss you and Mother
and the boys so orfalle.

His parents' replies ranged from the bracing 'I am so pleased to hear that you are in the choir (not spelt quier) and shall think of you tomorrow' from his father, to anxious sympathy from his mother. 'I should like to know one thing, my dear one, that is if you are really happy at school, – as happy as you can be away from home. Do tell me this in your Sunday letter'. Monier did his best to combine honesty with the reply he knew he was expected to make. 'I am very happy at school but not <u>nearly</u> as much as I am at home'. Several weeks elapsed before Sam and Ella realised that: 'The poor little man was very miserable his first term, as we found out when we went to visit him at half term'. In addition to being homesick, the boys were teasing him because of his stammer. Ella wrote to him as soon as she reached home.

> My pet, I can't help feeling you will be happier now. I think the worst is over, and do you know I am glad you had a good cry, and told us your troubles, for troubles always seem easier to bear when they have been talked about. Don't forget what Father told you about the swimming. Every day it got easier – and everyday school life will get easier. You will learn not to mind the chaff from the boys, and when they find you don't care, they won't chaff you any more. Be brave, and fearless, play your game and be very nice to the boys, even to those who teaze you. My own precious son, Father and Mother are very proud of you. Do you know my dear one, it is as hard for us to bear being without you, as it is for you to be away from us. We don't know how to bear it sometimes but we know it is for your good and we look forward to the holidays and to many other happy times together. And if you are happy and get on, it makes it all the easier to bear. Let me know in your next Sunday letter if you feel happier, and above all don't mind about your talking. You are much better in that way than you were, and if you are careful and talk slowly and gently you will soon conquer it altogether. Don't forget the text Mother marked for you in your Bible, Hebrews 13. 5.6. If the Everlasting Arms of the heavenly Father are under you, you need not fear what anyone may say or do. Oh, my little son, your Mother's heart is full of love for you and will pray often for you.

Monier-Williams' rhyme celebrating the moulding process hid its harsher aspects. Now they are laid bare. His mother's letter is a combination of comfort, sympathy, heartening advice to promote manliness and spirituality, all fortified by moral blackmail – and love.

Ella's letter crossed with one from Monier. 'Dear Mother and Father, I did feel so bad last night when you left me and erly *(sic)* this morning but I did not cry.' Monier had begun to learn to conquer himself. Was repression of his emotions the price he paid? It is impossible to answer categorically. Ninny had described him as 'sombre and sad'. His speech impediment did not improve and it was many years later, when he was happily married, that it at last disappeared. His children attribute it to their mother's patient coaching. He was the only son to be consistently unhappy at preparatory and at public school but, of course, being the eldest, meant he started each school without the support of a brother.

During Monier's second term at Summer Fields his parents' letters become more bracing. The word 'brave' begins to appear more frequently, and with it a hint that the time had come 'manfully to fight under [Christ's] banner'. The first letter from his mother is addressed to 'My darling brave boy' whilst his father's letter reminded him 'You do not need for me to tell you how often I prayed that God would bless my son and make him happy and brave and hardworking'. A few months later, Sam explained in detail what he meant. 'I want my dear lad to be bright and good tempered, to learn how to take a joke and how to bear a blow'. Writing about the funeral of Monier's great uncle, Charles Bignold, described earlier, he pointed the moral. 'Let all this remind you and me to be good soldiers of Jesus Christ. Play up like W G. Grace.' To the triple call of faith, family and duty was now added the need to acquire sterling qualities: bravery, cheerfulness, diligence and athleticism. Fortunately there was much at Summer Fields that Monier thoroughly enjoyed: cricket, association football, fives and Torpids, a 'bumping race' on the river. He was enthusiastic about the weekly two mile walk from Summertown to Alfred Street in the centre of Oxford, wearing his bowler hat decorated with a yellow and black Brasenose ribbon.

> Its [sic] very great fun on Fridays when we go to Gymnasium, we do dumbbells and sing songs to them as *Daisy Bell* and *After the Ball were over*.

Although he was not very fond of Latin, he liked mathematics very much, and often came top. He would become the one member of the family who was 'good at figures'.

Monier left for Rugby in 1896, the same year that Mrs Maclaren died. She was succeeded by her son-in-law, the Revd Dr. Charles. E. Williams who took over the scholarship class. From then on Summer

Fields 'became a veritable hot-house of classical scholarship ... in which encouragement was sometimes given by a generous use of the cane'. Under Dr Williams, Julian struggled, but academic Geoffrey flourished. Julian was entered for an Eton scholarship, but he 'made three bad howlers in his Prose ... he stuck to all the other papers with great pluck and determination and did so well that Dr. Williams had a little hope. However, he failed.' Geoffrey, to everyone's delight, for he had always been regarded as the cleverest child, 'a classicist to his finger tips' as his mother put it, won a £100 scholarship to Charterhouse. Unfortunately, there is little evidence as to how Geoffrey and Julian coped with the stricter discipline when Dr Williams became headmaster, but Ronald Knox, the future Catholic priest, journalist and translator of the Bible, was a contemporary of both boys. Ronald was regarded by Dr Williams as the cleverest boy he had ever taught and both he and his brother Dillwyn won scholarships to Eton. The Knox family records indicate, however, that the preparation of the boys for scholarships was only just within 'the borderline of sanity' and Ronald in middle age 'used to recall deliberately what it was like to be beaten for having an untidy locker, to remind himself how much better it is to be forty than eight'. Only one letter has been found from the Bickersteth children, and this is a joint one in which Julian rejoiced that 'nearly all the pipes here are frozen hard and it was awful fun this morning for we could not have a cold bath' whilst Geoffrey told his parents that he was 'top of the form'. Nevertheless, their parents were aware of what was happening, and regardless of scholarships, decided another school must be found for the three younger children. The entry in Ella's notebook was simple and to the point: 'We consider there is too much of the cane at Summer Fields.' Moral pressure was acceptable; excessive corporal punishment was not.

St David's, Reigate was selected for their fourth son, Burgon. The choice was again made with the safeguard of personal knowledge. The owner and headmaster was the Revd. William H Joyce, Vicar of Dorking, the father of Isabel Monier-Williams, one of Ella's sisters-in-law. Several of their Monier-Williams cousins were or had been pupils. 'The work results are not so brilliant at St David's', noted Ella, 'but we consider the smaller school better for our timid Morris'. Morris was next in line to start school, so if his parents accepted Joyce's offer of a place for Burgon, there would be a brother there, ready to look after him, in three years' time. Burgon, Morris and, finally, Ralph all had successful careers at St David's. Burgon won a scholarship to Charterhouse, and each in turn became school captain. Ella was delighted with the school.

'It is a real home. The chapel is lovely and every boy out of the forty joins in the anthem'. Sam, in his memoir of Morris, felt that 'perhaps his five years at St David's were the happiest time of the twenty-five years of his earthly life'. When Ralph left, 'laden with books and parting presents from every master at St. David's,' Ella and Sam felt that the school had fulfilled all their hopes.

> Certainly the boy has developed in a wonderful way, from a seemingly thoughtless, jolly child, into a strong bright boy seemingly born to be a leader, for never was any boy more popular with his fellows says Mr Joyce.

The leadership qualities, which they felt only a residential school could have instilled, were in place. The boys were ready to cope with the much tougher atmosphere of the late Victorian public school. Ella was very satisfied. The words that she had written in her diary about Monier when he left Summer Fields: 'His character is well-formed and he acts always from the highest principle' could, she felt, be used to describe all her boys.

It was in May 1896 that Monier wrote home to say that 'Dr Williams has decided that I was to go to Rugby' and in September Sam took him there to sit the entrance examination. A variety of factors drew Monier's parents towards that choice. Rugby had strong ecclesiastical links. A new headmaster, the Revd H A James, the son of an evangelical clergyman, had just been appointed. His immediate predecessor had been the radical Revd John Percival, 'stern, moral, spiritual, and intellectual' who had raised academic and moral standards before becoming Bishop of Hereford the previous year. Both the Archbishop of Canterbury and his predecessor had been masters there. The Bishop of London's sons, Frederick and William Temple were pupils and their father was a past headmaster. There were also the all-important personal connections. Ella's eldest brother had 'spent four very happy years' at Rugby and one of the housemasters, C G Steel, was a University contemporary of Sam. Equally important, his wife, Maud, was one of Ella's oldest friends.

As a result, Sam and his apprehensive son were invited to have lunch with Maud Steel before Monier sat for the entrance examination. It was a difficult meal. With irritated empathy Sam described it to Ella.

> I could wish he [Monier] was a trifle less silent. Maud's repeated efforts to get him into conversation all failed ... [she] had furnished an excellent lunch, of which Monier partook with

relish, though with restraint and wisdom … this experience is, though interesting, rather fatiguing from the two-fold sympathies which it calls out. Parental solicitude that the boy should do, and be, his very best is all awake, and yet parental sympathy with the ordeal for him, which all the novelty implied, is equally keen!

Despite his silence – perhaps this was his way of disguising the hesitancy in his speech – Monier passed and entered the Middle School, Lower Middle 1. He was followed by Julian, Morris and Ralph whilst, thanks to their scholarships, Geoffrey and Burgon both went to Charterhouse. Again, the records contain very little information about the Charterhouse boys, whilst the letters exchanged between Monier and his parents continue throughout his Rugby career. These naturally highlight only those aspects of school life which he felt could be shared with his parents. Swathes of school life are unreported. Bullying, for example, is never mentioned. Eddie Knox arrived at Rugby in the same year as Monier. His description of 'hacking, scragging, mauling and tripping [whilst] the prefects punished by making a wrong-doer run past an open door three times while they aimed a kick at him. Ribs got broken that way' bears no relation to Monier's letters. On the other hand, Knox was in School House and Steel's house may have been more relaxed. A slight clue as to the moral atmosphere is possibly found in a letter home at the beginning of his first year at Oxford, but it is no more than a throw-away comment which indicates little more than that the boys accepted without question public school sexuality as a part of life: 'The society in which I am mostly is certainly as pure as that of my latter days at Rugby. In fact I am really agreeably surprised'. Burgon reassured his parents in a somewhat similar vein soon after he arrived at Charterhouse. '… it is impossible not to hear very many unpleasant things, but in the changing room I am very lucky as I have a fairly quiet corner.'

Monier's reports of academic achievement are generally limited to form placements. Looking back on his schooldays, William Temple considered Rugby to be 'probably the most strenuous of schools … there is very little free time, except for boys who by working quick can make it.' Monier's comments are very different. In his second term, when he was taking consistently low places in his form, he asked his form master for 'some proses to do for him out of school as I have a good deal of spare time'. Towards the end of his Rugby days, Monier gloomily felt that he had 'improved in Latin Prose about up to the standard I was at when I came here' and that '[I] would undoubtedly [have known] more Mathematics now if I had been better taught'. However, unlike Temple, the Bickersteth boys were not academically inclined. There was no likelihood of any of the four reading Kant's *Critique of Pure Reason* in their free time as did Temple, or staying in their studies on a Sunday afternoon when everybody else was enjoying themselves out of doors.

All the brothers fell easily into the public school routine of Christian worship. Although historians have argued that attendance at chapel was merely part of public school routine, a social habit with no spiritual commitment, there is little here to support this view. Church attendance had, of course, been part of the boys' lives since babyhood and there is no evidence that, satiated with services, they now rebelled against them. Instead, they became sermon connoisseurs. 'Rather disjointed, but earnest' commented Monier dismissively in one letter home, but a visiting preacher 'gave a nice sermon this afternoon, pleading with the school to send out a few of their numbers as missionaries ... he also talked about Imperialism and God's empire.' Morris wrote home describing

> ... a most excellent sermon from the Bodger [nick-name for Dr James] ... 'Thy will be done' was his text. He said we did not ask what was God's will nearly enough ... Many boys come to a Public School intending to take Holy Orders, perhaps because their father is a clergyman or because their parents wish it, and have not really thought deeply about it. They begin to wonder, and then is the time to ask God's will and God's help.

Sam felt that there could be 'no question that Dr James' sermons were an asset of great spiritual value to the School. He possessed a noble voice and always put his ideals in plain words'. In contrast, Julian, whose devotion to Rugby was only equalled by that of William Temple, felt when he was a chaplain in France, that the public schools did not produce 'a type of man who feels any need for religion'. And to demonstrate the danger of making generalisations, Ralph, who tended to distinguish himself by being 'bottem' of his form and was a never-failing source of high spirits and mischief, asked 'if he might go into the Chapel at 3.15 and stayed there ... till 3.25 praying for Morris' who was away from school being confirmed.

All four boys were confirmed whilst they were at Rugby, though their father prepared them himself and arranged the services privately. Confirmation of Monier, as the eldest son, was an especially important occasion. On his fourteenth birthday Monier received a letter from his mother, reminding him that before his next birthday he would be

> admitted by Confirmation into the full Communion of our Church. You wish to be Christ's faithful servant and soldier, and God's grace in confirmation will help you to be so ... choose some one sin specially to fight against, and determine to stand up for what is noble, true and manly throughout all your school life.

Change can come slowly and almost imperceptibly. In 1838, Monier's grandfather had written to his thirteen year-old son, Edward (the future Bishop of Tokyo) in similar but slightly more admonitory terms: 'I think it would be good for you to tell me your worst sins. It may be a real help against falling into them'. Sam, as usual, was more reassuring:

> I trust that you have already had your heart drawn to God and that you know Him as our Creator, Redeemer, and Holy and Helpful Friend. If this be so, it needs that the history of confirmation, what it is and what it is not, should be made plain to you.

Together, Sam and Monier went to work on this in the Christmas holidays. It was no sinecure. Sam expected written answers to the points he raised. Monier's confirmation service in the Palace chapel at Exeter in January 1897 with his grandfather officiating was, Ella felt, 'a great reality to Monier'. He told her he wished to make a thank-offering in memory of the day, and gave 'some small altar vases for the Palace chapel.' Morris was partly prepared for confirmation at Rugby by the school chaplain who told his mother that 'he was the most spiritual child he had ever come across'. Ella's hopes rose: 'When he knelt before the Bishop he had the face of a little Angel. I felt sure he had given himself to the Lord and hope he may one day be a Minister of His Gospel'.

The other aspect of school life where the brothers must all have felt very much at ease was Bible study. It had a high priority at Rugby. Twice a year the whole school competed for the Buxton Divinity prize, an examination set by Dr James. The papers of the finalists were judged by outside examiners. Monier won it twice, and as he was presumably competing against William Temple, it was a real achievement. Dr James was in personal charge of scripture lessons and in 1897 for a whole term, Monier reported, all Rugby school studied Genesis. There is no evidence as to Dr James' approach, though Monier wrote to his father that he 'found [Genesis] very hard to understand in some places. I wish you would take it for our Bible lessons next holidays'. An indication may be found in a recollection of Eddie Knox's father, the Bishop of Manchester:

> One little incident occurs to me, worth recording as indicative of the cautious attitude which even schoolmasters of such a type as Dr. James, of Rugby, assumed towards Higher Criticism. I remember him consulting me as to introducing his sixth form to Sir G. Adam Smith's *Isaiah*, because it assumes the existence of a first and second Isaiah. That was in the 90's.

About Sam's reaction we know nothing. Although there are many accounts of holiday activities, they do not include Bible lessons!

If the boys were happily at home with public school religious teaching, the way they reacted to public school life is much more difficult to assess, limited as it is by what the boys were prepared to reveal and by what their housemasters were prepared to reveal to their parents. There is no doubt that Julian and Ralph were both very happy at Rugby. Monier and Morris, however, were much more vulnerable than their brothers: Monier through his speech impediment and Morris through his physical appearance and shyness. As far as can be judged, it was not the constraints which at that time public schools used to toughen their pupils – lack of heating, poor or inadequate food, cold baths – which caused their unhappiness. There is, for example, nothing in Monier's letters to suggest that he was enduring the 'godless world of cold, hunger, competition and endurance' described by some historians. Perhaps the regime at Summer Fields had indeed prepared him. Nor does his experience reflect the claim that there was frequently 'little kindness and less piety'. There is evidence that the masters were helpful regarding his speech defect. His best subject was 'Math' as that involved 'very little talking'. But, he added, even with other subjects, 'all my Masters are quite nice about it.' Yet there is no doubt that Monier was at times very unhappy. Although he mentioned his difficulty in his letters, it was not until the 1899 Christmas holidays, when he had been at Rugby for three years that he seems to have really broken his silence. What he revealed is unknown, but his mother described his mental state as 'desolation'. As soon as he returned to school, she wrote to him.

> Don't mind having broken down a little with your own Mother.
> … I know that all these feelings will pass away, and the burden
> will fall from your shoulders and you will never regret that you
> have borne the Cross for Christ.'

Whatever was happening at school, things did not improve. In
February, he was 'glad to say that so far I have kept myself out of any
bad fits of despondency, though I cannot yet see much diminishment
in "the funk"'. His mother tried to hearten him. 'Have no funk but
quietly correct yourself if you are wrong in your speaking … by prayer
and pains your Cross will surrender'. During the Easter holidays,
debilitated by mumps, Monier felt he could fight no longer. 'He opened
his heart to me' wrote Ella in her diary 'and told me how he suffered at
school … begging me to let him leave in the summer and go to Oxford
if possible … it was a sad Easter' It was agreed that he should leave at
the end of the summer term. Just before he left, he wrote home with
painful honesty 'I really feel quite sad at leaving, and wish it was not to
be, at least I do so now'. Dr. James told his parents that, in the words of
Tennyson, 'He has worn the white flower of a blameless life'.

It was a blow for Sam and Ella for they were both hoping that their
eldest son would take Holy Orders. Somehow he must overcome his
horror of speaking in public. Different elocution teachers were sought
and more lessons arranged. At the same time, he must be helped to
face his difficulties and conquer them. Ella decided that the best course
was for him to take family prayers. She and Sam would be away for
a few days helping with a Mission in Kent, so this would be a golden
opportunity for Monier, in a small, intimate setting, to 'conquer himself'.
A complete run of letters charts Monier's agony. The correspondence
from his mother echoes the letter she sent him when he was a small boy
at Summer Fields.

> My precious Son, I want you to do a thing which I know is hard,
> but which will be a real help in your future – namely take prayers
> while we are away. I love you so dearly, that you know I should
> not ask you to do this did I not feel certain it is right, right for
> Father and me to ask, and right for you to do. I only want you
> to read the prayers, not the lesson, and I implore you if you find
> it hard the first day, and actually hesitate over the words, still to
> persevere. It will be a moral victory which will do your whole
> nature incalculable good.

Monier replied by return of post.

I have not yet made up my mind about taking prayers tomorrow. I went and tried this afternoon, for about a quarter of an hour, to see how I got on. I did the prayers about *(sic)* as I did with you; I then tried tomorrow's lesson, but it was awful. Also in trying to read to Ralph tonight, I couldn't say half a dozen consecutive words from the book, but had to just put in some of my own. I do so wish you had not asked me to take prayers. I hope the Mission has begun well and that your colds are better for the change. I am, your ever loving son, Edward Monier Bickersteth. Oh! Prayers! *(sic)*

His mother's reply was robust.

My precious Son, Your letter went to my heart. And yet I know if you do overcome this dread, this difficulty, your life will be happier after ... when you have once climbed the mountain of difficulty you will look back and be surprised at all it has cost you. ... Do you think we want you to take prayers for our sakes? My own boy, no – it is for your own sake, that you may take your right place as eldest son. But don't worry. If you have not felt able to do it, leave it. Some day it will be easier perhaps, only you won't overcome your difficulties unless you face them. ... I am just back from my speech, God helped me, and thirty seven mothers joined the [Mother's] Union.

Even with his mother's example before him, it was too much for Monier to face, but he was brave enough to reply by return of post.

Dear Mother, I have not taken prayers, I really could not. I did go and practice by myself.

His parents could not disguise their disappointment. Ella replied:

I am quite certain that you gave it [taking Prayers] your most careful and prayerful thought. I can't help being sorry you did not make the effort for you would have faced your difficulty and had it behind your back, but now don't give it another thought. It is not worth making much of ... I thoroughly understand your feelings so mind you enjoy the rest of the fortnight, and look forward with hope and courage to your future life.

Ella claimed that 'she thoroughly understood' Monier's feelings. That is a rash claim for any mother to make. A few years later in 1907 she was completely baffled by Morris. What was the matter with the boy? He had done so well at St David's. She felt that 'he had learnt to rule and behind his timidity was a quiet power'. Admittedly his brothers had been worried about him earlier in the year, but that had been cleared up. So why now, aged sixteen, was he so 'terribly low' at the thought of returning to Rugby after the Easter holidays? 'Self-conquest' was sadly lacking. Ella rallied the family round to cheer him up.

> [Uncle] Stanley took him to the theatre to see *The Scarlet Pimpernel.* … We took him [next day] to see some moving pictures and then had tea at Peter Robinson [a departmental store in Oxford Street], but the tears rolled down his cheeks in the shop. In fact he did not show sufficient self-control.

The reason for his misery can only be teased out through ambiguous references in letters and diaries. At first, Ella was delighted that Morris settled in so well and easily at Rugby. She noted in her diary that letters from Maud Steel and Morris himself had been most encouraging. Her old friend wrote 'Morris is a constant pleasure to me and seems to be growing visibly in manliness and self-confidence'. Morris' letter was full of excitement at his House winning the Singing cup. He had sung soprano in the quartet and Dr. James had been most complimentary. Ella was so pleased that she sent both letters on to Monier, now a curate. His reaction was not what she expected

> [Morris] tells you how the Head of the House has taken him out to the Hunt Steeplechases, and let him off fagging, and how a man, called Rowden, in the VIth has let him off "study and toast" fagging for a fortnight and given him 2 big boxes of chocolates. Well this never ought to be, it is quite clear to me that Morris' popularity is not altogether owing to the singing.

Monier consulted Julian, who had only just left Rugby and was still in close touch. Julian told him that 'several things have been happening [in the House], none of them the least sensually immoral, but still things that ought not to happen.' Monier felt his father should write to Morris pointing out that

> it is not wise for a younger boy to receive presents from an older, as he may expect something in return which the younger cannot give. … Anyhow, one gentleman cannot receive presents from another without giving some back, which Morris can neither afford nor probably would wish to do.

It would seem that Sam thought it would be better if Geoffrey wrote instead. Morris was particularly close to Geoffrey, sharing the same artistic interests. It is not known what passed between them, but everyone was relieved when Morris was said to have responded with 'such manliness'. A month later, in the Easter holidays, Ella noticed that he was constantly receiving letters from Rowden. 'Certainly the boy has a most romantic affection for him. They correspond continually.' But any anxiety she may have experienced was put to rest by Morris himself. On the way to Church one Sunday, Morris had commented 'I spent nothing on cakes or sweets [during Lent], nor would I allow anyone to treat me.' Ella felt 'so thankful for this. Rowden gave him a number of chocolates, but he brought them all home, because he would not eat them in Lent'. Yet again he was upset at the thought of returning to school. Sam gave him a new cricket bat to cheer him up. Both parents called in at Rugby a few weeks later to see Mr Steel to check how things were going. The news was good. Morris had 'developed wonderfully … He fills quite a position in the house already and has every minute occupied with rifle corps, sporting, singing in the concert and cricket'. Matters came to a head a year later in the summer. Morris was to go to Camp, and all was settled when

> Mr. Steel wrote and said he did not wish him to go, stating that Morris was an absolutely good boy himself but he might be exposed to unpleasantness if he went. …We are sure Mr Steel acted unwarrantably, for a further letter showed that he kept Morris (the good boy) back, and let the bad boys go for fear of breaking up the battalion… Still, when you see what a big fellow he is, in his eighteenth year, one feels he could have taken care of himself in camp and been a good influence there. He has a sweet, strong, refined face.

All was eventually resolved. Morris returned to school in September

> … more brightly than we could have hoped for. Mr. Steel had learnt all the truth of what Morris suffered last term, and of the evil that was going on from another boy in the Sixth. One bad boy has left and Mr Steel will watch the other.

On reflection, in later years, his father felt that Morris had been made 'to plough a lonely furrow … never an exhilarating, though a not infrequent, experience at some time or other in the life of a Public School boy'.

Whatever worries Sam and Ella had about Monier and Morris, there were two aspects of Rugby life that not only did the boys enjoy in full, but their enjoyment was enthusiastically shared by their parents. Sport and service in the Rugby School Corps were the most exciting and enjoyable features of school life for all the boys – and ones which were also taken seriously by their parents. From preparatory school days Sam and Ella had cheered their sons at House football and cricket matches, ready to endure considerable inconvenience to attend. There were family rejoicings when the boys won their House caps, and greater celebrations when first Julian, and then Ralph, became Captain of Games at Rugby. At Charterhouse, Burgon was also playing soccer extremely well and Ninny wrote to him, giving a slightly different view of football than that of the rest of the family. 'I do think football a hateful game, but for all that I must congratulate you on your success as I know to you it means much, but you know I always was a very silly person'. She was, as she well knew, in a minority of one. Such was the importance attached to sport that among a list of questions which Sam suggested Monier asked himself as he prepared to take his end-of-term communion at Rugby, was 'In games, have I played fairly and patiently, and for the good of my side?' It was no longer sufficient just to 'play up like W G Grace'. The sports field was now linked to the altar.

Sam also wanted Monier to join the Rifle Corps. The Rugby School Corps had been formed in 1860, the first of all the public school Volunteers. It was Monier's inability to 'get out the orders quick enough' that persuaded his parents to send him to more elocutionists. As he pointed out, if his speech were better he might be able 'to take the lead in the Rifle Corps, Football and the House'. Monier became a Corporal, though whether he ever succeeded in 'getting the orders out quick enough' to be promoted further is not known. However, dressed in his red uniform and with his shining helmet, he was thrilled to march in the first battalion in the Public Schools Review to mark the Queen's Jubilee. His father was equally thrilled to see his son in the leading contingent. 'I think it must have been Father you heard cheering, for his loyalty was keenly excited and he cheered with all his heart and soul' wrote Ella. Sam only wished he had been given a similar opportunity when he was a boy. 'Just think how useful it would be to me, if I knew all about drill. If you should become a clergyman, Church Lads Brigade would sure to be yours' he told Monier. He was quite right. In 1907 when Monier was a curate in Lambeth he did become responsible for the Church Lads Brigade. All the boys joined the Corps, Julian becoming an officer and winning the tactical shield.

Even 'timid' Morris revelled in the excitement.. His father's memoir includes his enthusiastic account of a charge at a field-day.

> I captured one person, who refused absolutely to get up when I told him to. After a little arguing, not of the quietest, I took him by the scruff of the neck and pulled…. It was most exciting, and I felt charging was real and living. I hope I shall often have another chance of it on future field days.

But was it 'real and living'? On the contrary, it was contrived and fake. But the thrills it engendered were to motivate Morris and many of his public school contemporaries to rush to enlist in 1914 when the call of duty became a siren-song as well as a moral demand.

As the boys went up the school, they had increasing responsibilities for leadership in their House. Monier was amazed when, at evening Prayers, Mr. Steel said

> 'Roe, Hadley, Bickersteth and Hemp you had better come and sit up here.' I now sit at top table and use the VI form room where there is a fire and a library of books … in the dorm, Lanyon and I are head. We have hot water brought for us every night.

He had been chosen to have VIth Power. When the Sixth form in a House was small, some Fifth form boys were appointed by the housemaster to be responsible for aspects of House discipline. Monier soon found out, however, that his new position caused problems.

> It is a very difficult position to hold in one way, i.e. Men with whom I am on friendly terms with, take advantage of it, and think they can do what they like; also friends of the VIth, and it is jolly difficult to keep them in order without making enemies.

He and his friends found a solution:

> 'I am sorry to say we in the Sixth Form have whacked a boy … But I am sure it was necessary and has done good; because it has shown that although we are all new VIth yet we are not going to be rotted'.

In his future career, although he would not be able to 'whack' recalcitrant parishioners, early experience of the problems involved in leading would be useful. Sam must have been pleased that his eldest, conscientious and often anxious son, so like himself, was gaining the experience needed to become 'a leader of men'. When War came,

Ralph also found his VIth Power experience useful:

> I have just caught five or six officers chewing toffee or something.
> My hat! They will hear about it when it is time to dismiss!!! They
> occasionally try and play upon me like this – I suppose because
> they think I am young and innocent. I may be young, but I'm
> not so bloomin' innocent as they imagine, and they will soon find
> it out!!!

Morris also completed his Rugby career happily and gained VIth Power.
In his last term there is a letter from him to Geoffrey. He was having a
'jolly good time' and in it he provides a rare glimpse of brotherly rough
and ready camaraderie:

> I have had to have two or three executions in Dorm. The other
> night I came up rather late and ... a huge pillow fight had been
> raging. Luckily Ralph had not been in it – otherwise I should
> have claimed 2/6d from you and Burgon! Some people went to
> bed that night a little the worse for wear.

Public school education was certainly providing the boys with the
experience to become leaders, but it was also providing the social
connections so necessary to give opportunities to exert that leadership.
Sam and Ella were very aware that, in order to seize opportunities to
lead it was necessary to know the right people. Public school would
set their boys on the right road. The friends they made at Rugby and
Charterhouse might well influence their whole lives. When Archbishop
Benson died suddenly in 1896, Sam was delighted that Monier knew so
quickly that his successor was to be Frederick Temple, whose two sons
were at Rugby.

> Fancy your knowing all about the new Archbishop before we did.
> That comes from being at Rugby, the school, which has trained
> so many Bishops. Perhaps it is now training one in a boy I know.
> Who can tell? ... Do you know either of his two sons?

Unfortunately, Monier only knew that Frederick Temple's nickname
was 'farting Freddy'. However, Julian became a great friend of Frederick
Temple's brother, William. Through Julian, the Charterhouse brothers
also became friends with him, Geoffrey staying at Lambeth Palace.
Three years later the two families met together on holiday in the Lake
District. It was a huge party, made up of the Temples and the two sons
and five daughters of the Revd William Spooner, Dean of New College,
Oxford. The programme was typical of the Archbishop's Rugby days of

muscular Christianity. Eleven year-old Burgon described one day out. 'Today will be memorable as I climbed Easedale Crag, Sergen Man (*sic*) and Langdale Pike. We were walking from 9.45 a.m. to 8 p.m. We altogether had a very happy day. But some of us were rather tired.' Ella noted that 'Mrs Temple was especially attracted by Burgon. He certainly is a charming boy, full of life, energy, good temper, good looks and good spirits.' Ella was also delighted that the little Spooner daughters were in the party – at long last the boys could meet some girls! Burgon kept in touch with William Temple all his life. He became the brother who excelled at 'making connections'. He fulfilled his six year-old promise when 'he had a smile and the right word for all he meets'. Thirteen years later, he was at a Lambeth Convocation party with Monier. 'Both boys thoroughly enjoyed it .... Burgon would be introduced to all the Bishops he could' wrote Ella. Though it is arguable whether Summer Fields and Rugby helped or hindered Monier's leadership abilities, he also developed a confident ease in society, despite his speech difficulties. 'We took Monier to [the Lambeth Palace garden party] and very pleasant it was introducing him to all our friends. He makes himself so agreeable' wrote Ella happily.

It is hard not to agree with Ella that the public schools had fulfilled their parents' hopes. The huge sacrifices of time and money had been worthwhile. Their boys were independent and self-assured, but still held to the family values. All of them gained places at Oxford. Certainly Monier had not been happy at school, but it would be very misleading to assume that his school days were unadulterated misery. Some of his time at Rugby is related with great enthusiasm. Julian's feelings for Rugby were unequivocal. He loved it. The games, the drama, the Volunteers and the Scout camps were all a delight. Morris, in his last year, 'felt tired of being here although I am having a jolly good time this term'. Geoffrey and Burgon at Charterhouse had hard times, but when he was leaving Burgon wrote to his parents:

> It really was too awful saying goodbye to everyone at Charterhouse. ... However, all things must have an end – and I have had a perfectly ripping time here'.

Perhaps the most conclusive evidence that the boys considered their education, if not always wholly enjoyable, certainly advantageous, was that Monier, Geoffrey and Ralph all sent their sons to public schools, and the bachelor brothers, Julian and Burgon, helped pay their nephews' fees.

Background Reading

Aldridge, N *Time to Spare? A History of Summer Fields* Tallboy Publications, Oxford (1989)

Fitzgerald, P *The Knox Brothers* Macmillan (1977)

Usborne, R *A Century of Summer Fields 1864-1964* Methuen (1964)

Mangan, J A and Walvin, J (eds) *Manliness and Morality: Middle Class Masculinity in Britain and America 1880-1940.* Manchester University Press (1987)

Vance, N. *The Sinews of the Spirit: the Ideal of Christian Manliness in Victorian Literature and Religious Thought.* Cambridge University Press (1985)

Sources

In the Bodleian Library:

Letters to Samuel and Ella Bickersteth from their eldest son Monier 1886-1911

Letters to Monier from his parents Samuel and Ella Bickersteth 1890-1910

Diaries of Samuel and Ella Bickersteth

7

UNIVERSITY AND THE SHADOW OF WAR

I n 1911, Morris described his life at Oxford as 'unadulterated bliss'. 'They say there hasn't been a summer like this for years … I have played a good deal of tennis, a little cricket … and have been a certain amount on the river – enough to learn to punt.' He had captured the mood of the moment. Sunlight rather than shadow characterised the lives of the brothers during the fourteen and a half years they were undergraduates at Christ Church, Oxford, each in succession occupying the same rooms in Peckwater Quad. Absorbed in the nursery, reinforced by family tradition, augmented by their public schools and now to be consolidated by their university experience, their lives still followed the paths laid down by their parents, grandparents and great-grandparents. Their faith was permeated by a Bible-based evangelicalism, with its emphasis on conversion, redemption, activism, and the particular Bickersteth focus on sacramentalism. To an extent surprising to modern eyes, their parents continued in the training role that they had assumed throughout the boys' younger days, and Oxford saw the final stages in the casting of the mould which would be tested in the crucible of the Great War.

Monier went up to Christ Church, Oxford in 1901, each brother following him in turn. Ralph, arriving in 1913, stocked his wine cupboard with port, hock and whisky, confidently expecting that his 'Oxford time was going to be so very entertaining'. There were setbacks and failures, but finally Julian and Burgon gained a second in Modern History, Monier managed to get a third and Morris struggled to secure a pass degree. The academic white hope of the family, Geoffrey, obtained a second in Greats (*Literae Humaniores*). Ralph never returned to university after the war. Geoffrey, Julian and Burgon came to decisions about their future careers, and took the first steps in achieving their aims.

Travel and sport were the high marks of the 'golden years'. The climax was reached when Burgon captained the winning side in the Varsity Association Football match. His team beat Cambridge three goals to two. Next day the papers said he had 'played the game of his life', despite having one leg in bandages due to a pulled muscle. A 'large company of Bickersteths, Rundalls and Aglionbys' watched the fun and Ella found herself 'shouting "Oxford" with all my might'. She was not alone. 'The row of brothers made a good noise, and Father too'. Julian also had his sporting successes, and became captain of the Christ Church Rugby XV. Geoffrey was another keen footballer, but had the misfortune of breaking his collar bone in two successive terms which seems to have brought his sporting career to an untimely close. Morris, a keen cricketer, also became an expert bridge player. In the long vacations, their parents encouraged the boys to travel extensively in Europe and to learn to speak one language fluently. When they went to Germany, in order to improve their German, they stayed with contacts of their mother's elderly friends – the families whom she first knew when, as a young girl, she studied German with her father on continental tours. On holiday with his mother in Dresden, Morris and Ella went to the Opera every night and saw *Der Rosenkavalier*, *Mignon*, *Tosca*, the *Rheingold* and the *Valkyries*. All the brothers made visits to France, Switzerland and Italy. At the end of their university careers, they began to explore outposts of the Empire: Canada, Australia, India and South Africa. All over the world there was always a relative who could be relied upon to introduce them to the right people in the right circles – whether they were clerical, missionary, academic, or administrative.

The boys led full social lives: 'smoking concerts', the theatre, opera, London musicals, the June College balls, were enjoyed to an extent which sometimes perturbed their parents. Julian 'was walking down the High at 6 a.m.' after a Christ Church ball, whilst Monier went to so many dances that he 'only had six hours sleep during sixty' and had to admit that he was 'rather tired'. Julian was lucky not to be arrested after a grand bump supper marking Christ Church being Head of the River after sixty years. He and his friends had felt a celebratory bonfire would be appropriate, so they tried to pull down a temporary grandstand for fuel. The Fire Brigade and the police were called out. The result was that next day Julian was 'limping from a blow on his leg from a policeman's truncheon' – something that could hardly escape his mother's eagle eye. There is no doubt that the boys enjoyed a social life at Oxford which would have horrified their evangelical ancestors. Yet in many respects their university life had a great deal in common with that of their predecessors. In 1843, when the boys' grandfather, Edward Henry, had gone up to Cambridge, his father (Edward of Watton) was very conscious of the 'many peculiar snares and temptations of being thrown so much on your own free choice as to the employment of your

time'. Sam and Ella knew exactly what he meant; it worried them as
well. Their sons would be enjoying their 'own free choice' after their
strictly regulated school and home lives. The antidote was obvious:
more guidance would be needed, not less. Advice – moral, medical,
and marital – flowed from the Vicarage. It determined the subjects
the boys studied. On their father's recommendation, Monier, Burgon,
Julian and Morris all read history. There is no evidence that they were
particularly attracted to that subject, and strong evidence that Morris
would have preferred English literature. It extended to their leisure,
and the sports they chose. It flowed against a backdrop of parental
financial anxiety incurred by the privileged opportunities they wanted
for their sons. But its principles were fed from the evangelical well-
springs of the past, and the boys, whilst for the first time enjoying 'free
choice' in both leisure and work, responded if not always in tune with
those principles, always influenced by the underlying harmony of faith
and works instilled in the family throughout the generations.

Because each generation of Bickersteths tended to keep their
letters, it is possible to compare the boys' Oxford days in the light of
the principles listed by their great-grandfather half a century earlier.
Edward of Watton sent his advice to his son in lengthy letters setting
out the rules he wished Edward Henry to observe. He must not neglect
private prayer. The Sabbath must be strictly observed. He must look
after his physical health as well as his spiritual health. Friends must
be chosen with care and 'expensive habits ought on every account to
be avoided.' It was the same serious evangelical path that Sam and
Ella wished their boys to follow. Consequently, the letters they sent to
their sons were not dissimilar. Fortunately they were shorter. Edward
of Watton was still captivated by the novelty of the penny post – his
'new tool for evangelism' – and his letters could run to 1,500 words
and more. Nevertheless, they provide striking examples of continuity
in evangelical practice extending to the third generation. Cambridge,
in Edward Henry's time, was known as a centre for 'moral earnestness',
characterised by piety and religious zeal. In Oxford in 1908 piety and
religious zeal were still alive. Burgon belonged to a Bible Circle which
met on a Sunday evening and, although he 'came in quite by accident'
he seems to have attended regularly throughout term in 1908.

> We begin by an extempore prayer which I always think is rather
> a mistake unless it is well done – then each read a verse round
> of the Epistle to the Ephesians – it is that that we are doing now.
> Then Henderson, whose turn it was, spoke about the chapter
> and then we discussed it. The doctrine of predestination comes

rather into the first chapter – that we are pre-ordained etc – and this point was fully discussed.

When visiting preachers came to Oxford, they could be sure of a large audience if they were good speakers. In 1905 Julian went to a crowded meeting addressed by Dr John Mott, an American Methodist layman who was General Secretary of the World Student Christian Federation. Supported by the Archbishop of Canterbury, he had come to Oxford to recruit university men for ministry in the Empire. Night after night, undergraduates crowded into his meetings to hear him speak and to be enthralled by his call: 'the evangelisation of the world in this generation'. The address Julian heard: 'How may Jesus Christ become a reality to me?' was aimed at Christians who felt that the 'facts of their faith were unreal to them'. Because they might have 'spent several years in the study of Christ,' they now assumed that they had no need to 'exercise their minds upon Christ in order to keep Him real in their thought and experience'. It spoke to the needs of Julian in a way that Edward of Watton would have instantly recognised. Ella recorded in her diary that 'it was a vivid spiritual experience... which 'helped him a great deal to realize his faith in Christ'.

At Cambridge, ten of Edward Henry's contemporaries took Orders; three became great clerical headmasters; five became bishops. Sixty years later in Oxford the Bickersteth boys were contemporaries of George Bell, a future Bishop of Chichester, Henry Scott Holland, theologian and social reformer, and William Temple, a future Archbishop of Canterbury. Although it would be wrong to assume that the brothers moved exclusively in church circles, it would seem that the majority of their fellow students at Oxford had a church connection. Amongst the many names which occur in their diaries and papers, many of the young men had links with the Church – a father who was a leading Church of England layman, a cousin who was a bishop, a brother who was ordained. The boys shared the same staircase in Peckwater Quad as Neville and Gilbert Talbot, sons of the Bishop of Rochester. Gilbert was 'the little boy' who, years before, had taken Morris' place when he was too shy to present the bouquet at a Church bazaar. Neville and Gilbert both became Army chaplains. Gilbert died at Ypres and his brother, who was to become Bishop of Pretoria, founded Talbot House (Toc H) at Poperinghe in his memory.

The similarity throughout the generations is seen clearly in the way Edward Henry was instructed to conduct his life, and the advice of Sam and Ella to their sons. Edward Henry's father told his son never 'to neglect private prayer, at least morning and evening, and read daily in secret, in regular order, and with earnest prayer, the Holy Scriptures'. The first letters Monier received from his parents when he arrived at Oxford also gave him clear instructions: 'I want you to say your prayers in cathedral each morning and that will set a time to your day and life' wrote his father. His mother wrote by the same post:

> Have a plan for your day. If you begin with daily chapel, that means your getting up in good time. Then besides your morning prayers, have a short midday act of prayer.

And, like every generation of Bickersteth fathers, Sam added 'I daily throw around you the shield of our intercessory prayer'. Prayer, regular Bible reading, church attendance – all these had been absorbed by the boys throughout their lives. In diaries and letters, Sunday after Sunday, they noted attendance at Early Service and matins. Their ancestors would have had little cause for complaint.

In the same way, Sam and Ella wholeheartedly endorsed Edward of Watton's admonition to his son on the necessity for a 'well regulated plan of rising, study, and going early to rest'. In his turn, Edward Henry had kept a close eye on his son, Sam, when he felt he was 'over-working'. Sam still kept the letter:

> You must not scruple to take the bromide at the beginning of the night whenever you need it for the next few weeks ... I fancy you may be able to read all your permitted five and a half or even six hours a day, with frequent breaks of sleep or of at least lying back on an easy chair or sofa for ten or twenty minutes so as never to put any strain or constraint on thought.

Sam and Ella felt that exercise and Malt Extract were preferable medicines, though it was only too clear to Sam that nineteen-year-old Monier's difficulties with examinations did not arise from 'overwork'.

> I don't approve of the ball this week ... It tries you unnecessarily and preoccupies your mind. You have had a social life for four months following after the festivities of your first summer term, and now you ought wholly to concentrate on intellectual life and prepare for this coming examination [Mods] and pass it.

His mother was equally firm. Whilst his father emphasised the need for him to concentrate on his work, Ella did not allow him to forget that physical exercise was equally important. She enquired 'Can't you do both football and rowing this term? ... rowing is such a much better all the year round exercise'. Next day, she had second thoughts and wrote again:

> I advise and <u>wish</u> (*sic*) you to take Malt Extract for lunch. Order it from a grocer, and we will pay for it. But first take a good dose of opening medicine. Often at the fall of leaf one feels poorly. ... also, between ourselves, I fancy you were a bit vexed at Father's letter. ... You may say "but one dance won't endanger Mods" no doubt it won't ... but Mods are important.

Shortly afterwards eight bottles of Hoffman's Malt Extract were delivered. Monier passed Mods.

The precision which established who was to pay for the Malt Extract was typical of the family finances. Edward of Watton's advice that his son should avoid expensive habits was wholeheartedly endorsed by Sam. His financial position had not been improved by his move to Leeds, and to fund his sons for well over a decade at university was daunting. Money, or the lack of it, continued to be a major source of anxiety and was not a taboo subject in the Bickersteth household. The boys knew their father's income in detail, and that family money invested in Sampson Low, the religious publishing house, was now earning no interest and there was every likelihood that the firm would become bankrupt, which indeed it did. Sam's letters became peppered with regrets that he could not afford to visit Oxford, or could they find someone with whom they could stay, to avoid hotel bills. Rather desperately, one year even the annual summer holiday looked beyond their means. Did Monier know of 'a cheap farmhouse' as his doctor had advised against Sam having a working holiday as a locum? It is not surprising that each boy was given an allowance and expected to keep within it. Monier was allocated '£200 per annum which, including your allowance of £40, must cover all your expenses'. There was no argument about it. As Burgon cheerfully noted in his diary, describing a hectic day out at the university races:

> Crowds were there, coaches, brakes, motors and traps by the dozen, a whole row of bookies who did good trade, it seemed. I did not bet. I had no money. If I had, it does not amuse me. Guy lost and so did John Stainton, so I could chuckle over them.

As each boy moved through university, he was expected to find short tutorship positions. Some were luckier than others. 'Geoff and Julian have suddenly got tutorships and are off, Geoffrey to a Captain Tyler on the Chiltern hills to teach a clever Eton boy, Julian to Sandling Park to look after Arthur' wrote Ella. Arthur was the son of Alexander Murray, a partner in the Murray publishing house. Despite making a possibly useful contact in the publishing world, Julian had a 'dull time'. Geoffrey fared better: he enjoyed 'lots of motoring' and 'heaps of golf'. But both gave the money they earned to their father. Financial pressure meant that Burgon's entry to Christ Church had to be postponed for a year. He was sent to Leeds University which enabled him to live at home, but it was not a success. 'It would have been better to have left him in Dresden as French and German teaching at Leeds proved most disappointing' wrote Ella. It might also have been economical. Monier had recently spent six weeks in Frankfurt to improve his German. The cost had been £2 per week – perhaps because his mother had written to his host saying Monier 'did not mind simplicity'. Unless the records have been discreetly edited, there is no indication that any of the boys incurred debts at Oxford. The horror with which his mother recounts a lapse by Julian seems to confirm this:

> It was one of the saddest moments of our lives when our dear Julian wrote to say that at the Christ Church Steeple Chases he had succumbed to a sudden temptation and lost £6 at a card trick swindle, £2 of which was not his own ... the Fall may so humble him that his character may gain in the future, but his doing it is a mystery. He has never gambled, he tells us, or played for money before. May God bring good out of evil.

Sam, as so often happened, was a little more relaxed than his wife. He sent a telegram in reply saying 'We understand and feel for you'. He followed it up with a cheque – but only for £3.

Where Sam did part company with his forebears was in their judgement that 'a desire to associate with those of higher rank in life' was 'attended by many evils' whilst those in 'inferior circumstances may seek to gain advantages'. Sam was well aware that in the modern competitive world, good contacts were essential. Their home training would be a sufficient safeguard for his boys from anything which might be 'a corrupting influence'. They had sent them to Oxford partly in order to make useful friends and contacts and to cultivate those of 'higher rank'. Fortunately, the boys had led such social lives ever since they were small children that they were naturally gregarious. Even shy Morris, after some initial help from his brothers, was quite capable of maintaining an active social life of his own. In addition, they went up to

Oxford knowing boys from Rugby and Charterhouse who either had preceded them or went up at the same time. Friends of one brother became friendly with the other brothers, whilst sons of clergy that they knew well were to be found amongst several colleges. Throughout the period, a succession of Monier-Williams cousins came up to Oxford. Evelyn, Monier's contemporary, was President of the Oxford Boat club and stroked the Oxford Eight in the University Boat Race. Perhaps it is not surprising that Ella urged Monier to take up rowing as a sport, and understandable that he decided against it! Burgon kept a note in his diary of everyone that he met. In Hilary term 1905 there are over seventy different entries. Names which re-occur, and continue to re-occur during the Great War, include Hew Hamilton-Dalrymple, 9th Baronet of North Berwick, William Leveson Gower, a relative of the Duke of Sutherland, Philip Gibbs, the future war correspondent, and Stephen McKenna, who would become a popular novelist. It was a rare week which did not feature a party of friends sharing breakfast with him, or evening cocoa. Also in evidence are merry evenings where wine, rather than cocoa featured. At Lewisham, their father declared that he was 'a total abstainer, for six reasons. I have six sons'. He hoped his boys would follow his example. They appear to have ignored his advice. No letters of reproof have been found, though comments such as 'a little the worse for wear' or 'dined a little too well' only appear in letters and diaries that their parents would not have seen. One very positive result of all this conviviality was that, in France, there was rarely an officers' mess where Burgon, Julian, Morris and Ralph had not met some of the officers socially.

There is, however, no doubt that Edward of Watton would have been horrified to see one of his great grandchildren 'a little the worse for wear'. It was in these more mundane aspects of their lives that differences began to emerge and changes in attitude can be seen. Edward of Watton insisted on 'an entire separation of the Sabbath to its sacred duties. Let it not be a day of visiting, or of receiving visits.' Sam and Ella's views on the keeping of Sunday were a little more relaxed, but both Monier and Burgon found it a confusing subject. The first clash between parents and son came in Monier's second year. A series of letters record the dissension, triggered apparently by a casual comment that Monier included in a letter home. He had been to Holy Communion, morning service and then to friends for lunch.

> And then we went in the punt up to Marsden, when some of us walked back and Illingworth and I had tea with Sandeman which was very pleasant. He played us some Greig and Beethoven.

His mother could hardly believe what she was reading and wrote to tell him so. Monier, with some spirit, promptly replied:

> You understood my letter quite rightly last Sunday. I did go out in the punt on Sunday afternoon. I went with a good many other men, and we were not noisy – I do not think that there is any objection to punting so long as it is not turned into a rowdy concern.

This triggered a letter from his father:

> About punting on Sundays. Think twice and pray thrice before you make it your custom. In itself it is neither right nor wrong. It belongs to that large class of acts, which must be looked at in its bearings on a whole course of actions. I Cor. 6.12. ['All things are lawful unto me, but all things are not expedient'] Punting ... is in itself insignificant, but it is associated in men's minds with Sunday observance, one of the most potent forces in bringing about the salvation of man. Hence, dear boy, if you avoid it, it may make other men think, and enable you to be a witness for a great principle.

Monier replied next day, but thought it wiser to write to his mother:

> Please thank Father very much for his letter. But I cannot see the punting question in the way he does – of course if he or you or both say plainly you would rather I did not do it, I should not; but as it is I do not feel that I need stop it.

It would probably have been wiser for Monier to reply direct to his father. His mother, in terms that seem calculated to strike home, at once let him know her opinion, though she stopped short of issuing a ban.

> I want to tell you that I do feel very badly about the Sunday going on the river. I am quite certain you would not do it if you thought it wrong, but the chief cause of my disappointment is that you do not see that it is wrong, or rather that the principle does not appeal to you. We will talk it over when you come home, but I can hardly believe that you, who do live very near your Lord, could think the crowded river last Sunday was what He would like on His Day. ... I had rather you did not do it, but I would far rather you did not want to do it.

What was said during the holidays is unknown. One senses that, in the absence of an outright ban, Monier decided that discretion was the better part of valour. A generation later, he was not disturbed by his son punting and having rowing practice on a Sunday.

Three years later a similar situation arose with Burgon. He was in France, staying in the family of a French pastor. They all played tennis on a Sunday afternoon. Could he join in? Like Monier, Burgon had difficulty in accepting his father's argument. Sam was

> ... quite clear that a game rightly played on a weekday cannot be intrinsically wrong on a Sunday, but it would be contrary to the spirit of the Day, the Day is given for Worship and for rest and recreation, both of mind, body and spirit. On the whole games militate against both these purposes for which the Day is given to man. A walk with a friend does not.

Burgon could not see the difference.

> These people (the pastor and his sons] never think twice about it ... therefore what I cannot quite see is that, what difference it makes if I play tennis on a Sunday here. ... I go to my Holy Communion and I go to Matins at 10.30 – after lunch I play a game of tennis for an hour or two then a walk perhaps and then probably read or perhaps music in the evening. In that programme for Sunday I can see nothing wrong.

Neither did he feel that his argument clashed with the behaviour expected from a vicarage son. He was, after all, in France.

> .... in England I should not dream of doing it, least of all at Lewisham. There we are sons of the Vicar and we try to set an example and people would think it a very green thing to do – and naturally and rightly so! But here it is different.

Here the discussion was overtaken by the exciting news of Bickersteth's appointment to Leeds, and no more is heard of the argument. It would seem that father and son were both prepared to live with the ambiguities created by following the faith of their fathers.

Despite these divergences from what both Edward of Watton and their parents considered to be the way of virtue, both Burgon and Julian made contacts in Oxford which directed their lives along paths similar to those of their forebears. Dr John Mott, who had been responsible for Julian's 'vivid spiritual experience' was also responsible for turning his thoughts to youth work in Australia. Julian, on going down from Oxford had gone straight to Wells Theological College, a Leeds parishioner paying the fees. After ordination, he became a curate at St Andrew's, Rugby, and remained closely in touch with his old school, playing for the Old Rugbeians and becoming increasingly involved with youth work, with his holidays occupied with Scout, youth and Army camps. At the same time Mott, still looking for university men to go out to the dominions, met William Temple, and asked him to go out to Australia to see the work of the Student Christian Movement there and judge its potential. Temple returned full of enthusiasm about the opportunities he had seen, and recommended his friend Julian as the man best able to meet the challenge. The result was that by 1912 Julian had been appointed chaplain and assistant master in history to the Church of England Grammar School at Melbourne where Temple had lectured. Little is known about his years there, but there is little doubt that he thoroughly enjoyed the open air, sporting life and the free and easy relationship between masters and boys. At the same time, he had an uneasy relationship with his first headmaster and had grave doubts about the suitability of his successor, a Cambridge man whose brother, he knew, was 'certainly not a gentleman'. According to Morris, who spent about three months with him in 1914, he was also 'out of sympathy' with members of the staff. Perhaps he was prepared to preach on controversial subjects? The records are silent, but on one occasion the War Diary reveals that he was willing to tackle racial questions and preached 'condemning the White Australia policy and saying that the War must alter the relations between the white and coloured races within the Empire'. The whole experience must have been a cultural shock after his regulated upper middle-class life in England, though it did not dampen his enthusiasm for all things Australian. Morris felt 'he was doing a great work', but within months war was declared and within a year, Julian was returning to England, travelling at his own expense in the hope of serving as a chaplain with the British Expeditionary Force. He arrived home in January 1916 and found that Sam had been busy arranging interviews on his behalf. Three weeks later he crossed the Channel. He was now a chaplain and would be going straight up to the front line. He wrote home: 'I shall probably be in and out of the firing line all the time. So I am in luck's way'.

One of the contacts Burgon made in Oxford was also life-changing. The Revd W G Boyd, chaplain to the Archbishop of Canterbury, had been sent out to Western Canada on a fact-finding mission in 1909. Over 180,000 immigrants, mostly bound for Western Canada, were entering the country every year and there was little provision for their spiritual needs. The Church of England was noticeably lagging behind other denominations, and the need was great. As a result the Archbishops of Canterbury and York launched the Western Canada Mission Appeal, asking for men and money in the bluntest of terms: 'those who can, ought to give large sums'. Men who were 'strong, manly, gritty, and ready to adapt to new conditions' were urgently needed. Ordination was irrelevant. 'It is what he is as a man that matters, ... but he had better not go unless he is sure that the Lord is calling him, and then he will go in the spirit of humility and self-sacrifice.' Boyd called to see Burgon:

> Early in April 1910 I was sitting in my rooms in Christ Church, hard at work as my final examinations were uncomfortably near. There was a knock on the door and in came W. G. Boyd. I did not know him at all well ... the object of his visit soon became clear. Would I consider joining the Archbishops' Western Canada Mission when I had taken my degree?

After anxious family consultations, the answer was 'yes'. Burgon went off to Canada in 1911 with, wrote Sam, 'a few tears shed by parents who dearly love a most loveable son'. They were certain that he was 'fitted for work in a pioneer land ... as a fighting soldier of our Lord'. Even so, his mother was not happy that he travelled steerage. 'It was such a small ship and Burgon had a horrid under-berth in a cabin with three quite poor men.' He had refused to switch to the liner on which one of his friends was travelling. Burgon's two years in Western Canada were the beginning of his life-long love of Canada and Canadians. He relished the democratic atmosphere, so different from anything he had previously experienced. He rode, and trudged through the mud, ice and snow of the Western Trails, and along the new Transcontinental Rails up to the rail heads, living 'in my own shack in the mountains at 54 degrees below zero for two days, and at 62 below for a few hours'. He stayed in the construction camps, distributing newspapers and magazines in the bunk houses, watching over dying emigrants, preaching and hymn singing in the cook houses. His passionate interest in, and ability to identify with the roughest and toughest of the labourers shine through his letters home:

> One of the foremen shouted out, "Here, you fellow, come and give us a hand with the trams" which I was only too glad to do. So had you been there, you might have seen me sweating away

with one of the roughest bunches of men at that time in the West – a steel-laying gang being by reputation as tough a bunch as you would find anywhere ... I was covered with oil and dirt by the time we had finished ... it was highly interesting to gain a practical knowledge of the whole process of laying steel.

With the encouragement of the Governor General, Lord Grey, who considered 'Young Bickersteth a wide-awake fellow, full of vigour and enthusiasm,' the letters were published under the title *The Land of Open Doors*. To Ella's great delight, when the Mission held a public meeting at Church House 'the Bishop of London's reference to Burgon and his well-known book was greeted with loud applause.' Returning home in 1913, Burgon spent a year at the Sorbonne, perfecting his French, preparatory to returning to Canada to take up a lectureship in the University of Alberta. He had just bought his ticket when war was declared. Geoffrey dashed up to Liverpool to get his brother's money back.

Unlike his brothers, Geoffrey's career moved smoothly onwards in the academic world. He obtained a post of assistant master at Marlborough which enabled him to earn enough to gain further qualifications. By 1913 he was studying philology at Munich and Heidelberg universities and had published his first book, a selection of the poems of Carducci with translations into English verse. He was well on his way to the academic career he had always wanted and was expecting to return to Germany when war was declared.

As, one by one, their sons' university days drew to a close, Sam and Ella could feel that Burgon, Julian and Geoffrey had fulfilled all their hopes. It was the futures of Monier and Morris which gave them sleepless nights. Monier came down in 1904 having decided he was not fitted to become a priest. 'He felt no call, and his ideal of what a parson should be, being very high, he felt he could not attain to it' wrote his mother sadly. Unfortunately, he was completely undecided as to an alternative career. Disappointed though they were, his parents threw themselves into the task of finding other openings. They inundated Monier with advice. He must be careful when filling out application forms. His father instructed him to 'Write out all your answers on a sheet of foolscap and then copy them. Be careful of handwriting and spelling'. His mother felt he might become a Member of Parliament, or a First Division clerk in the Admiralty, and then, more realistically, join the Egyptian Civil Service. 'It seems a great opening for a distinguished career, and there is no doubt they are trying to get University men, and Gentlemen, and are not going on the system of competition'. She had correctly identified the one remaining branch of the civil service where there was no entry examination. His father thought there might be openings on the Canadian railways. Relatives were consulted, and members of the aristocracy 'carefully approached'. Sir Charles Bignold, Lord and Lady Cavan, the Leveson Gowers, Arnold Forster, MP, Lord Edward Cecil and Lord Mount Stephen were all contacted – with little success. An opening was finally found through a churchwarden having a friend, Mr Kemp, who was 'a partner in one of the biggest firms of Chartered Accountants' – Price, Holyland & Waterhouse, now PriceWaterhouseCoopers. Mr Kemp strongly recommended accountancy as a suitable profession. His reason must have been music in an anxious father's ears and a vindication for all his struggles with school and university fees:

> He says there is a great opening particularly for a Gentleman, who also knows his business. He laid great stress upon the 'Gentleman' and said also that your University friends would be useful as clients.

Sam consulted his brother-in-law, Monier Faithfull Monier-Williams, and promptly sought an introduction to Edwin Waterhouse, the senior partner. The result was that Monier, whose best subject had always been mathematics, signed his Articles. His father paid the premium, having raised the money on his securities and made it clear that Monier would be expected to repay it when he was independent. For two years, Monier lived at home in Lewisham, working in the City and helping in the parish. Yet thoughts of ordination were never far away and in 1906 he told his parents that he had decided to take Orders. On Easter Day, at early service, kneeling with his mother and all his brothers, 'he gave himself to the Ministry'. By July he was studying at Wells Theological College and from 1907-1911 he served first as a curate in Lambeth and then in Bedale in Yorkshire. In 1911 he was offered a living at Bromsgrove, Castle Bromwich. With a stipend of £250, plus a new house, marriage was at last possible, and he had loved Kitty Jelf 'as long as he could remember'. They had met as children at dancing classes in Lewisham vicarage. Dr and Mrs Jelf, old family friends, were delighted. So were Monier's parents. Kitty was ' not only pretty in face, but charming in character, very unselfish and accomplished – in fact, a darling' wrote Ella. The wedding was in June, in Christ Church Cathedral, with his father officiating alongside the Bishops of London and Rochester. It was a joyous occasion. Their proud mother commented: 'All my darlings were in black tail coats and high hats, finished off with grey waistcoats, ties and spats'. Within a few weeks Julian had sailed for Australia, and Burgon for Canada. It was inconceivable that this would be the last time all six brothers would meet together.

Ironically, it was Morris, whose life was to be so short, who gave his parents more cause for concern than all his brothers put together. He had to take Mods twice and at this early stage of his university life, wanted to become engaged. He had fallen in love with Dorothy Hepton – 'quite pretty and rippingly dressed' in the opinion of Burgon who always tended to admire his brothers' girl friends whilst dismissing all others as 'dull' or 'heavy'. Dorothy was the only child of Sir William Hepton, Lord Mayor of Leeds and a wealthy wholesale manufacturer. Although both parents were family friends of the Bickersteths they could not approve of the match. Lady Hepton's reaction, in particular, greatly surprised Ella. She insisted that her daughter was 'heart-whole' and, as a mother, she wished 'nothing said until Morris had some prospects'. 'I must say' commented Ella indignantly 'that I thought Lady Hepton would have encouraged any connection with a boy of ours'. Two years later, Ella asked her if the young people might at least correspond, but Lady Hepton again insisted that Morris must wait until he had prospects. Morris then made matters worse by failing his final examinations despite following his mother's advice and taking Sanatogen daily. Sam and Ella could, and did, take their sons to task over any failings, but were ready to defend them against all outsiders. Morris' tutor must have been, thought Ella, 'terribly to blame' and Sam wrote 'a strong letter to the Dean to complain of his neglect'. In response, the tutor, Keith Feiling, who would become Chichele Professor of Modern History, wrote 'a horrid letter to Morris'. Morris was despondent. He had no clear ideas about his future, though he had considered ordination and missionary service. His uncle Monier offered to pay for his articles if he wished to become a solicitor, but Morris had no inclination for a legal career. Perhaps a career in shipping might be his metier. As with Monier, his father began writing to all his contacts, whilst insisting that Morris return to Oxford to complete his degree. This time he successfully took the extra papers he needed for a pass degree, came home and proposed to Dorothy. The answer was 'no'. 'She did not love him in the way he wanted … it was piteous to see him' wrote his mother. 'I longed he should break down, but he struggled for self-control'. He still had no plans for the future and seemed poorly. 'What is God preparing him for?' she asked herself. A few weeks later he was admitted to hospital with appendicitis. The surgeon, Sir Berkeley Moynihan, a family friend, performed the operation and recommended a long, convalescent sea voyage. In February 1914, Morris set sail to visit Julian in Australia and then go on to South Africa. Ella was relieved: 'Well, change of scene and surroundings must widen his outlook, set up his health and turn him into a more useful man'. He was in Rhodesia when war was declared.

Within days of the outbreak of hostilities, Ralph who, as a Territorial, was at summer camp with the West Yorkshire Regiment, had volunteered. Morris enlisted with the Leeds Pals as soon as he arrived in England. Burgon had to be restrained by his parents from immediately travelling to Paris to enlist as a French soldier of the Line, but by September 1st he had 'taken the King's shilling' and was a trooper in the Yorkshire Hussars. Julian, in Australia, was trying unsuccessfully to go as a chaplain to the Australian troops who were being sent to the Dardanelles. Geoffrey, back home in the Leeds vicarage, was mortified that he was 'unable to serve in the army owing to bad knees, eyesight and a weak collar bone'. He had to be content to help find homes for the Belgian refugees being sent to Leeds, and to work for a B.Litt. He had left all his books in Germany as he had expected to return there in the autumn. It was 1919 before he saw them again.

The speed at which the whole family managed to put itself on a war footing suggests that they were expecting war to be declared. There is no evidence that this was the case. As far back as 1900, Monier had listened to Dean Farrar preaching at Rugby and warning that 'we are about to go through a European war or some other great crisis and are not likely to come out victorious'. The Dean may well have been thinking of the recent Balkan conflicts and, presciently, where they might lead. Monier dismissed it as 'a pretty good sermon, but very pessimistic'. Burgon had joined the Inns of Court Mounted Infantry in 1908 whilst he was at Oxford, but there is no indication that he did this because of the threat of war. The uniform, the company of friends, and the opportunities for summer camp and riding seem to have been the attraction, whilst passing the selection process was itself a cause for pride. Monier, on leaving Oxford, had also volunteered and was a lieutenant in the King's Royal Rifles. Like the Inns of Court Mounted Infantry it was a prestigious regiment, and the uniform, complete with helmet, was even grander than the one Monier had loved in the Rugby Volunteers. Rather than a training ground for war, it was for him a useful and pleasant way to gain the expertise he needed to drill the Church Lads Brigade when he was a curate. Their father had been honorary chaplain to the 2ⁿᵈ Kent Volunteer Artillery at Lewisham, and was now honorary chaplain to the 7ᵗʰ Battalion of the Leeds Rifles. Sam was deeply patriotic, but the position of honorary chaplain was regarded as almost part of the job for the Vicar of Lewisham or the Vicar of Leeds. Unlike some Church of England clergy, especially his good friend the Bishop of London, Sam

> was quite shy about putting on his uniform, but very soon got used to it and really looked remarkably nice … when we said good-bye to the Bishop, Father, unaccustomed to his uniform, did his utmost to get his cap off instead of saluting, much to Ralph's amusement.

So did war cast no shadow? Historians point out that the Great War did not occur 'out of the blue'. Some of the events that preceded it such as the Balkan wars, German expansionism and the arms race, were threatening clouds which could not have passed completely unnoticed by the brothers. On the other hand, they had all enjoyed so many continental holidays, as well as longer stays in Germany and France, and their mother had so many German friends, that, like so many of their contemporaries, they turned a blind eye even to its possibility. Yet at the same time, few boys could have been better prepared for war, ready to accept and even relish it. Brimming with health and vitality – Burgon, Julian and Ralph in particular seemed to have inherited the Bickersteth and Monier-Williams energy with its

Lieutenant Monier Bickersteth, King's Royal Rifles, Cadet Battalion. 1905.

love of non-stop activity – from nursery days they had learned to look after each other, the older ones shielding their younger brothers. They had absorbed love of country and pride in their family's record in the Armed Services. At public school they had been trained to lead. As they grew up, the newspapers they read, the books they had been brought up on, the songs they sang in the music halls, all implied that war was but a shadow on the path to glory. Patriotism was in their blood; the claims of country and Empire deeply embedded.

In other ways, they were remarkably ill-prepared. The mock battles they had so much enjoyed in the Volunteers did not bear much relationship to trench warfare. They had little knowledge of the men they were destined to lead. They knew that they had enjoyed a privileged life style, very different from that of private soldiers. In theory, they knew something of poverty and deprivation. It would have been strange if they had not read part of Booth's *Life and Labour of the London Poor*, as their father had been interviewed for the Religious Influences survey. Leeds had some of the worst slums in the country and both their parents were campaigning for better social conditions. But the boys were only at home during school holidays and then much of their time was spent staying with relations or with school friends or, at Leeds, with the local aristocracy and the wealthy manufacturers who were the patrons of the parish church. In the January school holidays in 1908, they enjoyed skating in the grounds of Lord Airedale and at Harwood House, where Lady Harwood was 'very nice', they attended the Lord Mayor's ball, and stayed on a private estate in the Lake District where they enjoyed shooting and golf. Ralph went to stay with the grandson of Lord Halifax. We do not know what misgivings Monier might have had when he drilled his Church Lads Brigade, but in 1914 only Burgon knew what it was to mix with men who were neither 'gentlemen' nor 'respectable' and, worst of all 'had no breeding'.

Nevertheless, they knew what was expected of them as vicarage sons and as Bickersteths. So when the first grim signs of the reality of war appeared – the invasion of Belgium and the sacking of the University library in Louvain, they did not hesitate. The war was just. Therefore there was no doubt about their duty. Had not their mother told them that it was essential to 'bury your will in the field of duty'? Their father's life demonstrated it. They joined all their public school friends in the rush to enlist. Who would get out to France first? In April 1915 Ralph won the race. His brothers wrote to congratulate him and wish him well. Their mother said simply 'Well, God will decide for my boys'.

Background reading

Bickersteth, J B *The Land of Open Doors.* University of Toronto Press (Reprinted 1977)

Mackie, R C *Layman Extraordinary. John Mott 1865-1955* Hodder & Stoughton (1963)

Parker, P *The Old Lie. The Great War and the Public School Ethos.* Constable (1987)

Sources

In the Bodleian Library:

Letters to Samuel and Ella Bickersteth from their eldest son Monier 1886-1911

Letters to Monier from his parents Samuel and Ella Bickersteth 1890-1910

Diaries of Samuel and Ella Bickersteth

Correspondence and papers 1838-1904 of Edward Henry Bickersteth, Bishop of Exeter

Correspondence and notebook belonging to Burgon held by the family

PART III

THE TESTING OF THE MOULD

8

THE GREAT WAR

'My eyes are glutted with the sight of bleeding bodies and shattered limbs'. Julian. Cambrai. December 1917.

Wednesday, 5th August 1914 saw Sam, Ella, Burgon and Geoffrey on holiday in the West Country. Opening the newspaper, they read 'the great flaring words we expected written right across the principal sheet: "War declared between England and Germany."' It was, they felt, 'impossible to suppress a sigh of relief. At any rate we had been true to our obligations.' They caught the first train to Leeds. Packed into a carriage crowded with reservists, Sam shared his *Times* and a map of the war with them. Burgon planned his next moves. He would go to London and try to see everyone who might help him get to France quickly. Ella decided to call a meeting of 'all the leading ladies in Leeds' for Friday afternoon at the vicarage. When they reached home, 'the telephone bell rang all day' as Ella arranged to provide overnight hospitality for 'ladies who are preparing a hospital at Chapeltown'. Friday morning they scoured the shops trying to buy Ralph's army kit as he was away at Army camp. The price of revolvers had rocketed and Leeds gunmakers were asking 'a most unreasonable sum'. In the afternoon, the 'leading ladies' arrived and Ella persuaded them that 'all the organisations they represented should work together and not issue separate appeals'. The next day their help was needed. Ella was asked to provide a 'hundred operating coats' and she 'parcelled out the work'. Sunday saw Sam preaching at the Parish Church, choosing as his text Revelations 19.11. 'The white horse, and he that sat thereon was called faithful and true'. The white horse was the badge of the Leeds Rifles. Afterwards, as chaplain, he marched through the City at the head of 7th Battalion of the West Yorkshire Regiment. Meanwhile, Morris in Salisbury, Rhodesia, was travelling non-stop by train for three days to board a ship at Capetown to return home, whilst Julian in Australia began applying for permission to serve as an Army chaplain. The call of duty had been answered by a whirl of activity. It had also broken one of the old evangelical shibboleths. The hunger for war news was just too great. The Bickersteths bought a Sunday newspaper. 'At least, Mother, Geoffrey and I did, and Father read it' wrote Burgon in the War Diary he had just started.

Over the next four years, the non-stop activity continued. In various stages, Ralph, Burgon, Morris and Julian arrived in France. Geoffrey, graded unfit for military service, eventually became an intelligence officer in the Admiralty, serving in the Royal Marines. There were some happy family events: Ralph and Geoffrey both married and Monier's family increased. He continued to have problems with his speech, so he decided to leave parochial ministry for a time, and in 1915 became the first full-time Secretary of the Jerusalem and the East Mission, opening their London headquarters and soon establishing it as one of the twelve recognised missionary societies in the Church of England. '£350 a year with a typist under him', Ella wrote delightedly in the War Diary. She had taken over responsibility for it from Burgon, circulating and then pasting in copies of the letters sent home by her family, so that not only would all the boys be kept in touch, but there would also be a permanent record. Together with press cuttings they would eventually fill nine large volumes, and Sam's secretary would have transcribed hundreds of thousands of words. All their sons wrote home, continuing their old school habit of Sunday letter-writing. Those from Burgon were frequent, lengthy and detailed, with vivid descriptions of the Front and reflections on Army strategy and the Church of England's response to the war, whilst Julian often used his as a form of catharsis – long, heart-rending descriptions of the horrors he was experiencing. Geoffrey kept his parents and brothers up-to-date with political news and London gossip.

Ralph was the first of the brothers to volunteer for overseas service. He was in camp with the Territorial Army when war was declared and, as a second lieutenant, was immediately mobilised. Even so, it was not until April 1915 that, after many false starts, he left for France with the 7th Battalion, West Yorkshire Regiment – the Leeds Rifles. His parents went to Gainsborough to see him off. 'The modern soldier presents a curious spectacle when everything is on', remarked Ella, as she helped him put on his knapsack and then 'hung on him' a revolver in a case, field glasses, two haversacks, water bottle, periscope, and wirecutters. 'Rather like a Christmas tree' suggested Ralph, as they tried to find space for his egg sandwiches and the pocket camera his father had bought him at the last minute. Then it was off to the parade ground for the leaving parade. Sam was asked to address the men and Ella described the scene:

When he had finished speaking, all caps were removed and the battalion joined Father in the Lord's Prayer, and he gave them the Blessing. It was a moving sight. Then the bugle sounded, the men fell in and with a quick clasp of my hand Ralph was at their head and I watched them march away.

Ella was left alone 'feeling rather in a dream' for Sam had marched with the men to the railway station. A few days later she received Ralph's first letter. He had arrived safely in France and spent the first night sleeping on the floor of a disused Iron Foundry, 'a most infernal place'. The next morning had found him sitting on the top deck of a London bus, facing the slogan: "Good morning. Have you used Pears soap?" The bus took him within seven miles of the firing line. Now he heard continuous gun fire, but could still write home next day with reassuring news. He had been talking to

> a chap who was wounded at Neuve Chapell. He says they all love the trenches. The Germans are absolutely beat, and everyone is very gay. Well, we are all certainly very lively.

Ten days later, in the trenches himself, but with a constant supply of chocolates, cigarettes and biscuits from his girl friends, he sent her even more reassurance:

> We fire about every five minutes and the German snipers' bullets whistle every now and then over our heads. I honestly never felt more comfortable, secure or happy with life in general as I do now.

His mother must have had her suspicions, for a few days later he is writing to her promising 'I won't be incautious, not even if we are in the trenches a long time'. He then rather spoilt the effect by adding:

> These gases are the blooming limit – but the appliances against them are perfectly adequate. Could you send me a bit of flannel to go over my nose and mouth?

By the middle of May he was spending four days in and four days out of the trenches and the continual gunfire was affecting his hearing. His ears 'sung all day long'. He was pleased his mother had sent him a respirator for the gas attacks for it was an improvement on others he had seen, but his battalion's casualties were mounting. On the 16th he 'lost two first-rate men' and the next day 'another excellent lad was shot dead'.

I think that just about put the lid on and I was fed up to the world absolutely, but I am getting over it by degrees... I don't quite know why I am so depressed. I'm not a bit really, but it is annoying to have one's men trickle away like that.

By the end of the month, the strain was beginning to tell, but so was his upbringing.

It makes one feel so helpless if one can't hear anything. Still, please don't worry – I don't, or try not to. I am very fit otherwise and my insides are quite alright which is merciful, but what Heaven wills has got to take place, so one has got to grin and carry on. We all wish Dad was out here with us. I wish he was, but I fear he wouldn't be allowed near the firing line – no parsons are, at least I've never seen one.

All his platoon were Leeds men, and all of them had met his father. The letters stop until the end of June, for his 'insides' were not 'alright'. He had developed peritonitis. His parents managed to travel to France and saw him in hospital at Tréport 'looking worn and tired, and very much older' and were made more anxious by the surgeon saying he 'feared the effect of the operation on Ralph after what he had gone through'. Sam found out what had happened and recorded it in the War Diary:

From June 17th to 20th he stuck to his post in the trenches like grim death in the face of constant pain, three sleepless nights, the whole time bombarded by the Germans. Maurice Lupton [a family friend, son of a future Lord Mayor of Leeds] meeting with a terrible death close to him, and he himself nearly killed by a high explosive, which only missed him by three feet. He would not give in, knowing that they were two officers short.

Sam and Ella were told that he seemed unable to sleep, though when his parents arrived he relaxed. Even so, as they watched over him, Sam feared that 'his dreams were of the trenches every night.'

In July, Ralph was back in England at Lady Evelyn Mason's hospital in London. Most of his relatives visited him – and so did most of his girl friends, and he became engaged to Alison Grafton. A year later they were married. His convalescence was far from straight forward, the surgery in France had been poorly performed, an abscess developed, and another operation was needed. His hearing, and especially the tinnitus, did not improve, and he suffered from neuralgia (severe headaches) and sleeplessness. In December he was temporarily graded as fit only for home service and appointed as an instructor for young officers. He had a flair for the work, was as popular as ever, and after long delays was eventually gazetted Captain.

The records reveal few details about his health, though Ella frequently noted 'Ralph is unwell' and felt that his training work, which could involve teaching during the day, and taking the men out on manoeuvres all night, was taxing him beyond his strength. She was probably correct, for by September 1918 he was 'very ill and in bed with a temperature and a nervous breakdown.' Alison 'so practical, cheerful and full of common sense' wrote to say that he had lost the use of his left arm and the doctors had said that he must be kept extremely quiet and see no-one. Ralph tried to write optimistically:

> I really am better, but a trifle thin, and I've had two good nights – the first for weeks. My head seems easier too and I'm not half so shaky – as I say, my left arm is the worst thing I've got and the Doctors say with treatment it will get all right but will take a long time. I cannot lift it at all, from the elbow joint downwards it is all right. Of course the nerves if touched are pretty painful.

After enduring endless medical boards where after one particularly unpleasant time he commented 'Their whole attitude towards me was vile', Ralph was finally invalided out of the army at the end of October 1918. A few days earlier he had celebrated his 24th birthday. 'What a lot he has been through in the last four and a half years' noted his mother, who could, at times, match Ralph for understatement.

Whilst Ralph was enduring intense bombardment in the trenches, his elder brother, Burgon, to his intense frustration, was safely playing polo. Although he arrived in France in May 1915, only a month after Ralph, he soon realised that, having enlisted in the Yorkshire Hussars and been appointed to the 6th Cavalry Brigade of the Royal Dragoons, he was unlikely to see much action. It was good to be a member of 'a crack regiment, with all the ésprit de corps and great traditions of a public school or college' but would there be any role for the cavalry in front line fighting? He doubted it. A year later he disgustedly summarised his service as

> two big shows and billets: Loos and the Hohenzollern Redoubt – nasty times no doubt but lasting a comparatively short time – and all the other months a quiet life, and on the whole a comfortable one, behind the line.

At Loos he had been left in charge of the horses, though it was neither an easy nor pleasant task. There were over 3,000 to look after, and they were all in 'regular and shelling range of the German guns'. His 'nasty time' at Hohenzollern – his first experience of trench warfare – was described by Philip Gibbs in the *Daily Telegraph*.

> A section of trenches was blown in, isolating one platoon from another. A sergeant-major made his way back from the damaged section and a young officer [Burgon] who was going forward to find out the extent of the damage met him on the way. 'Can I get through?' asked the officer. 'I've got through' was the answer, 'but it's chancing one's luck'. The officer 'chanced his luck,' but did not expect to come back alive. Afterwards he tried to analyse his feelings. 'I had no sense of fear' he said, 'but a sort of sub-conscious knowledge that the odds were against me if I went on, and yet a conscious determination to go on at all costs and find out what had happened.' He came back, covered in blood, but unwounded.

Burgon's reaction was similar to Ralph's: 'I am enjoying myself immensely'. When the war was over, he added a note to this entry in the War Diary: 'it was literally true'.

Nevertheless, he again returned to billets, though he was seconded to the Brigade's new machine gun squadron. He would be 'commanding about forty men and two guns'. It did not mean immediate action, and again he was frustrated by being so safely away from all danger, with a programme of work in the mornings and then afternoons free for golf or polo, and a full social life of parties and concerts in the evenings. He was now receiving copies of his brothers' action-filled letters which, he admitted, only made him feel worse. It was not until August 1916 that he was in the Front Line, in an attack at Thiepval, not far from Julian. The attack failed, but Burgon was involved in heavy fighting:

> everything was forgotten in the excitement of pressing that little double button of my gun. Through the smoke and above all the noise I could see the flame spurting from the barrel and hear the deafening rattle, as the bullets flew over to the German parapet.

At last, he could write home: 'How preferable all this is to billets'. To his intense annoyance he was then returned to billets and it was over a year before he was back in the Line and in the thick of the fighting. He was one of the officers leading an unsuccessful trench raid. The aim was 'to kill Boches and take a few prisoners' by crossing no man's land, through the wire, to the German Front Line. The whole manoeuvre was, considered Burgon, badly planned and went badly wrong.

He was fifty yards from the German trenches, with a severely wounded corporal and four men, when 'Henderson's hunting horn sounded withdrawal'. How were they to get back? With drawn revolver, Burgon covered their painfully slow retreat, for he would not abandon his helpless corporal.

I thought we should never get back – half a mile at a snail's pace. ...Just as we were getting near our outpost, heavy stuff began falling around. By the grace of God there was a small trench, and into that we scrambled; it was not more than three feet deep, but we lay at the bottom in the mud with the wounded man, and hoped for the best.

They were out in no man's land for an hour, but at 2.00 a.m. the barrage lifted, and stretcher-bearers arrived. Burgon was lucky to be alive; two of his fellow officers had died and one was badly wounded. He was the only officer to return unscathed and he was awarded the Military Cross.

It was not until 1917, at Arras, that the Army decided to use the cavalry. It was another failure; 500 men and 1,200 horses died. In driving sleet and snow, Burgon managed to get his section of the squadron out without any casualties, but it was, he admitted, 'a terrible experience'. In 1918, resisting the Ludendorff Offensive, the Royals again went into action as cavalry and, as Brigade Intelligence Officer, Burgon was now in the centre of the operation. It was 'open warfare' at last.

For four nights we practically had no sleep. I lived and slept at the HQ of the French Division ... and went backwards and forwards all day and all night.... I took the French General's orders down, translated them, and flew off in a car to my General ... It was a thing you could not afford to make a mistake over'.

In the months up to the Armistice, Burgon was in almost continuous action and he was awarded a bar to his Military Cross. Julian managed to find out what happened:

Apparently he took command of two companies of infantry at the moment when they were being counter-attacked, and reorganized the men to resist it, over the heads of two frightened and incompetent infantry subalterns; with this he combined the sending back of accurate messages to his General. The Corps Commander said that these were the only messages he got all day.

Burgon's war service of short spells of violent action, with long spells of frustration and boredom, gave him plenty of time to think. Letters, lengthy, detailed, analytic and often exasperated, flowed from his pen. To his parents and brothers, he described his daily life, his active service, his views on military strategy, the attitude of the Church to war and how it should change to meet the needs of the Peace. He had a gift for descriptive writing. Moving up to the front line, he wrote

> Nothing could have been more romantic. The endless column of mounted men moving snake-like over the countryside, which was bathed in a still silvery moonlight.

His next letter was more prosaic:

> The new budget is interesting. No more halfpenny postcards will make a difference to parsons I'm afraid. Did I tell you I have grown a moustache and am always called Bishop as at Oxford?

There is every indication that Burgon was ready to discuss church affairs in any officers' mess that he found himself. There is no indication that this was resented, and his nickname seems to have had no hint of sarcasm. He was a very muscular Christian; athletic, physically tough, able to relate to 'high and low' as he had done since childhood. In addition, he took with him to France his passion for all things Canadian, and his interest in history, literature and, above all, journalism. Not only did he write much of the *History of the 6th Cavalry Brigade 1914-1919* when he was in billets, but throughout the war he was in close contact with a leading group of journalists. Names of writers and war correspondents dot Burgon's correspondence. A typical entry reads:

> Sitting round the fire smoking their pipes were Philip Gibbs, *(News Chronicle)*, McCarthy *(Times)* and Percival *(Morning Post)*. Plumer and Valentine Williams (the latter *Daily Mail*) were away ... John Buchan went home in disgust after that last Loos despatch was so cut about by the censors.

Despite his reservations, he revelled in the social life behind the Line. When he wrote home to say that he had met 'loads of people that he knew' he was not exaggerating. He was constantly meeting Charterhouse and Oxford men. He made it his business not only to get to know fellow officers – from Generals downwards – but all their friends and relations as well. One letter to his mother is not untypical:

> Gibbs ... came to lunch. He is a Major in the 10th Hussars, and with him Francis de Tuyll. The latter is constantly over here and is a very nice fellow. His Mother is the Duchess of Beaufort, and the Duke his stepfather. His own Father is dead – Baron de Tuyll. I also met young Airlie whose sister Lady Helen Freeman Mitford was widowed a short time ago, also Lord Douglas Montagu Scott – a cousin of my friend David Scott.

Burgon was conviviality personified. He closed that letter with a request. 'We should all rather like some Wensleydale cheeses. Could you send us a few?' Doubtless, Ella obliged – her son was obviously following her advice given in more tranquil times to cultivate the best people.

When Julian arrived in France in February 1916, he also was delighted to find that he met 'men who know me or the family at every turn'. He was allocated as chaplain to a battalion of the London Scottish and to the 12th London Regiment, the Rangers. The officers of the London Rangers included his cousin Clare Monier-Williams, a senior Major who had been confirmed by Bishop Edward Henry, an adjutant who was a friend of Burgon and Geoffrey – and an officer's servant who had been a parcel carrier in private life and had delivered hats to Julian's aunts. Even better, he was told that he 'would be going right up to the Front ... the real thing straight away'.

It was on the Somme that Julian had his grim introduction to the horrors of a full scale offensive when, at Gommecourt, his 'beloved Rangers' sent in 'twenty-three officers and seven hundred and eight other ranks but only six officers and two hundred and eighty other ranks came out'. From early morning Julian was based at the Advanced Dressing Station (ADS), separating the seriously injured from the 'walking wounded' under a bombardment that 'rent the heavens asunder.... not a few died before or as they reached us ... but perhaps the most terrible thing of all was the laughter and tears of the shell-shock cases'. It was not until evening that he was sent off for 'a cup of tea and to eat some biscuits with hands stained with the blood of the dead and dying'. Then, as darkness fell, he went out to the trenches to help bring in the wounded, returning to the ADS just after dawn, to complete the evacuation by motor ambulance. After a couple of hours sleep, the next day was spent identifying the dead. He arranged for a mass grave to be dug, though he and the diggers had to lie flat within it for 'a very uncomfortable half-hour whilst the cemetery was bombarded'. And still the wounded came in 'now suffering terribly from exhaustion'. Then the rain started. Everything flooded. 'I didn't know there could be so much rain in the world. The trenches are waist deep in water and the mud indescribable'. That night he snatched a few hours sleep in a dug-out without any cover and under continuous bombardment. 'It is rather a curious feeling lying in a dug-out hearing these huge crumps and wondering where the next one is going to.' Next morning he was out again, burying and identifying bodies. Part of a chaplain's duty was the collection of body parts.

Like his brother, he was awarded the Military Cross, for stumbling and crawling through the mud in the trenches on the front line was the pattern of his life during the next two years. The little walnut box given him by the boys of Melbourne Grammar School would be in his pocket. He would prop it open on the firing step to reveal the silver crucifix. Not only did it provide a focus for a dying or wounded man, but, in a chaotic situation, when all connections with normal life had evaporated, it showed that some certainties remained. Around his neck was 'a silver pyx which held the Sacrament in one kind' (the wafer dipped in wine). Soldiers, Julian felt, 'were hungering without knowing it fully, for the Bread of Life' in preference to endless exhortations to good works or the expounding of scriptural texts. The sacrament of Holy Communion became pivotal to his chaplaincy and, allied with it, confession. When men were away from the Front Line he provided training in the faith, through confirmation classes. It was, he considered, his duty to 'warn our men of the "Wrath to come" as well as the Everlasting Love of the Father'. It was '... such difficult work. So much seems to be against you.'

His 'difficult work' culminated in his duties to minister to condemned deserters. The chaplain was required to stand alongside them when they were convicted and go with them to the Guard Room. Julian wrote home to describe in detail how he had supported a man in his 20's, who had lived on the streets of East London and served prison sentences, and now had no contact with his family. He had deserted on several occasions and had only twelve hours to live.

I took a chair and sat next to him. "I am going to stay with you and do anything I can for you. If you'd like to talk, we will, but if you would rather not, we'll sit quiet." Two fully-armed sentries with fixed bayonets stand one by the door and the other by the window. The room is only nine feet by ten feet. Anything in the nature of a private talk seems likely to be difficult.... So I sit on silently. Suddenly I hear great heaving sobs, and the prisoner breaks down and cries.... In a second in a low voice I talk to him. He still seems a little doubtful about his fate, and I have to explain to him what is going to happen tomorrow morning. I tell him about Morris and of how many splendid men have "passed on"; what fine company he will find on the other side.

There is little response. Julian then reads from the Bible, but to no avail. Trying to find a point of contact, he produces an Army Prayer Book which contains hymns, and asks the man to look through it and see if he can find a hymn he knows so that Julian can read it to him. The prisoner finds *Rock of Ages* and asks 'not if I will read it to him, but if we can sing it'. Julian is astonished, and very conscious of the sentries and the bizarre nature of the request, but he suggests they might sing it together before he goes to sleep. The prisoner makes it clear he wants to sing it now. This time, writes Julian, 'I had enough sense, thank goodness, to seize on "the straw"; and we sat there and sang hymns together – for three hours or more.' The last hymn chosen was 'God be with us till we meet again'.

He sang it completely unmoved... and then said 'We haven't finished yet; we must have God save the King.... the guards had to get up and stand rigidly to attention while the prisoner and I sang lustily three verses of the National Anthem.

A few seconds later the prisoner was asleep. All night Julian sat beside him.

I felt that the hymns, even if the words had not meant much to him, had been a prayer, or rather many prayers ... to him, hymn singing meant religion ... he found real consolation in singing hymns learnt in childhood.

At dawn it was time for the man to be roused, and whilst his breakfast was being brought up

we knelt together in prayer. I commended him to God and we said together the Lord's Prayer, which he knew quite well and was proud of knowing. Then he sat down and ate a really good breakfast.

At 4 a.m. it was time to go the 300 yards to the stake.

> I held the prisoner's arm tight for sympathy's sake.... the doctor blindfolded him. He was breathing heavily and his heart was going very quickly, but outwardly he was unmoved. I said a short prayer... and whispered in his ear 'Safe in the arms of Jesus' and he repeated quite clearly 'Safe in the arms of Jesus'.

It was soon all over. Julian's concern then was for the firing party – he spoke to them and handed out cigarettes – one of the very few mentions of cigarettes in all Julian's letters. The last task was to give a Christian burial to the body. 'I then went back to the Transport Lines and tried to get some sleep'.

What that sentence hides can only be imagined. But Julian had discovered the prisoner's strengths, and built on them. Faith held steady for both of them. In much the same way as a very different man, Julian's grandfather, Sir Monier Monier-Williams, recalled a childhood hymn in his dying prayer, it was an old evangelical hymn that provided comfort:

> Safe in the arms of Jesus,
> Safe on His gentle breast
> There by His love o'er shaded,
> Sweetly my soul shall rest.

Julian was required twice to minister to condemned deserters. But how responsible had they been for their actions? Was the death sentence appropriate for desertion for men under unprecedented nervous strain? Julian and his fellow chaplains raised the issue with their General who conceded that, in these cases, 'it was not always possible to say how far a man was responsible for his actions'. They pressed him further. Surely 'all cases should be investigated by at least one other medical man besides the battalion medical officer, and that that other should be a specialist for mental cases if possible'. It was a recommendation that one day would become part of mental health legislation when compulsory admission to hospital was being considered. It rebuts the claim that among the chaplains who supported condemned men 'there was no indication that they felt that the system of military justice which condemned [men to death] was inherently flawed'.

There is no doubt that Julian's service in France was harrowing and his letters home sometimes turned into an agonised tirade of anger at 'this devil's work', but when he was away from the front line, there were lighter moments. Like most chaplains, he did his share of arranging socials, concerts and setting up recreation rooms for the men, and was especially enthusiastic – characteristically in view of his background – about the Brigade Sports. It is at these sports that we catch a glimpse of him seen through the eyes of an onlooker. 'They laughed and cheered mightily at a bicycle race between padres and doctors riding on French boneshakers over the rough ground. It was won by a long-legged Church of England padre'. Julian had been issued with a bike soon after he arrived in France. He was not sufficiently senior to qualify for a horse or a car. Generally on long marches, he marched with the men. But it is pedalling furiously along on his bicycle that Julian comes vividly to life. Burgon described his arrival when he, Julian and Morris all met just before the Somme offensive:

> Pushing a muddy bicycle across the yard came Julian, complete
> in khaki uniform and steel helmet.... [He] looked extraordinarily
> well, and happy, and as usual made us roar with laughter. "Mud?
> My dear boy, mud, mud, you say? I plough through it, live in it,
> lost my bike in it coming here. Shrapnel! Ah, shrapnel, nothing.
> All round my head this morning. No more notice that rain".
> "How bl--dy!" "Hush, hush, my dear boy, you mustn't say that.
> I am a padre you know." All this in the same old strain. Morris
> and I in fits of laughter.

Only brief flashes of humour light up his letters, but the few people who still remember him recall that he was 'full of fun'. Letters from Burgon and Morris mention his popularity. 'Everybody adores Julian. He has a smile for every man; and every man from the General to the newest-joined recruit, has a smile for him.' Was there an element of sublimation behind his life-long devotion to the social, educational and spiritual needs of young men? If so, perhaps it gave him the sensitive affection which enabled him to comfort and sustain another boy condemned to death for desertion.

> He turned his blindfolded face up to mine and said in a voice
> which wrung my heart, "Kiss me, Sir, kiss me', and with my kiss
> on his lips and, "God has you in his keeping", whispered in his
> ear, he passed on into the Great Unseen.

Julian's letters reveal a man totally confident in his beliefs and therefore free from the need either to be all things to all men or inhibited in his reactions to the horrors which he was experiencing. As a result, he exposes his engaging volatility. He could lose his temper and hit a German prisoner who deliberately let a stretcher fall causing a badly-wounded soldier cry out in pain. He could be in the depths of depression: 'all those confirmed two Sundays ago have gone, with one or two exceptions, and under the most awful conditions', and a few days later be writing 'I am very well and try to keep a brave heart'. One moment he is certain that the war will continue for years. A few days later, he thinks it may end in months. Above all, throughout his letters, we see a 'long-legged padre' pedalling furiously on his bike as he tried to cram twenty five hours into twenty four.

Unlike their older brothers, Morris and Ralph were swept into war service straight from Oxford. Ralph's happy-go-lucky temperament made this a smooth transfer. Morris found it difficult. He had arrived back in Leeds at the end of August 1914. For the previous six months he had been touring Australia and South Africa, and his parents had been hoping he would have come to some decision about a career. That discussion was shelved indefinitely, though Morris rather favoured a career with the British South Africa Company in Rhodesia. Instead, he at once enlisted in the newly formed City of Leeds Battalion of the West Yorkshire Regiment, which would be known as the 'Leeds Pals'. The commanding officer was Lt. Colonel Walter Stead who, with the Lord Mayor, Edward Brotherton, was instrumental in raising 'a Battalion of Leeds business men, 1000 strong, to form part of Lord Kitchener's Second Army'. If Burgon was unfortunate in choosing to serve with the cavalry and thus ruling himself out of much front line fighting, Morris considered he was even more unfortunate in being required to serve under Walter Stead. Stead was a well-known Leeds solicitor and an old soldier who had previously been a Commanding Officer of the Territorials. There seems to have been general agreement that he was not an effective officer, added to which he had not seen active service. One of Sam's parishioners summed him up: 'If I bought Stead at my own valuation of him and sold him at his own, it'd be the grandest transaction I have ever made', but in Morris's eyes his chief fault – and the reason for all his failings – was that his commanding officer 'was not a gentleman'. He unburdened himself in a series of letters home: 'I have seldom seen childishness, pig-headedness, inefficiency, tactlessness and foolishness in such a degree in any bounder before, and I have met quite a few men in my life'. To make matters worse, he felt that the choice of officers also left much to be desired. Morris was a second lieutenant himself, and the adjutant, an old Oxford man, was 'really quite charming', but the doctor, like two of his fellow subalterns, was 'not quite a gentleman'. As for the rest, he reported darkly, they were 'all as I feared they would be'. Geoffrey visited and sympathised: 'His brother officers are Morris's greatest trial. There is only one among them who has the least pretension to any breeding and he is a Cantab.' Colonel Stead had himself appointed the junior officers and in fact most were former members of either the Leeds Grammar School or the University Officer Training Corps – but the university was Leeds. The family decided that there was only one way of solving the problem: Morris must get a transfer. Parents, brothers, uncles and cousins banded together to provide useful contacts in the Buffs and the Guards. Application forms were secured and influential House (Christ Church) men approached. It was all in vain: Colonel Stead frustrated every move. The problem was finally solved when the Colonel himself was transferred to a reserve battalion. The new appointment, Lt. Colonel Stuart Campbell Taylor, although retired, was a younger man and had seen active service in India on the North West Frontier. Much more important for the Bickersteth family, he was 'a perfect gentleman' and the son of an old Oxford friend of Ella, the late organist of New College. Morris settled down, concentrated on his training high up on the windswept Yorkshire Dales, found that he got on well with his platoon, and was proud that at a party he was hoisted on their shoulders as they rushed round the room shouting 'Hurrah for Mr Bickersteth'.

In December 1915, much to their surprise, the Leeds Pals were sent to Egypt to guard the Suez Canal. It was hot, dry and dusty and water was in short supply. Morris was cheerful: 'As for washing, well we don't.' An officer was 'lucky if he could get a glassful to shave with'. Much of his time was spent superintending the loading of supplies by camel. He explained to his family: 'Camel loading is a pretty difficult business, as every load falls off at least three times before it is finally fixed.' It was made more difficult because the 'native drivers ... did nothing but jabber at the top of their voices'. This was no problem to a young man with Morris's background. 'I always start proceedings by kicking the man as hard as I possibly can behind – generally lifting him two or three yards – this of course makes him furious, but obedient'.

The Leeds Pals were only stationed at Suez for about three months, but it was long enough for Morris to have an unexpected meeting with Julian who was travelling through the Canal on his way home from Australia. Whilst his ship tied up at Kantara, Julian caught sight of 'a smart young officer' standing on the opposite bank, looking up at the steamer. It was Morris, and they managed to spend the rest of the day together. Two months later they were to meet again – only in France, and in snow rather than sunshine. The Leeds Pals received fresh orders and arrived at Marseilles on March 8th 1916 and immediately began the long, slow, fifty-three hour rail journey north. The men were in cattle trucks but Morris shared a carriage with five other officers and 'we managed to do ourselves quite fairly well'. Safely in billets, Morris was elected Mess President and arranged a six course dinner for the General, but before long he was in the trenches where, he reassured his mother, 'the only thing that really bothers me is the rats, and they are legion'. In fact, he was glad when his first 'five days in' was over. He, who as a child 'would not even dare to go into a dark room by himself' had found that he could cope with the

> curious underground, and to a very great extent animal life, that we lead ... because practically our life consists of trying our hardest to kill as many Bosches, at the same time keeping as safe as one can oneself.

Then, unexpectedly, he was home for a few days' leave. He had a 'ripping leave' but admitted 'the longing to be a civilian again is sometimes tremendous, but still everyone else out here wishes for the same thing, and everyone is undergoing the same hardships, so why should not I?' Back in France, he returned to the trenches, but now with the welcome news that he had been transferred to 'C' company as acting second in command. 'It is a jolly good company. and certainly I must admit that it greatly adds to the interest of things ... But of course I am most awfully sorry to leave my men – and some of them have come to me and said how sorry they are that I am going'. However, it was not for long as so many officers were lost in his old company that he was transferred back, still acting as second in command. It meant that he had 'roughly two hundred and thirty lives to look after'. He was now in the front line 'six days in and six days out', and the bombardments were frequent and fierce. The great advantage was that when he was out of the line he was based in the vicinity of Julian and, later, Burgon. They even managed to meet. 'The first thing we did was to laugh for about five minutes, as it was so extraordinary all of us meeting together'. It was five years since they had last all seen each other at Monier's wedding.

They did not have a great deal of time for Morris's battalion was on Parade and being inspected by the General. Burgon and Julian watched Morris 'standing rigidly at attention in front of his company – red bow on his right shoulder – looking extremely smart and soldier like'. Burgon told his parents that they talked about the imminent 'Big Push' and Morris said that he

> wouldn't care one way or the other ... [about] getting over one's own parapet and making for the enemy's line. He wasn't so certain about his younger subalterns, some of whom were only just from England. This seemed to worry him a good deal. "The officers" he said "are nothing like good enough for the men – they are splendid."

There was no doubt, wrote Burgon, that although 'there was much that was uncongenial to him in military life ... commanding a company he undoubtedly enjoyed. He certainly did it uncommonly well.' It was soon time to separate, but, as Julian said:

> We've met once and we'd better arrange to meet, again. Of course, we can't arrange anything for certain, can we?' It sounded so naïve that Morris and I roared with laughter. I turned to Morris and said 'Well, I heard there was a bit of a war on somewhere, didn't you? 'I did hear something about it' answered Morris very solemnly.

The brothers shook hands, wished each other au revoir and good luck, Morris and Burgon going off on horseback whilst Julian 'mounted his bike and rode away fast down the hill'. It was June 29th. On the 30th Morris wrote to his parents. Whatever happened, he wanted them to 'rest assured that I shall be absolutely CONTENT (sic) as I know I am in His care, and what He wills must be right.' Next morning he 'went over the top' and died at about 7 a.m.

In his last letter home, Morris had added mysteriously 'Thank Geoff for his letter and tell him he is practically right in what he says but not quite'. What he meant will never be known, but of all the letters in the War Diary, Geoffrey's are the most violent. Whilst all his contemporaries were volunteering, Geoffrey remained at home, not fit for military service, completing his B.Litt. and helping his mother organise relief for Belgian refugees. Over a quarter of a million Belgian people fled their homes following the German occupation and 1,700 came to Leeds, the first 19 families arriving in late September 1914. 'A more piteous little company of human beings it would be hard to imagine' wrote Geoffrey. There were more offers of hospitality than there were refugees, but one family with four children came to stay at the vicarage. Soon more and more refugees arrived. The Belgian

Allocation Committee met at the vicarage, and Ella tried to co-ordinate all the many offers of help. It was not easy. Conflicting instructions would arrive from London. Told to expect 80 refugees at 5 p.m, a later telegram changed it to '600 or so at 8 p.m.' The special train ran late, and although 'inside the Town Hall everything went like clockwork', there was confusion in the Art Gallery 'owing to the lack of interpreters and to the long time taken by the police in registering the refugees who were to sleep the night there'. It was 2 a.m. before Sam, Ella and Geoffrey got to bed. Over the next few weeks Geoffrey was occupied in arranging accommodation. It could be bothersome: an 'old gentleman and middle-aged lady wanted to sleep in the same bedroom – wouldn't do at all'. In November, a new Lord Mayor entirely re-organised the system 'forming a strong Executive of a few people who can give their whole time to the work'. Geoffrey reflecting on the first two months felt he had taken part in an 'unparalleled instance in history – an entire nation being taken in as guests by another'. Most of the refugees found work in the new munition factories, returning to Belgium at the end of the war. In the meantime, Geoffrey returned to work on his dissertation, confident that the war would soon be over, for he 'knew the Germans well'. 'It is the condition of Germany that will bring the war to an end. The German working-classes would stop the war today if they could. In a few months time matters will have reached such a stage that they will be able to put their wishes into effect'. His reasoning was good; his time scale was as erroneous as that of the rest of the population.

Even so, he was anxious to get some kind of work which would help the war effort. Enquiries regarding munitions work in Leeds came to nothing, so in October 1915 he went to London to stay with his Uncle Stanley and 'put out feelers' for work in the War Office or the Foreign Office. It was through a Leeds contact, the husband of a friend of Ella's, that he was successful. Henry Birchenough was Chairman of the British South African Company and a member of the Advisory Committee of the Board of Trade. He introduced Geoffrey to Henry Penson (later Sir Henry Penson) who had given up Oxford professorships in economics and modern history to work in the Trade Clearing House of the War Trade Department. Ella described it as 'a sort of commercial Scotland Yard' where the work 'required only men of intelligence'. It was soon to become the War Trade Intelligence Department and Geoffrey was delighted when he was offered a position. It was, he reported back home, 'run by amateurs. There is not a single civil servant among them. There is an extraordinary mixture of men, barristers, solicitors, authors, Oxford and Cambridge tutors, etc. and all are gentlemen …

I couldn't possibly be among nicer men'. The work was secret, but he felt it was 'quite useful'. Hours were not too arduous: 10 a.m. to 6 p.m. with an hour and a half for lunch and 'tea is made by the women clerks, of whom there is a large number'. His salary would be £12 a month and the only draw-back was being office-bound in the afternoons: 'I miss exercise after lunch, to which I have been accustomed all my life'. He compensated by walking home each night to his room at Ingram House in Stockwell, a large YMCA development.

He had hardly settled in when he found himself, to his delighted surprise, in the Army Reserve. The Derby Scheme, introduced as a half-way house to conscription, was due to end. Under it, men had the option of enlisting voluntarily or 'attesting'. If they chose the latter they would be obliged to enlist as a private if, at a later date, they were called up. Civil servants like Geoffrey in 'starred occupations' were urged to attest, mainly, he thought, to improve Lord Derby's recruiting figures for as they were in protected, highly skilled jobs, it was very unlikely that they would ever be available for armed service. Geoffrey and three colleagues all attested at Caxton Hall, Westminster. There was, he wrote, 'a farce' of a medical examination. He passed and was issued with a grey armband with a red crown, and went back to work confident that was the end of the matter. Nevertheless, he could now write home triumphantly: 'I am a soldier! Which I never thought to be in all my life and I hope you are pleased, because I am – very'.

By the Spring of 1917, he was head of the 'post bellum department' working in the section's new premises in St. James's Park. The lake had been drained to accommodate the £30,000 building. In his private life, things were also going well. At Christmas he had become engaged to Jean Sorley, the sister of Charles Sorley the war poet, whom Geoffrey had taught at Marlborough. It was not until July that the blow fell. He was on holiday at his parents' country home when the War Trade Department notified him that he had been released for military service. The family was horrified. It meant that delicate Geoffrey would become a 'Tommy'. It was a shocking waste of his talents, and his health would never stand it. Immediately, Arthur Balfour, the Foreign Secretary, and Professor Sorley, the father of Geoffrey's fiancée, were contacted. Then, 'after much talk' wrote his mother 'we decided he and father should go to London and see what could be done'. Despite Geoffrey being thirty-three years of age, it was better that he should not go alone. Before they left, there was a telegram from Professor Sorley with news of an intelligence post vacancy at the Admiralty. As a result, as soon as they arrived in London, Geoffrey went immediately to see the Deputy Director of the Naval Intelligence Division. 'He seemed' wrote Geoffrey 'to think I should do all right because of my knowledge of German', but first the War Trade Intelligence Department must approve the transfer. Next day Geoffrey went with his father to see Sir Henry Penson. 'It was apparent to me' wrote Sam ' that such a man as Penson would not and could not fight to retain his men or advance their interests'. However, Balfour had spoken to Lord Wolmer, Assistant Director of the War Trade Department. As a result, Sir Henry merely congratulated Geoffrey for 'falling on his feet', and, armed with an official transfer letter, Geoffrey returned to the Admiralty.

> I was conducted to Captain James who read the letter and instantly had a commission form made out and telephoned to the Ministry of National Service to fix everything up. ... They are all charming and it is just like a club in the sort of social feeling, entirely without office red-tapey atmosphere which reigns throughout the Trade Department. There are several Oxford and Cambridge Dons, among them Willoughby, who coached Morris in German.

Captain James (later Admiral Sir William James) was 'extremely handsome and most charming' and was always known as 'Bubbles'. When he was four years old, his grandfather, Millais, had painted him wistfully blowing bubbles, one of the most popular paintings of the period. The work, added Geoffrey, almost as an afterthought, would be 'so confidential that I can tell no one anything whatever about it. Only it is absorbingly, fascinatingly interesting, and extremely responsible.' Geoffrey's brothers were delighted, Ralph writing at once instructing him to get a hair cut and learn the hornpipe. As for Geoffrey, 'the whole thing seems like a dream and too good to be true'. He would have a uniform 'exactly like an Army Captain's, but with a Marine's badge' and the Mess uniform would be 'dark blue with a thin red stripe down the trousers'. And he would be on a special rate of pay! Sam returned home, but not before calling at Carlton Gardens to give Balfour the good news. The family connection, stemming from Ella's Faithfull grandfather, so carefully fostered throughout the years, had not failed when it was most needed.

From Geoffrey's point of view, at long last he was in uniform like his younger brothers. For years it must have irked him, and if Burgon, when he was safely in billets, found Morris's, Ralph's and Julian's action-packed letters dispiriting, it must have been much harder for Geoffrey. As a result, he not only took a keen interest in the news, devouring the newspapers and passing on any gossip he heard in London, but was consistently much more belligerent than his brothers. When an American steamer ran down a German submarine and was preparing to take the survivors on board, a British naval vessel intercepted them and, it was alleged, shot all the Germans although they had surrendered. Geoffrey heartily approved. He wrote home:

> Actually I rather we deliberately killed men we might easily have saved ... the Navy do not trust the politicians to bring these criminals to the gallows after the War. They execute them red-handed. Do you blame them? If you do, picture to yourself the struggling forms of women and children as the waters closed over the Lusitania.

His brothers seem to have appreciated that Geoffrey's bitterness stemmed from frustration and sometimes in their letters went out of their way to try to compensate. Julian wrote that he was 'not a little proud of the splendid way [Geoffrey] has stuck it without complaining at the daily toil of the office – in spite of headaches and neuralgia. He has done, and is doing, his bit indeed'.

It was Morris who acknowledged that Sam and Ella also had a far from easy time at home. Not long before his death, he wrote: 'Your trench work is much more difficult than ours'. Sam's life revolved round the demands of his parish and his duties as chaplain of the Leeds Rifles. He tried, and failed, to be sent out to France with them – the fact that the Bishop of London received apparently unlimited permission to visit the troops was a very sore point with the whole family. Sam had to be content with heading recruiting campaigns, arranging services for soldiers returning on leave, and visiting the hospitals where wards were full of the injured men. Eventually, his long service as a chaplain, going back to his Lewisham days, was recognised and he was made a chaplain to the King. His election to the Athenaeum probably gave him almost equal pleasure. As a source of contacts, gossip and rumours it was unequalled. Within Church circles, his hopes for the formation of a Leeds bishopric were crushed. With the outbreak of war, the decision was postponed *sine die*, and priority given to the formation of a Bradford See. Hope rose again as his name was canvassed as the new Bishop of Sheffield, and Press reports made it look like a certainty. Instead, their family friend, Sam's contemporary at St John's, Oxford, and distant cousin, was appointed: Leonard Henry Burrows. Sam's sons were appalled and reacted characteristically. Julian felt that the collapse of the Leeds campaign was 'a wonderful testimony to the splendid work done by you, Father, as Vicar of Leeds. You have performed all the administrative functions of a Bishop for ten years and more with such conspicuous success that from that point of view the local magnates see no need for a Bishop who would cost more'. Burgon admired his father's 'true sporting spirit in deciding to put no difficulty in the way of Bradford' and Geoffrey felt that 'in one way I should be rather pleased to see Leeds humiliated in having to take second place to Bradford'. They were all unanimous in their pleas for Sam to take life more easily, for his frequent spells of illness were now complicated by increasing deafness. Later that year, following the death of Morris in France, he was offered, and accepted, a Residentiary Canonry in Canterbury Cathedral. The appointment was kindly meant, but even so was disappointing. 'It was rather a bombshell and not quite what we expected to do when we left here. It seems such a contrast to our active life', wrote Ella. A bishopric still eluded her husband and would continue to do so. Their new home, Meister Omers, became an open house to a steady stream of servicemen, arriving from or returning from France, who called in with news from the Front.

The outbreak of war had brought a wider sphere of influence for Ella. As the wife of the Vicar of Leeds, she had a responsible and no doubt at times challenging role in co-ordinating the war efforts of the many women's organisations in Leeds. She became increasingly involved in the Girls Friendly Society and in the National Union of Women Workers. She was a member of their central committees, travelling regularly to London, despite air raids, for meetings over two or three days. In Leeds she started a women's luncheon club timed so that working women could attend. 'We want the women of the Labour side to feel that others of their own sex are waiting and anxious to learn something of their life so there may be established that rich bond of sympathetic and knowing fellowship which the trenches have taught the men'. In 1916, she could report:

> We were crowded out and representatives of every class of women were present from the Lady Mayoress to the Women's Labour League. Miss Grier gave an excellent address on "Women in Industry", and there was an animated discussion taken part in by all classes.

Her sons took a keen interest. Burgon wrote from France asking for details, whilst Geoffrey wanted to know members' reaction to a speech at the TUC Congress. When she moved to Canterbury she let them know that she was starting an NUWW branch in the city and had invited representatives of about forty different societies to join. 'I am certain we shall in this way draw all classes and creeds together and prepare the way for reconstruction after the War. Our scheme is to form a Citizens' Association and at once start instructing women on how to use their vote'.

The move to Canterbury coincided with the launch of the National Mission of Repentance and Hope, an attempt by the Church of England to respond to the spiritual needs of the nation in wartime and at the same time to urge the necessity for a new way of life to prevent further wars. During the summer of 1916, with three sons on the Somme, Ella threw herself into preparations for the Mission. Writing in her War Diary just after the death of Morris, she reported that

> We have started prayer-circles in Leeds and many of our women and girls have been to retreats and Quiet Days. The Mission itself is to be only a few days in each parish, when the Bishop of each Diocese sends his messenger, but the preparation for it is the real matter of importance. ... Itinerant clergy are being sent two and two through the country districts and women are going from place to place on a pilgrimage of prayer ... we are trying to prepare for a better England when the men return'.

In retrospect, the Mission is considered to have been ineffective. Yet for many of these women, including Ella, it must have brought comfort as they witnessed their belief that their loved ones had not died in vain.

For four long years, the lives of Sam and Ella had been overshadowed by the possibility of death and the likelihood of sudden death. More often than not it seemed that as one son came out of the Front Line, another son went in. By the first Christmas of the war, three of the boys' cousins had died. Montie Rundall, whom Burgon had 'looked after' at Charterhouse was killed with his older brother, Lionel, in the trenches of Festhubert, waist deep in mud. Geoffrey Ottley, aged 18, had been posthumously awarded the DSO. 'Never have we spent a Christmas Day less like Christmas' wrote Ella. Cheerfulness was, however, the order of the day when her sons came home on leave. Always theatre visits would be arranged, for she had noticed 'how thankful men who have been at the front are for the distraction given them by a good laugh at the theatre'. In the War Diary she made a careful note of the best anecdotes that she had heard. It was all the better if they had an ecclesiastical nuance, and better still if they had a dig at Winston Churchill. In 1914, he was rumoured to have been in the trenches at

Antwerp wearing the uniform of an Elder Brother of Trinity House. 'At any rate' said a Cabinet colleague 'he informed the Belgian enquirer that he was dressed in the costume of the Frère Aîné de la Trinité, to which the astonished man replied, with a bow, 'Mon Dieu!'

As more and more of the extended family joined up, Sam and Ella's lives became a roller-coaster of good news, bad news or, worst of all, no news at all. Of the children in the Bickersteth and Monier-Williams large group photographs on pages 22 and 23, twenty-two were in the armed services, and three were killed in action. They served in every theatre of the war. Between them, they won three DSO's and eight Military Crosses. But if the news of awards were occasions of great pleasure, the family letters also frequently told of injuries and 'near misses'. Visits to relatives were not always easy. 'It was so nice to see Florence's radiant face and her boy safe out of that awful battle with a 'cushy' wound. ... it needed all our faith and self-control not to long that the same fate had befallen our Morris'.

Morris had died on Saturday, July lst, leading B Company of the Leeds Pals. Today it is estimated that 504 men and 24 officers were lost. Morris was therefore one of many. The pages of the *Yorkshire Post* were black with the names of those who fell. 'The 15th West Yorkshire, having been nearly wiped out, brings sorrow into hundreds of Leeds homes' recorded Ella sadly. She and Sam received their telegram on Wednesday, July 5th. Only one response was possible for the family – the response which Sam made when he was at his most depressed at Lewisham – 'to work, to work'. There was much work to do in Leeds. His first task was to prepare the sermon he would preach on the following Sunday. After the service, more news of the Leeds Pals began to emerge as parents, who had received letters from their sons on the eve of the battle, began to get in touch. For some months, Sam had been acting as an unofficial 'clearing-house' of news from the Front for relatives of the men in Morris's battalion and now that link became even more important. There were endless visits to be made and sorrow to be shared. Nor must Ralph be forgotten, for his wedding was due to take place within two weeks, so they had a duty to keep as cheerful as possible. 'I could not wear mourning for Ralph's sake' Ella confided in her diary. She bought a new dress: 'black chiffon over apricot with coral embroidery'. The wedding was the happy event that she and Sam wanted. On the Saturday evening, Ralph and Alison arrived with 'a gramophone in a box with all the latest music hall records'. Uncle Monier's daughter was a bridesmaid, though she said she felt 'like a stuffed canary' in her white and yellow dress. Amongst the wedding presents was a silver centrepiece with the inscription 'To Ralph and Alison from Morris'. Sam performed the marriage ceremony, Ninny noticing that 'Ralph did answer well, and looked so smart'. Only then could Sam and Ella go away to stay with relatives at the Deanery, Wells, for a few day's rest and quiet. Ninny wrote to Burgon: 'They are very crushed at the loss of Morris but they were brave at the wedding'. Burgon, like Julian, was in France.

Mourning for Morris was long and heart-felt, but not bitter. Like all the bereaved parents in Leeds they yearned to know every detail of his death. On July 3rd, Julian managed to snatch a few hours to cycle from Gommecourt, where he had been working under fire non-stop for seventy-two hours, to look for Morris's body. It was impossible, but he could tell his parents that he had managed to talk to an eighteen year-old private who had been close to Morris when he died and was certain that he died instantly. At the end of July, Morris's orderly, Private Bristow, called at the Leeds vicarage. He could give Sam an hour-by-hour account from the evening of Friday, June 30th to the moment of Morris' death. Sam recorded every detail.

> A high explosive burst and a large portion struck the back of his head, making a very bad wound, and the impact must have stunned him. It was certain that he would have no real feeling of dying or of pain, although both his legs and hands worked for a minute or two. Bristow was lying about two yards to the side of him, but such was the machine gun fire that he could only creep round to the side of Morris from behind.

It was a great comfort to Ella to know that her son's face was undamaged. But it was also certain that his body would never be recovered, nor the exact spot where he had fallen identified, though a burying party had found and buried a body which had a pocket handkerchief marked Bickersteth.

In their grief over the death of Morris, the whole family followed the path taken by their predecessors. From the death-bed of Edward of Watton in 1850 to Julian's anguish at the slaughter in Flanders, the response was consistent. Generation after generation faced death 'in sure and certain hope of the resurrection to eternal life through our Lord Jesus Christ'. Edward of Watton had died confident that he would now 'see Christ'. He asked his family and congregation not to pray for his recovery; he wanted no delay in meeting his Maker. Eventually they would all meet again. In old age, frail and confused, Bishop Edward

Henry had a moment of lucidity when talking to Sam: 'It is all as the Master sees best. He wills. He knows best.' Morris, returning to the Front in 1916, gave a letter to his brother, Monier, to be passed to their parents if he died. Morris now only feared death in the sense that it would be something he had never before experienced. Apart from that, death was

> ... simply a gateway though which one passes into Life ... Whether it is sooner or later can really matter very little to any of us. Simply because in thirty or forty years the whole family will be together for ever in eternal life.... If you look at it in this light, death has no terror, and really very little sorrow or grief attached to it. ... At any rate this is what I believe.

It was also the conviction of his brothers. Julian, worn out with the horrors of clearing a battlefield and burying the dead, found words of resurrection going round and round in his head.

> 'The living, the living shall praise Thee'. I can't tell you why these words came, but I couldn't get them out of my head and I was not anxious to, as they comforted me with the thought that these whose bodies are here are not dead – they are alive – 'the living shall praise Thee'.

His much more restrained younger brother, Burgon, could only reveal his feelings through poetry. Sorley's *Two Sonnets*, he felt, expressed some of his deepest feelings 'in the simplest and therefore the most moving way.'

> And your bright Promise, withered long and sped,
> Is touched, stirs, rises, opens and grows sweet
> And blossoms and is you, when you are dead.

Ralph felt it was particularly appropriate that Morris should have been killed on his Baptism day 'How beautiful – the day he was enrolled on earth and now enrolled in Paradise'. For all the family the hope of resurrection stayed sure and certain, and in resurrection the family would be reunited.

Not everyone shared such simple faith. Both Sam and Julian had to face the doubts of believers and non-believers who had no such certainty. On the first Sunday after July 1st 1916, Sam chose as the text for his sermon in Leeds Parish Church 'More precious than gold'. (That the trial of your faith, being much more precious than of gold that perisheth, though it be tried with fire, might be found unto praise and honour and glory at the appearing of Jesus Christ. 1 Peter.1.7) He wanted to try 'to comfort the bereaved by the Christian doctrine that characters purified by self-sacrifice are of eternal value in the sight of God.' On the Sunday before the start of the Somme attack, Julian preached on 'joy'. He spoke, according to his prosaic description, with 'the sound of guns now insistent and becoming stronger, and becoming louder'. In fact, it was the greatest bombardment the world had ever known, and could be heard across the Channel. His message was that there was 'joy in self-sacrifice, joy in showing forth love which Christ Himself showed on the Cross, a joy in which we are called upon to join with Him, that "Love casting out fear" might be ours'. A few months later, preaching on All Souls' Day, his cousin, Father Cyril Bickersteth of the Community of the Resurrection, was quite clear that 'It was impossible to believe that the many who die without faith or absolution went to hell'. The Bickersteths were moving away from orthodox evangelical belief that salvation came only through Christ's sacrifice and closer to the Roman Catholic position that atonement could come through personal suffering.

When peace was eventually declared on the 11th November 1918 Sam had preaching engagements in Folkestone, so Ella was alone in the house when she heard a rumour that the Armistice had been signed at 5 a.m. and that hostilities were to cease at 11 a.m. Her response was characteristic.

> Issie Aitken came to tell me it was true. I was glad to have her with me, for I broke down after the long strain and anxiety. Then I pulled myself together.

She put out the flags and the whole household went to Canterbury Cathedral for a Thanksgiving Service. Julian was in the front line until the end, burying thirty men on November 9th and still not confident that peace was certain. On the 11th, his comment was simply '*Laus Deo!*' Burgon was at Leuze in Belgium and took part in a ceremony in the town square at 11 a.m. Bickersteth had the thrill, as a chaplain to the King, of preaching at both Westminster Abbey and the Chapel Royal on the first Sunday after the Armistice. '... the dignified people who formed the congregation [at the Chapel Royal] listened very intently to a sermon from Father on 'This God is our God for ever and ever, even over *(sic)* death' (Psalm 48.14) His message was one of continuity and certainty. But was the future certain? His sons had their doubts. Would life ever be the same again?

Background Reading

Bickersteth, J (ed) The Bickersteth Diaries 1914-18. Leo Cooper (1995)

Creighton, L (ed) *Letters of Oswin Creighton, CF* Longmans, Green & Co. (1920)

Jalland, P *Death in the Victorian Family* OUP (1996)

Snape, M *God and the British Soldier* Routledge (2005)

*Talbot, N S *Thoughts on Religion at the Front* (Macmillan 1917)

*Tawney, R H *The Attack*

Wilkinson, A *The Church of England and the First World War* SCM Press (1996)

Sources

The War Diary 1914-1918

Bickersteth, S *Morris Bickersteth 1891-1916*. Cambridge University Press (1931)

9

NEVER THE SAME AGAIN?

'It will be strange indeed if this war does not create the proper combination of psychological currents to produce a great poet'. Geoffrey. War Diary. February 1915.

G eoffrey, classified as unfit for military service, was the only brother with time to think in those early days of the war. With memories fresh of his days at Heidelberg, he realised only too clearly that it might well be his brothers' duty to 'put a bullet' in some of his academic friends. His conclusion was, of course, accurate and also ironic in that he did not know that he was to marry the sister of the War poet, Charles Sorley, who was killed in the same year. By 1915 Sam also felt unease, though for very different reasons. When visiting Ralph in hospital he saw that there were several men in the officers' ward who had been promoted from the ranks. They were being nursed alongside officers 'from the Black Watch and others of equal birth and breeding' and he noticed that 'it was not very easy for these different elements to amalgamate'. 'It will be rather a puzzle' he meditated, 'after the War is over to know what to do with these officers promoted from the ranks'.

Only a few months earlier, in the sunny autumn of 1914, everything had looked very different – and very simple. The war was for a just cause, lawfully declared and the means being used were in proportion to the ends it sought to achieve. The Church's message was clear, simple and united: there was 'a solemn duty laid upon the nation by God; it was a divine punishment for a variety of national sins.' The Bishop of London, Arthur Winnington-Ingram, always a favourite of Ella, could not have put it more clearly. He called the nation to band 'together in a great crusade – we cannot deny it – to kill Germans. To kill them, not for the sake of killing, but to save the world'. Any hesitation that the family may have felt was swept away with the sacking of the library at Louvain by the German army. The destruction of so many priceless books and manuscripts was evidence that German high culture had itself been destroyed by the barbarian Hun. That gratuitous desecration would 'only be wiped out by the destruction of some beautiful German city', wrote Julian, in the white heat of anger. Sam preached on war 'as a day of judgement'. His sons echoed his feelings: 'As to the Germans! May God help them! We shall win this war because God cannot allow such scum to exist'.

Nevertheless, over the next four years, doubts steadily increased. Was the war 'just'? The brothers disagreed with their father once they began to experience the reality of trench warfare. Burgon wrote from the front line, pointing out that he 'did not in the least feel thrilled at being faced with "the enemies of all that is fair and beautiful and of good report in Europe" as Father suggests, merely excitement at being so close, and a determination to stop them.' The romance of war, which he sensed in 1915 'in spite of burrowing and trench warfare' had faded completely by Easter 1918. 'A corporal killing 'fifty [Boches] in much less time than it takes me to write this sentence' was, he felt, 'a little difficult to reconcile with Good Friday'. Julian agreed with his brother. 'This war may bring out some of the good qualities in man, but the evil it does is incalculably greater. The whole thing is utterly devilish and the work of all the demons of hell.'

Ella had never been quite so certain as her husband about the war. Like Geoffrey, she had good friends in Germany, and could not regard their sons as 'scum'. As early as September 1914 she mused that 'probably they feel towards us just as we do toward them. They think their cause is just and the War has been forced on them by England out of pure jealousy of Germany's prosperity.' When the gas attacks began and Ralph was in the trenches experiencing them at first hand, she was very doubtful as to whether the British should use gas in retaliation, even though 'the account in the papers of the horrible deaths the men die after inhaling these obnoxious gases is enough to make one ill. All the same, I cannot myself think that we ought to retaliate in like manner, as two blacks do not make a white.' Even in 1917, a year after the death of Morris, she could still be 'horrified at vindictive feelings against the Germans.' She described 'meeting a lady who shall be nameless who not only wanted "Germany wiped out" but also "the women and children slaughtered." I ventured to suggest her feelings were not those of a Christian, but I fear they are held by many Englishmen and Englishwomen.' By 1917, Sam was probably the only member of the family who was not in favour of peace initiatives, for Ella recorded that 'Geoffrey and I wholly agree with Burgon that to stop the war now would probably bring more advantages to us than to continue it.'

The vigour with which Burgon and Julian expressed their changing views in their letters are the only clues that their arguments were being heard at home by reluctant ears, for the replies sent by their parents have disappeared. Unfortunately, as in their school days, when there was a real difference of opinion between sons and parents, it was thrashed out face to face rather than in correspondence. It is likely, however, that if the opinions of their sons as to whether the war was justified or not caused some dissension in the vicarage, their changing views on the class system which had enfolded their entire lives until 1914 must also have disturbed their parents. In France, their sons had left their privileged, closed circle and met and shared with ordinary men the worst conditions ever known to modern warfare. They found, to their surprise and subsequent anger, that the working man was worthy of respect as well as care, and that it was essential that this should be recognised in post-war society.

At first, however, there is no indication of a clash of views. In 1914, Sam and Ella must have read Julian's scathing descriptions of the enlistment of new 'Australian colonial contingents' (the Australian Expeditionary Force) with complete understanding. Nothing else could be expected. The Australian Socialist government had, they agreed, taught the working classes 'to think only of themselves and their own wages and gains'. 'Higher and nobler' matters were beyond them. How right Julian was in ascribing the drunken and undisciplined behaviour of the Australian volunteers to the fact that the 'colonial contingents [were] not officered by Public School men.' And when he dismissed Australian-educated Public School men as inferior to the British product, this was even more vindication for the sacrifices Sam and Ella had made to ensure that their sons attended the best Public Schools.

It was not until 1916 that Julian, now a chaplain with the British Expeditionary Force, first saw the 'working classes' in action. His experience during the Battle of the Somme, marked the beginning of a complete change of attitude. 'The courage, self-sacrifice and endurance of countless numbers of these men will be an inspiration to me for all time' he told his parents. As the war progressed, his passion for the private soldier steadily increased. When his regiment, the London Rangers, was broken up due to an Army reorganisation, his anger was palpable. '[One] fact alone helps them through – the comradeship of men who have shared countless hardships and dangers together; and now even this has been taken from them.' He railed against the Army hierarchy: 'the man in the infantry is the only man out here who is worthy of the fullest possible consideration, and he gets the least'.

His experience in the Front Line put him 'into closer touch with the sufferings of the infantry than was possible for Staff Officers' and he began to relate this to civilian life. In future the 'cleavage' that he saw between Army Staff officers and the infantry must not be replicated in employer/worker relationships in peacetime. He warned his parents that 'socialism or socialistic ideas grow apace in such an atmosphere as that which I have lived in recently'. Burgon, whose experience in Canada had given him first-hand experience of working men, felt equally strongly. He had more time to think dispassionately than Julian, but he came to similar conclusions. In 1917 he considered that he remained 'at heart, a Tory in Church and State' but he was appalled by the ignorance at home to the changes that the war was bringing about. 'The average man of my class, and of the churchwarden type, is entirely indifferent, neither knowing nor caring to know the most elementary facts of the situation'. Those who thought like Julian and himself were looked upon as 'dangerous disturbers of [their] peaceful outlook, politics-mad or red-rag socialists'. By 1918 he had moved further to the Left and, convinced that 'the majority of men of our class are ignorantly playing on the edge of a volcano', was seriously considering standing for Parliament as a Labour candidate.

Both brothers argued, with increasing exasperation, for change within the Church of England. They were not alone. Other chaplains were thinking on similar lines. A friend of Geoffrey, E C Crosse, who had been a master at Marlborough was now a chaplain and had been awarded the DSO. They had dinner together, perhaps at the vicarage, for Ella entered a summary of their conversation in the War Diary.

> Crosse considers the gulf between the church at home and the church at the Front is daily widening ... Unless the Church at home is willing to profit by the experience of the Church at the Front, when the Chaplains come home after the War, and entirely alter its ways in many radical respects – goodbye to the Church of England. After nearly three years of War and endless experiments and constant failure the Church at the Front is at last beginning to really get into touch with the British Nation (in the trenches) while the Church at home goes on bickering in the same old way.

Against this entry, Julian added at some unknown date, 'I agree with this statement'. Burgon tried to tease out its implications. He asked his parents: 'What is essential to the [Church's] creeds, her organisation, her procedure, and what is not?' Returning soldiers, he felt, would expect their spiritual leaders to resemble their commanding officers and 'speak in no uncertain voice'. They should give a clear lead on 'great burning problems like the Sacraments and the Reservation of the Sacrament ... and re-union ... questions [which] are being discussed in France with all the vehemences of a political question'. The Church should preach 'an understanding of the present demands of Labour. ... The speaker ... should be a Christian who is necessarily a firm and intelligent sympathiser in the problems of the people.' If, in the process, the Church 'lost the upper classes' and 'gained the working classes' Burgon would be content because 'in so doing, she will control what will shortly be the ruling classes'.

But in what setting should this radical message be preached? Oswin Creighton, another chaplain and son of an earlier Bishop of London, was an old friend of all the vicarage family and a colleague of Burgon in Canada. He had dinner, when leaves coincided in 1916, with all four brothers. For him, although religion in itself presented no difficulties, the 'formal method of its presentation' was unclear. He wondered whether paid clergymen should be abolished and church buildings abandoned. Like Burgon, he asked 'How are we to get men to look at the Church as a society ... rather than an extraordinary institution run by a peculiar caste?' Oswin was killed in action in 1918. There is no indication that Julian or Burgon shared his extreme views, but they were no doubt influenced by them although Burgon disassociated himself from the 'comparatively small party of out and out socialist clergy, keen on disestablishment, eager that the Church should embrace lock, stock and barrel Socialist principles.' But he was sure that congregations should be told 'in and out of season that it is their duty as Christians to have a well-balanced, intelligent opinion on these questions'. Julian had a great deal of sympathy with the views of another distinguished chaplain, Neville Talbot, who felt the approach of the evangelical chaplains left much to be desired. The Biblical literalism of the evangelicals was a 'dead weight', and they concerned themselves 'almost solely with the next world'. Julian certainly considered that the approach of the evangelical chaplains he met was unhelpful and, when most exasperated, he felt they were 'generally in the way' when there was work to be done. He regretted, with a fervour matched by his parents, that the evangelical Chaplain-General generally appointed men of his own way of thinking. Sam and Ella had themselves crossed swords with him when he tried to prevent soldiers attending morning Holy Communion in Canterbury Cathedral. He preferred all the men to be present at Church Parade which made Burgon want to know 'why the Chaplain-General is making such a confounded ass of himself?'

It would be reasonable to expect that, exposed to so many fresh influences, and with so many reservations about the Church of England in which they had been born and bred, the brothers would also begin to question their faith. Of that, there is no indication whatsoever. The simple evangelical certainties held good. For them, God did not 'die in the trenches'. There is no hint that the German soldiers and their chaplains who were certain that God was 'on their side', caused them any heart-searching. Julian, like other chaplains, saw daily that men who had no allegiance to any church, who were, at best, indifferent to the Christian faith, exhibited many Christ-like qualities. The commandment to 'love thy neighbour' had passed them by, yet in the comradeship of the trenches that love was in action. It has been described as 'the ultimate mystery of the first World War'. But Julian had no time to meditate on these theological ambiguities, and perhaps little inclination. Instead, he tackled the needs which were close at hand: 'burying the dead, visiting the living, writing to the bereaved, eating, sleeping, reading a little, praying a little'. In the same tradition as his forefathers, philosophy took second place to pragmatism.

After the Armistice, exhaustion set in. Julian and Burgon were both drained from their experience in France. Ralph had already collapsed with a nervous breakdown. Sam and Ella, now well-established in Canterbury, were still mourning the death of Morris. Ella called her sitting room 'Morris's room' and kept there the treasured crayon portrait given her by his brothers. When the rest of the family came together, a gap was either left in the group photograph or filled by this picture. Yet in her grief, she could not help noticing, and worrying about, the changes in Julian and Burgon.

Julian, she felt, had returned to England with 'all the faults of a young Reformer, wishing to sweep everything away, church establishment and privilege of all sorts, forgetting that a perfect whole is best attained by things both new and old'. He also returned home, in her opinion, as 'a <u>very</u> (sic) high churchman'. He was a real puzzle to her. He was so popular wherever he went, always the 'life and soul of the party', yet when she tried to discuss Geoffrey's marriage with him, he dismissed the subject because 'he understood none of those things'. She feared he was 'more likely to join the Mirfield Community than marry'. The Community of the Resurrection was a celibate Order, where his cousin, Father Cyril Bickersteth, was a founder member. Then, feeling she was being rather harsh, she added in her diary 'I want to record what a beautiful character Julian seemed to us to have attained – so calm, so devout, so earnest, so self-denying, so pleasant in temper – in fact there was the nobility of a real religious life stamped on every line of his face'.

Burgon was also changed. The last few months of the war had seen him in constant action and danger, during which time he was awarded a bar to his Military Cross. Now all his energy had faded. He had 'lost his keenness' and was, wrote his mother 'very unlike himself. 'He has got very cynical and thinks there is so little real religion in the world'. He made enquiries about standing as a Parliamentary candidate for the Labour Party, and saw Sir Arthur Henderson's secretary, but did not follow it up. Eventually he returned to Canada to the teaching post at the University of Alberta which he had refused in 1914 in favour of returning to volunteer in England. After two years, he felt that a lectureship was not for him, and decided to return home, still unsettled as to his future.

For Julian, change came suddenly and unexpectedly. An English advisory committee recommended him for the post of headmaster of the Anglican Collegiate School of St Peter, Adelaide on the grounds of his 'impeccable clerical background, public school education, colonial experience, war service, earnest Christianity and social qualifications'. When the letter arrived, Julian was 'overwhelmed' wrote his mother. The contrast between the life of the Community of the Resurrection and £1,500 a year and a house of his own, was dazzling. As long ago as 1910 he had told his mother that 'work among boys in England attracted him very much, and he had thought he should like to be a schoolmaster'. His experience at Melbourne Church of England Grammar School in the years before the war had proved to him that he had a vocation for teaching and enjoyed colonial life. In 1919 he sailed to Australia and over the next thirteen years built up pupil numbers at St Peter's, and using the Rugby model, introduced the House system and compulsory games. It was a highly successful headmastership, though not without controversy. His churchmanship led to difficulties, especially his emphasis on confession. On the other hand, he guided many of the boys towards ordination. Using the British model, he founded the Headmasters' Conference for Australian Independent Schools, and helped found the first residential college of Adelaide University. Thoughts of sweeping everything away including church establishment and privilege seem to have faded, although not his high church views.

It was not until 1922 that Burgon finally identified what was to be his life's work. On his way home after his unsatisfying years in Alberta as a lecturer, he passed through Ottawa. Calling on the Governor-General, an old family friend, he heard about Hart House, a new centre for extra-curricular studies which had just opened at the University of Toronto. A warden was needed, a unique job with a huge potential to introduce European culture to the young men coming to Toronto from the farms and small towns of Ontario and the Canadian West. Initially, Burgon showed little interest, but a few months later, on holiday in Switzerland, he received a cable offering him the position. 'Then set in', he said in an oral history interview, 'the enormous pull which [Canada] exercises. Suddenly I felt I would like to do it'. His enthusiasm returned; the next twenty-six years were the happiest of his life. His never-failing energy, the social contacts so carefully fostered in previous years, all came into their own. He modelled Hart House on the Junior Common Room of Christ Church, Oxford. From the Prime Minister, Mackenzie King, and the Prince of Wales downwards, he invited Canadian friends and visiting Europeans to meet and talk to the students. Burgon was determined that they should have the same opportunities to hear leading thinkers, such as Arnold Toynbee and Bertrand Russell, as had happened when he was an undergraduate.

The prestige of Hart House grew and spread and it became known for its theatre, its art exhibitions and its concerts. At a time when radio and the gramophone were in their infancy, opportunities for students to listen to music were few, so Burgon persuaded celebrated musicians, when they visited Toronto, to give recitals at Hart House. 'Bicky was a tremendous civilizing influence' recalled an early student, remembering in particular the evening coffee parties, modelled on the pre-war gracious living with which Burgon was so familiar, to which he would invite small groups of men. He 'would talk of books or art or of the history of London, or of his own student days in Oxford or Paris, or his experience in the West, to boys who had likely never been outside Ontario in their lives, and who until that moment might never have thought of it'. The need to educate the working classes which he had seen so clearly in France continued to drive him. Some of his radical fire was subdued but he could still say, in words which would cause some disquiet today, 'My heart leaps whenever I behold an undergraduate'. If the working classes were to be masters, as he had forecast, then he would do his utmost to ensure they were cast in a traditional upper-middle class English mould. It was the mould he knew best. It was not very different from the mould in which he had been reared.

Sam and Ella had been faithful to Grandfather Monier-Williams's rhyme that their children should be moulded as 'children of the Lord'. How had that early training in the home and then at school and university withstood the impact of the Great War? In 1918 Sam and Ella had good reason to view the results with satisfaction. The education they had provided had given the boys self-confidence, but they were, at a deeper level, self-assured. They were Christian gentlemen who, in the words of the psalm their parents had taught them, 'did what was right'. Moreover, their upbringing had given them the certainty that they knew what was right. War had tested that certainty, and had not destroyed it. It had enabled them to serve their country well. A century later, the picture is more disturbing. Today the brothers often appear as self-opinionated snobs, their penchant for social climbing being particularly offensive. Their disciplined upbringing with its emphasis on muscular Christianity seems harsh. How could it have been as happy as they maintained? The sexuality of Julian, Morris and Burgon would today be a matter for prurient comment. Yet they were of their time. Worldly success depended a great deal on knowing the right person, and the Bickersteth family had to make its own way in the world. Their childhood was the norm for their class. To be one of 'nature's bachelors' was an acceptable and fulfilling way of life; male friendships could be chaste. Julian and Burgon's passionate commitment to young men and boys was sublimation enough and, for them, their mother was the 'only woman in the world'.

In terms of their daily life and careers, the mould had served them well. Yet that is only half of the story. Sir Monier Monier-Williams, evangelical to the core, would have expected that his grandsons would be 'children of the Lord' in the evangelical tradition. Neither Sam nor Ella would have disputed this. The evangelical mould: Bible-based and activist, with redemption and conversion at its heart, had been the mould of the Bickersteths for generations. But moulds confine, whilst the spirit ranges free. Early in the reign of Queen Victoria, in many parts of the country, when the division between the clergymen of the Evangelical Revival and those of the rising high church Oxford Movement ran deep and wide, Edward of Watton, 'that most colourful and godly of the evangelical clergy' had begun to change the mould. Through his emphasis on the sacraments and the inclusivity of the Gospel he dared to bridge the gap between the two movements. It had driven him to Africa and missionary work, to pioneer the Church Missionary Society and to work with societies outside the Church of England through the formation of the Evangelical Alliance. Through the generations, it was his model of evangelicalism that the Bickersteth family followed and within which the Bickersteth boys were reared and which was subjected to the test of the Great War. Was that mould 'never the same again'?

For Sam, the Bickersteth mould continued to serve him well; still sacramental, still a popular visiting preacher, cherishing still the great days of his episcopal father at Exeter, the move to the sheltered cloisters of Canterbury, surrounded by clerical friends, bishops and archbishops, was a recipe for happiness and some compensation for the lack of high office. For Ella, the mould in which she had been formed so many years ago, had already been broken. She had left far behind the image of the wife as 'the angel in the home', nor did she want to be judged, as Dean Burgon had wished, by her ability to serve spinach appetizingly. The Great War consolidated her different model: evangelical, activist, politically aware. How far his experience in the Great War pushed Julian towards the Anglo-Catholic position he maintained for the rest of his life is debateable. In essence it was similar to Edward of Watton's position, but strengthened by his war experience. It is now generally recognised that chaplains without a strongly sacramental ministry found their chaplaincy particularly difficult. Certainly Julian was certain that there was a place for ritual. Confession and absolution was, he felt, 'just what the men needed' before they took the Sacrament, knowing full well that their days were numbered. By placing the crucifix in front of the eyes of a dying man, he could convey a message which had no need for words in situations where verbal communication was often impossible. It is likely that the passage of years, new experiences, new insights moved him further along the Anglo-Catholic path. Certainly, his life-long insistence on the value of the sacraments of confession and absolution was not part of the Bickersteth mould. Sam considered that 'private absolution may convey greater comfort, but never greater grace' and private confession should be restrained 'to those exceptional cases which alone seem to me to be contemplated by our Prayer Book'. Julian differed, but shared his father's respect and love for the Book of Common Prayer.

Perhaps it is best to consider Julian's stance using his own words. In 1917 he came away from a Chaplain's School in France envisaging a ministry composed mainly of men 'who came from the Catholic school, or have been much influenced by it' and were 'neither spikily High Church nor Protestant in the accepted meaning of those terms ... nor deaf to the claim of non-conformity to recognition'. Later, again in France, he described his faith as 'a fervent Evangelical Catholicism ... a clear exposition and insistence upon the importance of Sacraments

– shot through with a burning love for the Master'. Unwittingly, he was echoing Edward of Watton – who would have loved those adjectives – and thoroughly approved of Julian's modification of the rigid, early evangelical mould.

It is often claimed that the Great War was a watershed. The papers preserved by the Bickersteths are more ambiguous. Julian, writing from the heat of battle in France, predicted that he and his friends, who so wanted change, would be too exhausted to take an active part in a battle of minds when the war was over. It was not until there was another war, and another peace, that Julian and Burgon, semi-retired, found the energy and the time to return to the need 'to educate the working classes' which their War service had so forcibly impressed upon them. To a great extent the brothers returned to their old segregated world of solid, upper-middle class respectability, within a Church which itself showed rather more unchanging durability than they and some of their chaplain friends in France had wanted. All remained communicant members of the Church of England. Nor did the Great War destabilise the family. The 'golden chain' of mutual care and brotherly affection, so instilled in them from nursery days, held good to the end.

Soon after arriving in France and waiting to go up to the trenches for the first time, Ralph, with mixed feelings, settled down to write to Sam and Ella. He was bubbling with excitement but there was also trepidation. He wanted to express what he felt about his home, but how to find the words? Typically, he used the slang of the day. He wrote: 'We are a priceless family'. Then he hesitated. Would his parents know what he meant? So he added: 'You know how I feel, and if I can't write it, you must try to understand it. Can you?' Almost a century later, the 'intimate records', which Philip Gibbs was so anxious should be preserved, reveal at least something of what he meant. They are permeated with what can only be described as 'Bickerstethness': a family focussed on the Church of England for a hundred and fifty years, completely predictable as to its principles, always ready to get up off its knees and roll up its sleeves, supremely self-confident about its place in the world and its duty to those beneath it in the social scale, yet at the same time not taking itself too seriously. If thoughts like these were hovering at the back of Ralph's mind it is hard to disagree with him. His family was 'beyond price'.

Background reading

Craze, M R *A History of Felsted School 1564-1947*. Cowell, Ipswich (1955).

Sources

The War Diary 1914-1918

Diaries of Ella Bickersteth 1881-1919 in the Bodleian Library

Montagnes, I *An Uncommon Fellowship. The story of Hart House.*
University of Toronto Press (1969) Includes oral history interviews.

EPILOGUE

*'In the Bickersteth family every day is Stir-up Sunday'.
Archbishop Runcie. 1975*

1918 was far from the end of the story for Sam, Ella and their five surviving sons. All lived to a ripe old age, Sam serving for twenty years as a Canon of Canterbury Cathedral and Chapter Librarian. Gradually the grieving for Morris was 'softened and subdued by time', helped by the visits they made to France, with Ninny, to see the place where Morris had fallen. Looking across the devastated country from Albert to Ypres, and seeing at first hand how Morris and his comrades had 'absolutely no chance' against 'such hopeless odds' brought them some consolation. They felt it helped them 'more easily to give up our son, who with others had died to put a stop to such horrors'. Later, they were able to enjoy two world tours, Ella at last indulging to the full her delight in overseas travel. All over the Empire, there were relatives and friends to visit, and in Japan Sam could meet the people and visit the places where his brother, Edward, had been bishop.

Meister Omers, a thirteenth century flint and stone house in The Precincts, Canterbury, now part of the King's School, remained the family home until Sam's death in 1937, with sons and grandsons returning to share in a changeless way of life. Every morning started with family prayers, with Ella playing the hymn on the organ, and Sam, gowned, taking the service which the domestic staff and the family, including visiting grandchildren, were expected to attend. Did he recall how he had been almost 'unable to keep back [his] tears' when his youngest son, Ralph, left home for boarding school? Now his home was again often filled with small children, and this time there were some girls! The old games could be played again, and the children sent to search for the chocolate drops he had hidden on his bookshelves. Ninny, as in the old days, was again helping the little ones at bath-time. Then, in 1931, all the family converged on Canterbury to celebrate their parents' golden wedding anniversary with a thanksgiving service in the Chapel of Our Lady, The Undercroft, Canterbury Cathedral. Five years later, Sam finally retired. Aged seventy-eight and now so deaf that communication was very difficult and struggling with depression, described by Geoffrey as 'melancholia', he admitted that he 'felt the need of serving under MAY, instead of under MUST or OUGHT *(sic)* ... the exit door needs to be opened into a quieter life.' He died a year later; the old evangelical impetus to continuous activity – the 'to work, to work' from his Lewisham days, having remained with him until almost the end. Ella lived on, with increasingly failing sight, to survive another War, evacuation and the bombing of her home in New Dover Road and, with the help of Burgon, to compile another War Diary.

All the old anxieties of the days when one son seemed to come out of the Front Line just as another son went in were renewed. Monier and his family were at Chiddingstone, Kent, living in 'bomb alley', whilst Ralph's office in Lombard Street was in the heart of the City blitz. Burgon, back home from Canada, was in Canterbury in the Home Guard. Both he and Julian would make the slow and difficult train journey to London, which resulted in Ella being read vivid – perhaps too vivid – descriptions of the devastation of the London docks and of the nights Burgon had spent in air-raid shelters in order to experience the life of East Enders. More hopefully, Julian could write telling her of post-war hopes: discussions with Rab Butler (R A Butler, MP, and President of the Board of Education) who was working on what would become the 1944 Education Act which would change the system of secondary education and open the way to higher education for women and working class children. Now the letters from her sons were supplemented by those from her grandsons. Edward, John, Tony, Julian and Peter, the sons of Monier, Geoffrey and Ralph, were all old enough to serve in the Armed Forces. They could tell her the too familiar tales of the monotony, the thrills and excitement and the dangers of Army life in Burma, France, Greece, Germany and the Sudan. There was also again the old heartbreak when Geoffrey's son, Julian, died on active service in 1945.

The War over, Ella returned to Canterbury to a cottage near the cathedral in The Forrens. Despite almost total loss of sight, she remained alert, interested and active until the end, welcoming visitors from all over the world. Her ninetieth birthday was celebrated with her immediate family, but she received letters, cables and telegrams from friends and relatives at home and abroad. Characteristically, she replied to the toast to her health by again reminding her children of the prayer of Jabez and adding:

> I pray then, that God will bless you indeed and that His hand may be with you all, keeping you from evil and granting you day

by day opportunities of serving others. You may be certain, too, that if I pray this prayer for you while I am in this world, I shall continue to do so in the Land Beyond.

Ella died in 1954, within two weeks of her ninety-sixth birthday, having received the sacrament from her son, Monier, on the morning that she died.

Both Julian and Burgon came to live close to their mother. Julian had returned to this country in 1933 to become Headmaster of Felsted School, Essex, an independent boarding school founded in 1564. When war broke out, he evacuated the school to Goodrich, Herefordshire, fully expecting to return to Essex when the war was over. In 1942, however, William Temple became Archbishop of Canterbury and asked him to come to Canterbury as Archdeacon of Maidstone. The governors of Felsted released him and Julian, as a residentiary canon, came to live within a few yards of his mother and his brother, Burgon. It is thought likely that Temple's intention was to make his old friend a bishop. If so, the plan was foiled both by Temple's sudden, unexpected death and the new archbishop not being in sympathy with Julian's anglo-catholic views. Made a chaplain to the Queen in 1953, Julian retired in 1955. Unsurprisingly, his retirement was an active one. He became chairman of the Archbishops' School in Canterbury and saw it through its first five years as a successful comprehensive school, and was also involved in the siting and funding of the new University of Kent. He worked tirelessly for the cathedral, undertaking several tours of Australia and America to raise funds for the mother church. He died suddenly, aged seventy-seven. having suffered a stroke whilst sitting at his desk, writing a sermon for St Luke's Day, 1962.

When war broke out in 1939, Burgon was still at Hart House but obtained permission from the University to return to Britain for the duration of the war. He was appointed Personal Adviser and Assistant (Education) to General McNaughton who commanded the First Canadian Army and so Burgon travelled all over the south of England arranging lectures and concerts for servicemen. In 1942 he switched to work for the British Army and was appointed Director of Army Education. His brief now was to prepare men for civilian life after the war, and within the Army Bureau of Current Affairs he was responsible for preparing pamphlets to encourage discussion on post-war reconstruction. His *British Way and Purpose* series has been credited with contributing to the Labour landslide in the 1945 General Election, as a high proportion of servicemen voted for the Labour Party. Burgon returned to Canada briefly after the war, but retired in 1947, aged fifty-nine, recognising the need for a younger man to be appointed to lead Hart House into the future. Whilst in Canada, he had been offered some glittering opportunities for a career change. Mackenzie King wanted him to come to Ottawa and take over the prime minister's department with a view to forming a cabinet secretariat, similar to the British model; the *Times* wanted him as their London representative in Canada; Sir John Reith asked him to consider becoming his deputy at the BBC. Nevertheless, he came home to Canterbury and spent the next thirty years devoted to the things he considered the most important: his mother, his brothers and their families; the Church of England; and those whom his father, Sam, would have called 'the casualties of life's battlefield'. Scarcely a day went by without him visiting his mother, holidays were spent with Julian visiting family members and friends world-wide and generally included a visit to Morris's grave in France. He studied palaeography, worked in the cathedral library as Sam had done before him, and provided guided tours for his endless stream of visitors from all parts of the world. For twenty-one years he was an assiduous prison visitor. His life-long interest in people meant that the ability to be a good listener never left him and he became 'greatly loved from Dartmoor to the Scrubs'. He died at Canterbury, aged ninety-one, still maintaining his passionate concern for the Church of England through weekly telephone catechisms of his nephew, John, who by then was Bishop of Bath and Wells.

John was the younger son of Monier, the eldest of the Bickersteth brothers. Ordained before the Great War, Monier's speech impediment had made a parish ministry very difficult. Happily married, his wife enabled him to overcome his speech problems – was she helped, perhaps, by her close friendship with Sybil Thorndike, which dated from their school days? In 1935 he returned to parish work, becoming Rector of Chiddingstone, Kent and subsequently an Honorary Canon of Rochester as well as an Honorary Canon of St George's, Jerusalem. He then served as Rector of The Orchestons, Salisbury from 1950 until his retirement in 1959. Like his younger brothers, retirement did not mean inactivity. For twenty years he was Chairman of the Missions to Seamen, and his passion for missionary work in the near and Middle East never waned. For thirty years he edited *Bible Lands*, the magazine of what became the Jerusalem and Middle East Church Association. He died, aged ninety-three, a few months after attending the enthronement of his son, John, in Wells Cathedral. At last that deepest desire of Sam Bickersteth had been realised in his grandson. The little boy who had been so sure that he was made of 'inferior dust' became the father of another Bickersteth bishop.

Much less is known about the other two brothers: Geoffrey and Ralph. Geoffrey left the Intelligence Department in 1919 and was appointed lecturer in English at Glasgow, where he remained until he was appointed Professor of English at Aberdeen University in 1938. His special field was the relationship between Italian and English literature and his translation of Dante's *Divine Comedy* is still used today. Happily married to Jean Sorley, they had three sons and two daughters. The death of his second son, Julian, towards the end of the War in 1945, hit him hard, bringing back memories of the death of his brother, Morris, in the Somme. Three years later, the loss was reinforced again by the tragic death of his eldest son. Tony had survived a dangerous war fighting with the Gurkhas in Burma, to die in an accident whilst climbing in France. Geoffrey died in Chichester, living near his daughter, aged ninety. Ralph, the baby of the family, lived on until 1989. A successful business man, he was director and later chairman of the City insurance company, A W Bain. During the Second World War he worked closely with the Ministry of Food, and was a keen member of the Home Guard. In retirement, he 'looked after' his older brother Burgon who was eleven years his senior, going with him on holiday and acting as his chauffeur. He is remembered as a fun-loving grandfather, and for many years served as a churchwarden of East Grinstead Parish Church.

The deaths of Sam and Ella inevitably brought the family reunions to an end, but with the passing of years, the next generation took the lead. In 1987, Sam's grandson, John, organised a mammoth family reunion at the Palace, Wells and one hundred and eighty seven members of the extended family attended. Today, amongst the direct descendants of Edward of Watton, eighteen members have been, predictably, ordained to the Church of England ministry but they also share with him an unpredictability of churchmanship. Four anglo-catholics, one liberal catholic, five low churchmen and eight evangelical clergy of varying shades, including 'John of Ashburnham' who in 1958 founded the Ashburnham Christian Trust, and established a Christian conference and prayer centre, make up the tally. Amongst the wider family, the descendants of Edward of Watton's brothers and sisters, the count, up to 1918, is even more astoundingly high. A very rough calculation reveals eight bishops in varying parts of the world, and at least forty-two clergymen, eighteen lawyers, seventeen doctors, and seventeen academics and school teachers, some of whom were no doubt also ordained. Yet that is not the end of the story. When Edward of Watton went out to West Africa on behalf of CMS, he baptised many freed slaves. They were given a Christian name at baptism, but for a few years it was also the custom for them to take the surname of the man who baptised them. In 1816, Edward wrote in his journal: '... there was a nice-looking lad today whose face I did not sufficiently recognise to remember his name, so I asked, and was surprised by his reply "Bickersteth".' At least two clergymen have been identified amongst these 'black Bickersteths' who have now spread far and wide across West Africa, the USA and this country. But for Sam, Ella and their sons, their own close family was the one nearest to their hearts, and there was one family member above all to whom their thoughts returned: Morris. Every year, on July lst, the brothers placed a notice in the *Times* commemorating his death. It appeared until July lst, 1976 when the oldest brother was ninety-three, and the youngest eighty-two years of age.

Background reading

Smart, N (ed) *The Bickersteth Family World War II Diary. Dear Grandmother*. Two vols. Mellon Press (1999)

Sources

Edward of Watton's journal. Held by CMS

Conversations with Bishop John Bickersteth, 2008/10.

Index

Introductory Note

Entries are in word-by-word filing order. Illustrations are denoted by page number followed by illus, photographs by page number in square brackets. Titles of works are in italics.

Reference to the Bickersteth boys refers to the 6 sons of Sam and Ella Bickersteth.